Doing the Dirty Work?

The Global Politics of Domestic Labour

Bridget Anderson

Zed Books

LONDON AND NEW YORK

Doing the Dirty Work? The Global Politics of Domestic Labour was first published
in 2000 by
Zed Books Ltd, 7 Cynthia Street, London N1 9JF, UK,
and Room 400, 175 Fifth Avenue, New York, NY 10010, USA
zedbooks@zedbooks.demon.co.uk
http://www.zedbooks.demon.co.uk

Distributed in the USA exclusively by St Martin's Press,
Room 400, 175 Fifth Avenue, New York, NY 10010, USA

Cover designed by Andrew Corbett.
Set in 9.6/12 pt Monotype Photina, by Long House, Cumbria, UK.
Printed and bound in the United Kingdom
by Biddles Ltd, Guildford and King's Lynn.

A catalogue record for this book
is available from the British Library.

ISBN 1-85649-760-7 hb
ISBN 1-85649-761-5 pb

Library of Congress Calatologing-in-Publication Data
Anderson, Bridget
  Doing the dirty work? : the global politics of domestic labour/Bridget Anderson.
    p. cm.
  Includes bibliographical references and index.
  ISBN 1-85649-760-7 -- ISBN 1-85649-761-5 (pb)
  1. Domestics. 2. Alien labour. I. Title.

HD8039.D5 A53 2000
338.7'6164046--dc21   99-087818

Contents

Acknowledgements

One of the purposes of this book is to make domestic work more visible. I have four children and my experiences of negotiating the public/private 'divide' have informed much of my work. Nona, Liam, Roisin and Patrick have made me think deeply about the nature of theory and practice. To have the time to research domestic work I have relied heavily on paid and unpaid childcare, in particular the work of my mother who drives hundreds of miles each week to care for her grandchildren. Without her I would not have been able to write this book. Thanks, too, to the informal East Oxford network of parents who do emergency pick-ups, childcare and sleep-overs, and to the many Waling Waling members who over the years have cared for my various babies while I have interviewed and worked in the office.

Domestic labour is one of those subjects that almost everybody – except those men who have freed themselves from it completely – has a position on. I have developed my ideas by talking to friends, neighbours and academics, who have also invariably ended up looking after the children, often on a regular basis. For this all-round support thanks, especially to Robert Lemkin, Brida Brennan, Fe Jusay, Joanna Sephton, Nicki Marriot, Jacqueline Sánchez Taylor, Jo Child, Laura Brace, Astrid Grafe-Vertovec, Sue Brownhill, Rosemary Harris and Paul Grant. Carol Wolkowitz introduced me to Hannah Cullwick and moved the project on. I particularly thank Julia O'Connell Davidson and Susan Khin Zaw for their intellectual rescue work when I was down and almost out.

Members of the domestic workers' organisation, Waling Waling, have been a constant inspiration to me – Gemma, Evelyn, Vivian, Gladys, Rita, Maria, Ramchandra, to name but a few. No one who works with Margaret Healy will be allowed to retreat to an ivory tower – she keeps me going.

Acknowledgements

The national and international contacts of Kalayaan and the international office of the Commission for Filipino Migrant Workers in Amsterdam have been invaluable. These organisations and Annie Phizacklea, Francoise Mulfinger and Louise Murray recognised the importance of investigating and publicising the work of migrant domestic workers. This was supported financially (the crucial bit!) by the Equal Opportunities Unit of DGV of the European Commission, the University of Leicester and the Economic and Social and Research Council through its Transnational Communities Programme.

Finally, thanks to Maureen Byrne and Diana Holland of the Transport and General Workers Union, Lucy Rix, the brilliant European project officer at Kalayaan, and all those involved in the RESPECT network of migrant domestic workers in the European Union for continuing to struggle for justice in these bleak times.

1

Introduction

Political Fictions and Real Oppressions

Domestic work is vital and sustaining, and it is also demeaned and disregarded. Feminists have tended to regard domestic work as the great leveller, a common burden imposed on women by patriarchy and lazy husbands. There has been remarkably little problematising of paid domestic labour with respect to such an analysis, yet its use enables (predominantly) middle-class women and men to avoid the conflicts of interest inherent in the gendered division of labour and the challenges, both personal and political, that this poses to the 'nuclear family'. Paid domestic work in private households is disproportionately performed by racialised groups. To omit paid domestic labour, then, is to ignore the divisions of race and class in reproductive work. Paid domestic labour poses real challenges on both a philosophical and a practical level to feminism and political theory, as well as to community groups and women's organisations.

This book offers a contribution to theory that is based on empirical research into the living and working conditions of migrant domestic workers in five European cities – Athens, Barcelona, Bologna, Berlin and Paris – in 1995 and 1996.[1] It also draws extensively on my experiences as a member of Kalayaan, a UK-based group campaigning for the rights of migrant domestic workers, and on research funded by the Economic and Social Research Council through its Transnational Communities Programme. At an empirical level it begins to map the employment of migrant women in domestic work with a particular focus on Europe. It describes their recruitment, work, salaries, hours, living arrangements and employment relations, and I use this empirical information to test the hypothesis that workers' immigration status (relation to the state) and whether or not they 'live in' with their employer (relation to employer)

1

are key variables in determining their living and working conditions. At a theoretical level I necessarily address the inadequacy of conceptual tools designed to describe more 'traditional' forms of employment (that is, those traditionally of concern to white male sociologists) or to describe the experience of 'women' within the domestic sphere (that is, the experience of white middle-class women). Referring to the literature on women's unpaid work in the home and on paid domestic work, I argue that the paid domestic worker, even when she does the same tasks as the wife/daughter/mother, is differently constructed. The domestic worker, whether 'cleaner', 'nanny' or 'servant', is fulfilling a role, and crucial to that role is her reproduction of the female employer's status (middle-class, non-labourer, clean) in contrast to herself (worker, degraded, dirty). I assert, with particular reference to the caring function of domestic labour, that it is the worker's 'personhood', rather than her labour power, which the employer is attempting to buy, and that the worker is thereby cast as unequal in the exchange. This is important to our understanding of the 'slavery' of domestic work, and helps explain why domestic work is so often undertaken by racialised groups, whether citizens of the state within which they are working or migrant workers. For racist stereotypes and the reproduction of such stereotypes, as well as labour cost and supply, play a crucial role in determining demand. Racist stereotypes intersect with issues of citizenship, and result in a racist hierarchy which uses skin colour, religion, and nationality to construct some women as being more suitable for domestic work than others. The position of domestic workers in relation to the formal sense of citizenship (what passport a person holds) illuminates the broader debates on citizenship and demonstrates that the relationship of domestic workers to the state encourages and reinforces the racialisation of domestic work.

While the applying of employment contracts to domestic workers in private households and the professionalisation of domestic work may seem to offer some way forward and to counter some of the abuses associated with all these factors (such as the selling of personhood, and overt racist discrimination) there are serious difficulties in applying employment contracts to the private domain, both theoretically and in workers' real experiences. An analysis of the experiences of migrant domestic workers, then, demonstrates the inadequacy of many of the conceptual tools developed by liberal political theory, including notions of contract and citizenship. In particular I wish to draw attention to two political fictions that are revealed as problematic: that of property in the person, and the public/private divide. One must tread carefully when dealing with these and other political fictions: on the one hand they are constructed, not real; but, on the other, they order social relations, thereby forming the basis for real oppressions. 'Race', for example, is not a real category, but this does not mean that people do not experience racist violence and oppression. To understand a political fiction one must both work with it and move beyond it.

Property in the person

> [E]very man has a property in his own person. This nobody has any right to but himself. The labour of his body, and the work of his hands, we may say, are properly his.
>
> (Locke 1993: 274)

This idea that there is an intimate relationship between the body, property and labour has proved crucial for Western political philosophy. But there is a profound tension in the idea of property in the person, despite its 'obviousness'. Locke signalled this in his acknowledgement that a man does *not* stand in the same relation to his body as he does to any other type of property (*contra* Pateman 1988: 56) because the body is sacred:

> For men being all the workmanship of one omnipotent and infinitely wise maker, all the servants of one sovereign master, sent into the world by his order and about his business, they are his property whose workmanship they are, made to last during his, not one another's pleasure.
>
> (Locke 1993: 264)

So a man does not have the right to kill himself, or put himself into slavery, because he is the work of God. Put another way, there is a contradiction between the idea of the body as an integral part of personhood and the idea of the body as property.

This has particular resonance for women: at the time of Locke's writing of the *Second Treatise of Civil Government*, for example, married women in England were chattels, the property of their husbands. Women's continuing demands that their rights over their own bodies be recognised, particularly around questions of control over physical reproduction and male violence against women, may be seen as a struggle to apply the concept of property in the person equally to women and to men. But the tension between body as personhood and body as property has not been explored fully. The migrant domestic worker slips into the analytical space between body as personhood and body as property. For the domestic worker is selling, not her 'labour power' (the property in the person), but her personhood. I illustrate this with particular reference to the payment for care, which strains the political fiction of property in the person to breaking point. But it is property and its disposition by contract that have

formed the foundation of civil rights for Western political theorists from
Locke onwards.

Public and private

It is not new to point out that the public and private are inextricably
connected. As Pateman put it: 'the dichotomy between the public and the
private is ... ultimately, what the feminist movement is about' (Pateman
1983, cited Okin 1992: 315). But despite this there continues to be an
assumption, both in sociological theory and in common sense, that there
is in reality a sharp divide between the regulation of the public and the
private. The private/public polarisation implies and relates to other
dualisms. Thus:

Private	*Public*
traditional	modern
paternalistic/authoritarian	bureaucratic
personalistic	materialistic
customary relations	civic relations
affective	instrumental
primitive	civilised
irrational...	rational... etc.

It must be remembered that this division is a fiction. Indeed, the
experiences and employment relations of migrant domestic workers
suggest that the commonly accepted transition from traditional to modern,
from unfree labour to free labour, is incomplete. Migrant domestic workers
are, I will argue, defined in a very real sense by their social relations,
characterised by personal dependency on the employer often reinforced
by immigration legislation. Like individuals in Marx's pre-capitalist world
'their subjectivities are inseparable from their social position' (Sayer
1991: 18). But the relations of the private are more than a blip, a feudal
remnant, for the work of the private has a crucial relation to capitalist
production. It 'produces' people who make choices about the commodities
produced in the public, and the home is an important locus of consumption.

That the public and the private are not real does not mean that one
cannot be caught in the gap between them. Indeed, it is the very imagining
of them as two separate spheres that creates the gap. The domestic
worker, like the prostitute, occupies the imaginary space between the two
worlds, symbolically ordered and imagined in very different ways. Female

employers on the other hand, have their movement between the public and private facilitated by the domestic worker; she is their bridge between the domains. The employment of the paid domestic worker is one of the means by which some women are able to adopt the masculinised employment patterns that now characterise the work histories of so many European female workers, and migrant domestic workers are increasingly taking on the privatised responsibilities of the welfare state. It is by slipping between the two imagined domains of the public and the private that the employer consolidates much of her power: the worker may be treated as 'part of the family' (governed by customary relations) when it is a matter of hours and flexibility, and as a worker (governed by civic relations) if she becomes too sick to work.

The private/public divide has been recognised as highly gendered, with women predominantly responsible for the private and consequently often unable to participate fully in the public. Feminism has done much to challenge the divide, and authors such as Pateman have shown how these dualisms reflect, support and reinforce patriarchal power. When one considers the case of domestic workers, however, one must deal with the fact that women can move into the public (for there is nothing fixed about these categories) if they make alternative arrangements covering the loss of their reproductive labour. In tying women to the private and men to the public many feminists have assumed a homogeneity of oppression, and ignored the other kinds of power – not just patriarchal, but class, racialised, national, etcetera – reproduced by such dualisms. For the case of migrant domestic workers it is particularly useful to examine the concept of citizenship, tightly tied to participation in the public, with an emphasis on the formal exclusive meaning in terms of what passport one holds and where one can work.

Key

Women and power

We must first acknowledge differences between women in order to make connections. This is particularly important given the tendency among white middle-class feminists to universalise their experiences, effectively erasing the experiences of most women. bell hooks's observation is as applicable to Europe as to the USA:

> In America, white racist ideology has always allowed white women to assume that the word woman is synonymous with white woman, for women of other races are always perceived as Others, as de-humanised beings who do not fall under the heading Woman. (hooks 1982:138)

differ btwn women –
Not essential

5

This erasure has meant exclusion and privilege rather than unity, but it has also led to serious defects in the analysis of women's oppression and struggles – so that the cultural, economic and political struggle around reproductive labour, which surely contains the seeds of profound, revolutionary and anti-racist feminist change, is resolved for some middle-class women by employing a domestic worker. It is important, then, to acknowledge differences between women. Our theory must allow that some women hold power (and exercise it) over other women (and men). These differences are extremely complex (though immigration and citizenship legislation do a lot to simplify them!).

Orlando Patterson (1983), following Marx, distinguishes between the pre-modern, personalistic idiom of power, and the materialistic idiom of power under capitalism. In the personalistic idiom, power is openly exercised, its unequal distribution and created personal dependencies acknowledged, but an attempt is made to humanise power relations through social strategies such as gifts and fictive kin. In the materialistic idiom, relations of dependence are concealed, the power relationship is depicted as power over commodities rather than power over persons. The employer of the migrant domestic worker exercises both forms of power: the materialistic because of the massive discrepancy in access to all kinds of material resources between the receiving state and the countries of origin of migrants; the personalistic because the worker is located in the employer's home – and often dependent on her not just for her salary but for her food, water, accommodation and access to the basic amenities of life. The employer uses both these idioms of power, and both idioms are given to employers and reinforced by the state. The materialistic idiom is an expression of global capitalism, of the global exploitation of the poor by the rich; it can reinforce the personalistic power through immigration legislation criminalising migrants who work, or making them dependent on their employer for their immigration status.

In unravelling the complexities of the relations between female workers and employers, one must also acknowledge differences in workers' experiences. While some endure slave-like conditions, rape and beatings, others get on well with their employers and have no complaints about wages, work or treatment. I have attempted to analyse some reasons for these different experiences, but one also has to allow for the different contexts in which domestic workers are employed, and in particular for dominant attitudes towards women and towards 'foreigners'. One must also allow for the different psychobiographies of workers. This was a source of much discussion among workers themselves: to what extent could they improve their situation by being, not just politically organised, but more assertive personally. 'But it's still very important for migrant

6

workers or domestic workers to really assert themselves to their women employers ... 'It's still very important that change should come from us as migrants' (Debbie Valencia, Kasapi organiser, speaking at seminar for migrant domestic workers, Brussels, 5 June 1996).

This research is 'messy' in the same way that work on prostitution is – there are contradictions and tensions in individual experiences as well as theory. Domestic workers are as influenced as anybody else by prevailing discourses on the public and private, domestic work, immigration. While some feel their work is honourable, many more feel degraded and ashamed. O'Connell Davidson has cited E. P. Thompson's appreciation of the tensions within 'social consciousness' that give rise to:

> experience – a category which, however imperfect it may be, is indispens-able to the historian, since it comprises the mental and emotional response, whether of an individual or of a social group, to many inter-related events or to many repetitions of the same kind of event ... experience is valid and effective but within determined limits: the farmer 'knows' his seasons, the sailor 'knows' his seas, but both may remain mystified about kingship and cosmology.
>
> (Thompson 1978, cited in O'Connell Davidson 1998: 115)

The contradictions around domestic work, paid and unpaid, are expressed in the 'social consciousness' within which domestic workers and their employers struggle and negotiate. The polarities and pairings of private and public, of madonna and whore, are not isolated or autonomous. Each contains the other within it, and each refers to and implies other dualisms.

So difference does not necessarily mark separation. Throughout this work I have emphasised the role of female employers in exploiting and oppressing 'their' domestic worker; how the female employer raises her own status by degrading her domestic worker. But it should always be borne in mind that ultimately it is men and capitalism that benefit. It is easy to scoff at the employer who complains in her list 'What she does, what he does':

Me: Hire and manage cleaner
Him: Grumbles when shirts not ironed
Me: Hire and manage nanny
Him: Tells me to tell the nanny what not to do.
('The things men do (and don't)' *The Independent* 13 May 1998: 16)

But, as an Ethiopian worker in Athens put it, 'men do not share house-hold tasks. They will not accept that. Ethiopian and Greek men are the same. If the Greeks can afford they will hire, otherwise the woman will do it.' We need to acknowledge and recognise constructed 'difference' as binding as well as separating us. The realities of power are complex. We need to recognise difference in order to heal fractures between us and in order to know where to insert our crowbars!

Note

1 This research was funded by the Equal Opportunities Unit of DGV, the European Commission's Social Affairs Unit, and by the University of Leicester.

2

Dr Jekyll and Mrs Hyde
Defining Domestic Work

In general theorists have taken two approaches to domestic work. The first focuses on women's unpaid work in the home, the second on paid domestic labour. The former received attention from the turn of the century, but it was only in the 1970s that domestic labour became a key feminist issue. The relationship of women's unpaid work to production and to capitalism was the subject of much debate, with particular emphasis on 'wages for housework' and women as an economic class.[1] Interest in unpaid domestic labour has flagged somewhat in academic circles, although in the press the gendered division of labour continues to provoke comment and the importance of domestic work to the economy is now receiving some attention from European governments.

Writing on paid domestic work is voluminous but fragmented. Historians, anthropologists, sociologists and journalists have all written about paid domestic work, as have domestic workers themselves.[2] These autobiographical accounts are both historical and contemporary. One of the most interesting of the historical sources is the diaries of Hannah Cullwick (1833–1909) (ed. Stanley 1984), who began working as a lower servant when she was eight years old and worked as a maid of all work for much of her life. She recorded her daily activities for Arthur Munby, a middle-class man with whom she had a relationship for many years and whom she married in 1873. The fact that they were written not for herself but for Munby, a man who was undoubtedly titillated by degradation and servitude, arguably makes them a less reliable source for descriptions of the daily life of a Victorian domestic worker, but they are extremely revelatory of the expression of social and in particular gender and class relations through the institution of domestic service.

Autobiographical and biographical accounts of domestic workers –

those that are easiest to locate, at least – are notably from Europe and the USA. Indeed, most historical explorations of domestic work have focused on the USA and western Europe, although there has been some work on Latin America, Asia and Africa.[3] Historical work on the USA, in particular, is often concerned with issues of race, ethnicity and immigration. Palmer's *Domesticity and Dirt* (1989), for example, on the relationship between employers and domestic workers in the period 1920–45, examines women's complicity in maintaining the gendered construction of house-work, their different experiences of domestic work, and the meanings associated with housework depending on their 'race'. Glenn (1986; 1992) challenges what she calls the 'additive model of race and gender oppression' through an examination of the racial divisions of reproductive labour which highlights both hierarchy and interdependence among women. She demonstrates a continuum between domestic service in private households in late nineteenth-century USA and contemporary domestic work in public settings, showing how in both cases black women do heavy, dirty, "back-room" chores' (Glenn 1992: 20). Historical interest in these questions has continued to inform analyses of domestic labour, in both the USA and Canada,[4] but constitutes a serious gap in the European literature.

The relationship between migration and domestic work has also been explored in the USA and Canada,[5] and has received some attention from Asian writers, who have tended to focus on the situation of domestic workers as female migrants – unsurprisingly, since the area is such an important source for migrant domestic workers both within Asia and to Europe and North America.[6] Paid domestic work in African countries seems to have been examined least. The exception is South Africa, where the interlacing of racism, sexism and pass laws under Apartheid has been explored by Cock in a well-known study of South African domestic workers which demonstrates the need for more international exchange on the subject. It draws many comparisons between the situation of domestic workers under Apartheid and Victorian domestic workers in the United Kingdom, but is not at all informed about the living and working conditions of contemporary migrant domestic workers – which, because of their racialised experiences and the role of immigration laws and lack of citizenship rights, offer far more scope for comparison. Immigration policies in such varied cases as Canada, Greece, Hong Kong, Malaysia, Singapore, the Gulf States and the UK (Bakan and Stasiulis 1995; Anderson 1997a) have reinforced the dependence of migrant domestic workers on their employer through employment and settlement restrictions, with deportation as the final control, and this is very similar to the system under which domestic workers in Apartheid South Africa

10

worked, subject to pass laws and one-year renewable contracts.

In Europe the relationship between paid domestic work, immigration status, 'race' and ethnicity has received relatively little attention. Yet domestic work constitutes a significant area of employment for migrant women in Europe,[7] where their often extremely harsh living and working conditions are compounded by an 'illegal' immigration status. This is confirmed by a general report on the situation of black and migrant women in the European Community:

> black and migrant women's organisations point out that as white women improve their situation through campaigning and social change, some of the roles that they are leaving behind are being filled by black and migrant women – instead of being taken up by publicly funded services. As a result, many white women across a range of EC member states, have black and immigrant women as nannies, maid servants, cleaners and domestics.
> (European Forum of Left Feminists 1993, Summary: iii)

Although domestic work in private households is acknowledged as an important area of employment for migrant women, very little is known about the living and working conditions of migrants in this sector, and what studies have been done are localised and not comparative.

With some notable exceptions (Rollins, Glenn, Palmer, Davidoff), the literatures on women's unpaid work in the home and on paid domestic labour are largely uninformed by each other. By drawing on both, and applying them to the experiences of migrant domestic workers in the Europe of the 1990s, I hope to give some insight into why paid domestic labour seems to be on the increase in Europe and why it is that such a large proportion of the workers belong to racialised groups.

What is domestic work?

Attempts to describe what domestic work actually is have been very problematic: it is very difficult to describe what domestic work is in terms of tasks performed. As Glazer-Malbin (1976) pointed out, 'shopping', for example, can include such various tasks as drawing up the list, purchasing, putting things away and throwing out old food. Shopping can also involve childminding (taking the baby along with you, dropping the children off at school on the way) or taking the dog for a walk, for it is characteristic of domestic work that it often involves performing several tasks simultaneously – caring for a child, washing up and cooking lunch may all be done at the same time. Rather than a series of tasks, then, domestic work is better perceived as a series of processes, of tasks inextricably linked, often operating at the same time (Schwartz 1983).

11

But domestic work is more than the sum of these processes, for it is not just physical work (which may in itself be highly skilled) – cooking lunch may also involve mental and emotional work: what do I cook that is nutritious, enjoyable, ready in ten minutes and uses the ingredients in the cupboard? It is worth emphasising that domestic work is highly skilled both in terms of time management and what is actually done – a friend recently commented that she can always tell when a man has hung out the washing! It is therefore often difficult for men, untrained as they usually are, to take over. Which is not to say that men cannot be trained, or that they do not use a deliberate hopelessness about the house to escape household work, but if we are to allow that domestic work is skilled work, then the handing over of it is not simply a question of men doing their fair share. They must be taught how to do it – and women teaching men how to do something as lowly and 'unskilled' as housework is difficult to negotiate. Rather than 'nag', women will do it themselves. When men do unpaid household work, they, like children, help by task; it is women who manage the process – again making it difficult for men to insert themselves into the domestic labour of the household. The management of processes is crucial to ensure that they all run smoothly. The 'housewife'[8] has a dual role, as manager and as labourer.

The unproductive/productive/reproductive debate

Many of the 1970s debates around the relationship between domestic work and capitalism were concerned with housework's productivity. Clearly the notion that domestic work is unproductive downgrades its social and economic contribution and excuses its invisibility. In order to centralise domestic labour some feminists have argued that it produces a commodity which is absolutely central to capitalism: labour power itself. Marx signalled this critical relation between unpaid work in the home and capitalist production in his theory of surplus value. 'What, then, is the cost of production of labour power? It is the cost required of maintaining the worker as a worker and of developing him into a worker' (Marx *Wage Labour and Capital*, 1847, R. Tucker (ed.) 1978: 206). Engels interpreted this:

> According to the materialistic conception, the determining factor in history is, in the final instance, the production and reproduction of immediate life. This, again, is of a twofold character. On the one side, the production of the means of subsistence, of food, clothing and shelter and the tools necessary for that production; on the other side, the production of human beings themselves, the propagation of the species.
> (Engels 1884: 4)

12

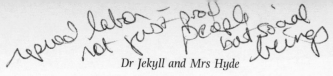

The notion of 'production of human beings themselves' is broader than simply the production of labour power, and is a more accurate description of household work. After all, not all household members can exchange labour power: children may grow up to be unemployed, the elderly are no longer working. While some domestic work may be necessary to survive, much of that basic survival work (the manufacture of clothes, the growing of food) is now done outside of the home in many states, particularly those receiving international migrants. The confinement of tasks to those merely necessary for survival would enable most productive workers to service themselves. But reproductive work is not confined to the maintenance of physical bodies: people are social, cultural and ideological beings, not just units of labour. The washing of clothes is not necessary for survival, but most human beings find wearing unwashed clothes for a long time unpleasant – although precisely how often one changes one's clothes is very much culturally determined. How a house is ordered, what food is cooked, how children are brought up and the elderly cared for are in part a personal expression of the household, and particularly of the (female) household manager. Reproductive work – mental, physical and emotional labour – creates not simply labour units, but people.[9] Domestic work is 'reproductive work', necessary for social reproduction, defined by Brenner and Laslett as including:

> how food, clothing, and shelter are made available for immediate consumption, the ways in which the care and socialisation of children are provided, the care of the infirm and elderly, and the social organisation of sexuality. Social reproduction can thus be seen to include various kinds of work – mental, manual, and emotional – aimed at providing the historically and socially, as well as biologically, defined care necessary to maintain existing life and to reproduce the next generation.
> (Brenner and Laslett 1989:382–3)

It is important to emphasise that social reproduction is not confined to the family. It refers also to the perpetuation of modes of production and social reproduction with their associated relations such as those of class, 'race', gender and generation. Education and the media, for example, are clearly socially reproductive institutions. Production and social reproduction in this broad sense are bound up with one another. It is not just that reproduction is a necessary prerequisite to production, but that much of what is produced has labour added and is used/consumed in the home. As Delphy and Leonard (1992) point out, in the First World, at least, the objective of production is no longer just survival; it is consumption.

In a recent television news report on refugees the reporter explained that 'Living in crowded conditions these women know that hygiene is vital', over shots of women washing clothes in a river. The scene changed to a woman sweeping the space outside her tent, where she had placed a rug and two chairs, while the reporter went on to say how the camp's inhabitants were struggling to maintain some dignity in their lives. I was struck by the sophisticated grasp of the functions of domestic labour implicit in these words: domestic work is necessary work in that without it humanity would not continue. We need to accommodate the raising of children, the distribution and preparation of food, basic cleanliness and hygiene in order to survive individually and as a species (which is not to say that domestic work cannot be organised collectively), hence the clothes washing in the river. But the ordering of our space is also distinctively human – without domestic work we would, literally, be living 'like animals'. Apparently paradoxically, given the low status of domestic work, the woman's sweeping of the ground was presented by the reporter as giving her and her family some human dignity. Whether it would have been so presented if the sweeping had been done by a man, however, is another matter. This aspect of domestic work, the maintaining of order (in our space, between genders) is not crucial for survival. Particularly for the middle classes of the industrialised world, it is bound up with the reproduction of life-style and, crucially, of status. Nobody has to have stripped pine floorboards, handwash-only silk shirts, ornaments that gather dust. All these things create domestic work, but they also affirm the status of the household, its class, its access to resources of finance and personnel, and the adequacy of its manager, almost invariably a woman. These two functions cannot be disentangled. To take the example of clothes washing, in some circumstances washing clothes is necessary for survival, but even when it is not most people across cultures would agree that stinking clothes can constitute an offence to human dignity – and then, such matters as exactly how often they are washed, and whether they are ironed, rapidly become issues of status.

Domestic work as social reproduction is profoundly rooted in community. Through the doing of domestic work we literally reproduce our communities and our place within them. In the doing of domestic work, particularly in matters involving the care of children and the elderly, we forge our communities. The organisation of our homes and their accoutrements demonstrates our position within wider social relations. As reproductive work is concerned with the social and cultural reproduction of human beings, the actual doing of the work – who does it, when and where – is a crucial part of its meaning (Romero 1992). More than a reflection, it is an expression and reproduction of social relations, and in particular of relations between genders.

14

What is paid *domestic work?*

The problem of the definition of domestic work is not simply a theoretical one. It is experienced by domestic workers as a lack of job description with serious implications for their working conditions. The International Labour Organisation (ILO) uses the following job description for a 'domestic helper/cleaner':

Domestic Helpers and Cleaners
Domestic helpers and cleaners sweep, vacuum clean, wash and polish, take care of household linen, purchase household supplies, prepare food, serve meals and perform various other domestic duties.
Tasks include –
(a) sweeping, vacuum-cleaning, polishing and washing floors and furniture, or washing windows and other fixtures;
(b) washing, ironing and mending linen and other textiles;
(c) washing dishes;
(d) preparing, cooking and serving meals and refreshments;
(e) purchasing food and various other performing related tasks;
(f) performing related tasks;
(g) supervising other workers.
(*Source*: ILO *International Standard Classification of Occupations* Geneva 1990)

This description completely fails to describe the jobs done by migrant domestic workers. When I asked them what they did, workers frequently responded 'everything': 'We have to do everything, do the garden, clean the garage, clean the car, take the goats out for work, the children, there is nothing we are not told to do' (Irene, a Sri Lankan working in Athens). Their work covered all household chores and more, including cleaning their employers' workplaces, cleaning the houses of friends and relatives of their employers, chopping firewood, fetching water, looking after pets and houseplants, and tasks too many to list. But the crucial omission in the ILO definition, as far as migrant domestic workers in Europe are concerned is caring work. Childcare and care of the elderly are often the principal responsibilities of such workers.[10] The ILO definition should alert us to the fact that commonly paid 'domestic work' is not held to include such caring work, which is more likely to be professionalised as nannies and personal nursing assistants. But it is, in fact, an important component of the jobs of migrant domestic workers. This may be acknowledged even by states. For example, in 1998 the UK government announced that non-nationals entering the UK as domestic workers had to have responsibilities which exceed the ILO requirements, termed 'basic levels'. Examples of such duties included childcare and 'personal attention to a sick, elderly or disabled member of the family'.

Why employ a domestic worker?

Many women of all classes are faced with the problem of how to combine paid employment with caring for young children when state-provided services are minimal or non-existent. As the imagined domains of the public and private are kept apart, the huge tasks of social reproduction are rendered invisible, and arrangements often privatised. The employment of a domestic worker is often presented as a strategy for enabling middle-class women to enter 'productive employment' (Hertz 1986). In Europe many employers needed childcare while they were working, or care for an elderly relative. Given a declining welfare state, families that are increasingly nuclear with no support available from kinship networks, a growth in middle-class female employment outside the home, with a pool of cheap, flexible labour, it is scarcely surprising that the employment of a migrant domestic worker is regarded as a suitable strategy for families in need of full-time carers. Employers often refer to domestic workers as their substitutes: 'the domestic worker is a double, the other self one leaves at home doing those things that traditionally you, as a woman, should be doing.... I felt it in my own flesh, this other self who freed me so I could perform my other roles' ('Leila', quoted in Pereira de Melo 1984).

But workers do not simply substitute for the work of their female employers. They often perform tasks it is unlikely that any woman *with a choice* would be prepared to undertake. Take Irene's employers, for example:

> They have a very big house, and everywhere, white carpet. They have three dogs. I hate those dogs, with long, long hair. Even one hair will show on the white carpet.... They have another working for them. She is a Filipina and she comes in twice a week to clean the big big mirrors.

Would her employers have both white carpet and dogs if they (or, most likely, the female employer) had to clean the house themselves? One suspects that only if the husband were particularly brutal or oppressive would this be the case. This kind of pointless work is typical of the demands made of migrant domestic workers:

> Every day I am cleaning for my madam, one riding shoes, two walking shoes, house shoes, that is every day, just for one person ... plus the children, that is one rubber and one shoes for everyday school, that is another two.... And that is other shoes for the children. Fourteen shoes every day. My time is already finished, I'm cleaning the shoes. I said, 'Why don't you buy like this, the machine?' but they said 'It's very expensive'.... You will be wondering why she has so many bathrobes, one silk, and two cotton. I say, 'Why madam has so many bathrobe?' Every day you have to

16

hang up. Every day you have to press the back because it is crumpled. (Francia, Filipina in Paris)

The servicing of life-styles that would otherwise be difficult, if not impossible, to sustain forms an important component of paid domestic work. Among workers I have spoken to this is reflected in a sense that they are being required to do work that employers themselves would never consider doing. 'It's not fair, you wouldn't tell your fellow human to do something you would not be happy to do. But they don't respect' (Joy, a Ghanaian woman working in Athens).

This clearly brings us back to issues of status, to domestic work as an expression and reproduction of social relations. Placed within this context, paid domestic work poses a serious challenge to the analysis of domestic work as a common burden shared between women:

> When wives have servants, even part-time cleaners a few days a week, they may appear to do less domestic work, and they are certainly often reviled as lazy parasites when they rely on paid help with childcare and housework even if they are in full-time employment. But women are actually only given servants or au pairs when their workload simply cannot be carried by one person ... or when their husbands want their time to be shifted elsewhere.
> (Delphy and Leonard 1992: 235–6)

But waged domestic labour indicates that women have different experiences of housework, mediated by differences such as class, age and 'race' (Palmer 1989). Indeed, in certain European countries domestic labour may also be undertaken by migrant men, effectively degendered by 'race' and citizenship. The employment of a domestic worker is not only a coping strategy, and often its purpose is not to free up a worker from the demands of caring and housework to take on productive employment. Cock's South African study, for example, found that just over a quarter of the married female employers were employed outside the home, while for the majority the employment of a domestic worker facilitated leisure activities and a high-status life-style. Unlike those in Cock's study, the majority of workers I have spoken to are working for dual-income families, but this is not always the case:

> with my employer the only thing I cannot do is go to bed with her husband. If only I can go to bed with her husband maybe she will ask me to because I am doing everything. She is sleeping in the morning, and she wakes up at one o'clock. She doesn't work since I was there I do everything. She doesn't go out. She is sitting, drinking, smoking, telephone ... if only I can wash her peepee maybe she will ask me for her.
> (Teresa, a Filipina working in Paris)

The recruitment of overseas domestic workers in Taiwan was halted in March 1995 because only 11 per cent of the 13,286 women who had been given licences to hire domestic workers had entered the job market. Moreover, while one could argue that childcarers free women for the labour market, for example, could one really say that of cleaners working for a few hours a week? Time-consuming as cleaning a house may be, there are not many women forced to make a decision between, for example, employment outside the home and housework. Whether their employers were working or not, domestic workers often worked at sustaining an otherwise unsustainable life-style.

There are clear parallels between the servicing of life-styles by contemporary domestic workers and the work of domestic servants in England in Victorian times. Davidoff's work on the role of domestic workers in reproducing gender identities in Victorian households (1974) throws new light on the role of migrant domestic workers. She explores how nineteenth-century divisions and polarities – such as male/female, middle-class/working-class or urban/rural – were played out in the household. At a time when reproductive work multiplied – not just because of demands made on wives to be good companions and mothers but also because of the increased size of houses and objects – middle-class women could, through managing the labour of domestic workers, be 'domestic' without being 'dirty'. The employment of domestic workers meant women could negotiate the contradiction between domesticity, requiring physical labour and dirtiness, and the cleanliness and spirituality of feminine virtue. 'Ladies' need servants. The idealisation of white middle-class women as the pure, pious, moral and virtuous centre of the household required a splitting of women and their functions into two mutually dependent but antagonistic stereotypes: pure/dirty, emotional/physical, madonna/whore, each drawing their identity from their opposite, and these stereotypes were expressed and reproduced in the employer/domestic worker relationship. Servants met manual demands, freeing wives to meet the emotional demands of husbands and children. Once established this relationship worked to maintain difference: workers proved their inferiority by their physicality and dirt, while female employers proved their superiority by their femininity, daintiness and managerial skills. Male employers proved *their* superiority by never having to consider domestic drudgery, while enjoying the home as a refuge, a well-deserved rest from the stresses and strains of productive work.

This division of labour continued beyond Victorian times (Castro 1984; Palmer 1989). Victorian polarities have 1990s resonances and accretions. For example:

'Madonna'	*'Whore'*
wife	domestic worker
clean	dirty
spiritual	physical
moral	immoral
placed on a pedestal	doer of dirty work
companion	servicer

Gregson and Lowe's finding in English households in the 1990s – that the employment of a cleaner was often justified by the parents' desire for 'quality time' with each other and their children to assist in their social, emotional and educational development – implies a similar duality, non-gendered for the employers but not for the (inevitably female), cleaner. The issue is often one of gender relations: unwilling or unable to argue with a male partner and children over sharing domestic chores, and unable to manage the house to everybody's satisfaction, the woman employs a domestic worker. So gender and generational conflict over domestic work is averted (or often transferred to relations between female employer and female worker). There is another option, of course, which is to tolerate untidy rooms and dusty shelves, but there is pressure to maintain acceptable 'standards' from relatives, friends and others who visit the household, from the internalisations of the woman herself, and, crucially, from the husband.

> she doesn't do ironing, because she's particularly slow, I'm particularly quick and my husband is very fussy about his ironing, he likes his shirts ironed just so.... If I wasn't working at home I'd have to ask her to tidy up because my husband couldn't bring back his client if there was mess everywhere, but because I'm around I can tidy up.
> (Helene, employer in Paris)

It is women who bear the brunt of the public/private distinction – as housewives, confined to the 'private' and unrecognised workplace, and as workers who must juggle the double day, working around childcare and domestic duties. The employment of a paid domestic worker enables the negotiation of contradictions, not just the public/private divide, but gendered identities and the consequent tensions and demands placed upon women. The employment of a paid domestic worker therefore facilitates status reproduction, not only by maintaining status objects, enabling the silver to be polished or the clothes to be ironed, but also by serving as a foil to the lady of the house. The hired reproductive worker is reproducing social beings and sets of relationships that are not merely not her own but also deeply antagonistic to her own interests. Her presence emphasises and reinforces her employer's identity – as a competent household manager, as middle-class, as white – and her own as its opposite. Perhaps Leila is right: her domestic worker is her 'other self', but rather than a mirror image the worker is the Mrs Hyde to her Dr Jekyll, the two woven into mutually dependent female stereotypes. A European 'housewife' does not just labour, she (usually) has some control over the management of the process, retains an emotional stake in the household, and often derives economic and other benefits. The well-kept house, children and husband are a tribute to her managerial skills. While wives may gain status and privileges from relations with their husbands, domestic workers do not (Glenn 1992).

A domestic worker may be employed to act as a carer or to service a life-style, though in practice the two functions are difficult to disentangle. While female employment may create a demand for childcare, it may also be presented as a choice made by women citizens opting for higher-status paid employment rather than low-status reproductive labour: 'Now the girls, the Greek girls, they want to be secretaries. They go to university. Who will go to university and then clean homes?' (Caritas volunteer worker in Athens). While a family may 'need' a worker to look after their children, they do not need a worker to clean the children's shoes every day. But the relation between a domestic worker and her employers, and in particular her female employer is inevitably one of relative status, while men's ultimate control over the household remains unchallenged. As one French employer put it:

> My husband has been well brought up by his mother to be sensitive to dust and to notice that kind of thing, so ... he'll say, 'Here's a cobweb, when you see Madam C you must tell her to clean there'. Then I pull the cobweb, and he says, 'No, you don't do it, that's for her to do. That's her job.'

The very hiring of a domestic worker lowers the status of the work she does – the employer has better things to do with her time. Moreover, while the housewife is acknowledged as manager and labourer, the domestic worker is simply a labourer, the 'hands' (Davidoff 1974) (though in reality she, like the housewife, is constantly managing processes) who is managed by her female employer. The hard work of the domestic worker redounds to the credit, not of herself, but of the household manager, who has demonstrated her skills in such a marvellous find. What women have in common is the management of the processes of domestic work, but most women have to both manage and labour, while some predominantly manage. This makes for very real conflicts of interest between women as household managers and household workers, as the manager seeks to extract maximum hours and minimum wages – thereby having an interest,

Key

in her capacity as household manager, in devaluing household work.

A domestic worker, then, is not just a person who does a job: like the 'mother' and the 'wife' she is performing a role within the family. In the final analysis, domestic work is not definable in terms of tasks but in terms of a role which constructs and situates the worker within a certain set of social relationships. Even when her tasks are ostensibly the same as those performed by 'mother' or 'wife' – though often not, they are cast as such – her role is different; she affirms a household's status, and in particular affirms the status of the woman of the household.

How to value domestic labour?

value / wage

Domestic workers that I interviewed in European cities were clear that there was no such thing as a 'fair wage' – and this raises the broader issue of how to value domestic work. Domestic labour is not included in national accounts. If a meal is cooked in a restaurant, it is reflected in GDP; but if it is cooked at home, it is invisible. Some attempts are being made, however, to acknowledge domestic labour officially. In the UK, for example, the justifications given for the omission of household production from the system of national accounts in 1993 were:

1   that household services have limited repercussions on the rest of the economy, and the decision to produce a household service entails a simultaneous decision to consume that service;

2   that there are no suitable market prices that can be used to value such services, because they are typically not produced for the market;

3   that imputed values have a different economic significance from income available in cash, so that if household members could choose between producing services for themselves and producing the same services for another household in return for cash, they would probably choose the latter because of the greater range of consumption possibilities it affords.

In 1997, however, the UK Office for National Statistics attempted to produce a Household Satellite account:

> the term satellite is an unfortunate analogy. By almost any measure the household industry is probably larger than that of any of the main single digit heading industries within the production boundary. The accounts could be seen more as twin planets rather than earth and moon. None-theless, difficulties in valuation outweigh these concerns and justify the use of a satellite.

(Murgatroyd and Neuburger 1997: 65)

As is apparent, the Household Satellite report rebuffed the claim that household services have limited repercussions on the rest of the economy. Indeed it found that, depending on how one values domestic work, in the UK it accounts for between 40 per cent and 120 per cent of GDP. The practical problems of valuation outlined in points 2 and 3 nevertheless pose real difficulties. Moreover, point 3 is far from being as simple as it purports to be – there are all kinds of reasons why one would prefer to bake a cake for oneself and one's loved ones rather than sell it on the market. Consumption possibilities are far from the only or indeed principal consideration, and this is of the essence in domestic work. Should we attribute the same value to housework in all households irrespective of the earning potential of their members and of the level of household capital equipment? Or if, for example, a barrister chooses not to work in chambers but to look after her children, should it be valued at £250 an hour, since that is what it is worth *to her*?

The issue becomes even more complex when we attempt to recognise the value of paid domestic labour. If we allow that domestic workers enable the employment of female household members, should we argue that the domestic worker who facilitates the employment of the barrister should earn half the hourly wages of her employer, since without her the barrister could not go to work? But rates of pay in this case will depend directly on the status of the employer and be completely independent of the worker's skills, needs and costs; and the domestic worker who works for a primary school teacher would earn substantially less than the barrister's worker for doing the same job. Or what should we make of the argument that, since most women work for nothing in the home, no one should be paid to do it?

> I had a helper. She said she was coming at 8 am. She comes at 9.30 am. I have already started to do the work of course. I am afraid to give her a machine because maybe she doesn't know how to use it, so I do that. Then we clean out the fridge – together. So I do half the work. So half the money is mine. So if we take foreigners it is because we want to help them.
> (Employer in Athens)

And what about the monetary value of caring work? While motherhood is priceless, when we pay for childcare we are eager to explore the cheapest options, as if mothering and nurturing were separate functions (Rothman 1989).

The young and domestic work

In many countries of the world domestic work is regarded as suitable employment for children and young people, particularly young girls. It is,

22

according to Anti-Slavery International (ASI), one of the most common forms of child labour. In many countries of the south children may be seen performing reproductive tasks considered too arduous for children (or even adults) in the north. Children of five and six care for babies, collect water, make fires and cook. It is not unusual for children to be sent to live with other, wealthier members of the family – one source of my own interest in domestic workers in private households was my grandmother's recollection of her Burmese mother's taking in of poorer relatives who were responsible for childcare and housework in return for her finding them suitable husbands when they grew older. Today such arrangements are increasingly commercialised; children may end up very far from family and home, under the control of adults who do not even have to pretend that the child's well-being is their priority. There are large numbers of children working in such circumstances throughout the world. In Haiti, for example, large numbers of rural families send their children to work in the homes of towndwellers, and in Port-au-Prince alone there are an estimated 40,000 *restaveks* as they are known. Similar systems have been observed in Bangladesh, Philippines and Senegal. They can result in grossly exploitative practices and in poor conditions that impact particularly badly on children, such as lack of adequate physical and emotional care, loss of parental contact and affective relations, and lack of recreation and education. Many children end up in situations like that of Demsee, taken from her village in Sierra Leone to work in Freetown when she was about eight years old. She was handed over to a Lebanese family by her father in exchange for the use of a two-room shelter. Every day began at six o'clock. Apart from being nurse to two young children she had to look after two schoolboys and do all the house cleaning, as well as being at the beck and call of the gardener, chauffeur, cook, watchman and houseboy. She was given only leftovers to eat. 'I was always being beaten. I was beaten so much that after a while I didn't really feel it any more'. Her male employer raped her from the age of nine, and when she was ten he forced her to be circumcised. She put up a fight, but to no avail. Demsee was brought to London by her employers seven or eight times from the age of twelve. She was kept isolated but managed to make friends with a woman whom she met in Regent's Park. She helped her run away, and so Demsee started a life on the run as an 'illegal immigrant'.

In Europe the more typical form of allocating domestic work to young women (though not to children) is the au pair system. This cultural/educational exchange agreement was formalised in Strasbourg in 1969 among some European countries. An au pair, generally speaking, is a young person (almost always, but not exclusively, a young woman) who comes to a foreign country to learn the language, and lives with a host family, helping in their house (often with small children) in return for pocket money. The au pair is not constructed as a worker, and legally can work only a certain number of hours per week. She is not covered by regular social security. Rules governing au pairs (age ranges, hours worked, sum payable and countries of origin) vary from state to state. In the UK, for example, unmarried persons (until July 1993, unmarried 'girls') between 17 and 27 can enter as au pairs providing they are nationals of Malta, Cyprus, Turkey, Bosnia-Herzogovina, Croatia, Slovenia, Macedonia, the Czech Republic, Slovakia and Hungary. They may stay for a maximum of two years. They are supposed to be living as 'part of the family' and 'helping' for no more than five hours a day, with two free days a week. The Home Office suggests up to £35 a week pocket money. The potential for exploiting the young woman under this system is clearly considerable. Au pairs I have spoken to talk of working full days, of being permanently on call and subjected to sexual harassment. Many of the difficulties au pairs encounter in terms of hours, responsibilities and negotiating relationships with members of the household are shared with live-in domestic workers. Au pairs, too, have a sense of being of a lower status than other people in the house. As one Czech au pair put it to me: 'You are part of the family, but you are low, lower than them.' My chats with local au pairs scarcely constitute a scientific survey, but it does seem that what is not shared with migrant domestic workers is the vulnerability to physical abuse, imprisonment and maltreatment. I am not saying that this never happens to au pairs, but in general they feel that, in the worst case, they can return home. The immigration restrictions in the UK mean that, for the most part, the young women do not have small children dependent on their earnings and that going home is not unduly expensive – particularly since au pair agencies often run special cheap coaches between London and the au pairs' countries of origin. When this is not the case, those defined by immigration regulations as 'au pairs' are clearly as vulnerable to abuse and exploitation as those defined as 'domestic workers'. Au pairs in the Netherlands (which is not a signatory to the Strasbourg agreement), for example, must be aged between 18 and 26 and may work for a maximum of one year. It would appear, however, that the au pair system is being used to bring in domestic workers, in particular from the Philippines. In a statement by the Philippine embassy on the au pair issue issued in The Hague on 9 March 1999, it is stated that the term 'au pair' only appeared in the Philippine Overseas Employment Administration in 1994, and then under the classification 'Household Workers'.

This means that from that year the au pair, as far as Filipinos are concerned, has been understood to mean domestic helper – not cultural exchange visitor as originally envisaged by the 1969 agreement.
(Philippine Embassy statement, published in *Philippines News Briefs*, February–March 1999, Netherlands)

In the Philippines, women are charged a placement fee from 10,000 (£165) to 45,000 pesos (£750), while host families in the Netherlands are charged a mediation fee of up to NLG 1,000 (£340) which is often passed on to the au pair. This, combined with the cost of flights to Europe and the fact that they are earning only 'pocket money', means that many of the women have not paid off their debts by the time their permit has expired, and must then become 'illegal'. Adela, a single parent from the Philippines with the immigration status of au pair, found her work intolerable: 'I was like a slave. I had to attend to my employer, her baby, their two dogs ... . Prepare food for my employer's factory personnel ... do the laundry, clean the house and attend to the baby when he cries especially at night' (interview with Fe Jusay, Commission for Filipino Migrant Workers, Netherlands). She was paid 500 guilders at first, and then nothing at all. Unable to endure this treatment, and needing the money for the support of her child in the Philippines, Adela ran away from her employer and is now an undocumented worker. According to the embassy statement,

> the concomitant irregularities and complaints have come about, such as under-compensation, excessive hours, over-work, culture shock, etc. There have been reported cases of abuse, discrimination, runaways and even prostitution.

Nor is this restricted to the Netherlands: such cases have been reported in other European countries, in particular Scandinavia. The au pair system, then, is as open to abuse as any other when the workers it places are vulnerable.

Conclusions

Paying for reproductive labour raises challenging issues, particularly when it is being performed in the employer's home. It is not simply paying for work that the employer does not have time to do. Nor is the paying in itself what makes it distinctive – after all, many domestic workers, particularly children, do not get paid at all. What is peculiar about the position of the domestic worker in terms of work is, first, her role in the household; and, second, her lack of power and authority within the house. Being unable to set limits to her own tasks reinforces her role as the doer of 'dirty' work: 'to my surprise I had to bring also the dog outside at 12.30 in the evening and after that I had to wash the anus of the dog if he shit' (Lourdes, Filipina working in the Netherlands). This job does not have to be done by anyone. To force another person to do it (Lourdes was undocumented and not paid by her Dutch 'employers') is surely only to exercise power by demeaning other people. Not all domestic workers have to perform such degrading tasks, but the boundary between Lourdes' work and that more typically performed by domestic workers is not clear. Indeed this lack of clarity is one of the key difficulties in analysing the experiences of domestic workers, even when one limits the field to the experiences of migrants. The same task may have multiple meanings, depending on the context. While some migrant domestic workers feel that they are paid adequately, and have no complaints about their living and working conditions, others are exploited and abused. It is important, therefore, to have some means of analysing the heterogeneity of their experiences.

Notes

1 See, for example, Benston 1971; Berk 1980; Gardiner 1975 and 1976; Gardiner, Himmelweit, and Mackintosh, 1975; Dalla Costa and James 1972; Gerstein 1973; Vogel 1973; Harrison 1973; Seccombe 1974; Coulson, Magas and Wainwright 1975; Himmelwiet and Mohun 1977; P Smith 1978; Fee 1976.

2 Brooks 1986; Buechler and Buechler 1985; Grosvenor 1972; Harrison 1975; Keckley 1868; Brown 1984; Workman 1985. Also 1933 domestic workers' correspondence with the Roosevelts and with the Secretary of Labor, Frances Perkins, referred to in Palmer 1989.

3 Fairchilds 1984; Katzman 1978; Davidoff 1974 and 1983; Maza 1983; Turkovic 1981; Keat Gin Ooi 1992; Dudden 1983; Sutherland 1981; Katzman 1978; Palmer 1989.

4. Dill 1988; Colen 1984; Palmer 1987; Romero 1992; Rollins 1985; Glenn 1992; Bakan and Stasiulis 1995; Cohen 1987.

5 Cohen 1987; Katzman 1978; Arat-Koc 1989; Bakan and Stasiulis 1995; Macklin 1992; Ruiz 1987; Romero 1992.

6 Lycklama and Heyzer 1994; Lim and Oishi 1996; ILO Equality and Human Rights Coordination Branch 1995; Gulati 1993; see also Anderson 1997(a).

7 The project was focused on first-generation migrant workers who were 'Third Country Nationals' i.e. from outside the European Union. It did not include migrants from within the European union, although migrant women from Spain, Portugal and Greece used to work in the private households of Northern Europe in the 1960s and 1970s. Almost all of these women now work in hotels or as concierges, and those who continue to work in private households are living out. As European Union citizens these workers have rights that Third Country Nationals do not. 'Migrant' is an extremely elastic term, and the complexity of different national definitions and legislations make comparative work on migrants in the European Union a complex

matter (Salt, Singleton and Hogarth 1994). So, for example, while in France until 1996 all those born in the state were automatically French citizens, in Germany a third-generation German born baby of 'Turkish' parentage counts as a migrant of one day's stay. Although my original interest arising from the situation in the UK was in the relationship between immigration legislation and domestic work, this could not be disentangled easily from the racialisation of domestic work in the European Union. I therefore decided that the emphasis in the project would be laid on first-generation migrants, irrespective of their immigration and citizenship status. I was particularly concerned that there was some representation of undocumented migrants, because immigration status in the UK had proved so crucial to the continuing dependence of workers on their employers. Domestic work is largely 'undocumented' in that, when paid for, it is usually on a cash in hand basis, undeclared by worker and by employer (Gregson and Lowe 1994). I use the term 'undocumented', however, to refer to migrant workers who are working without a work permit.

8 I am conscious of the limitations of this sexist and ethnocentric term. Much of the literature on women's unpaid domestic work is cast within this framework, however, and it is the dominant European paradigm.

9 Brenner and Laslett1989; Glenn 1992; Ehrenreich and English 1979; Rubin 1975; O'Brien 1983; Chabaud and Fougeyrollas 1984.

10 See e.g. Bakan and Stasiulis 1995; Cock 1989; Colen 1984; Anderson 1997(a).

3

A Foot in the Door

The Social Organisation of
Paid Domestic Work in Europe

live in or live out

Domestic workers in Europe classify their employment, not by type of work done (whether caring for children or cleaning a house), but by whether it is live-in or live-out. Live-in is often, though by no means always, associated with caring for children, the elderly or the disabled; live-out can be working for a single employing family, but more usually means working for several employers and is generally more task-orientated (cleaning, collecting children from school, ironing, etcetera). Live-in work is more common in Athens, Bologna and Barcelona, but workers in all five cities I visited felt that live-out work was becoming more scarce, and that the expansion in domestic work was for live-in workers. The other key distinctions drawn were country of origin and legal status, documented or undocumented. The experiences of migrant domestic workers vary from city to city, even within Europe, but to dwell on such fragmentation does not help us answer the broader question of why such a large proportion of this work is being done by racialised groups. To negotiate our way around such differences we need to pick out the key variables that order the experiences of migrant domestic workers and to examine how the social organisation of domestic work allows these variables to operate.

The migratory process

Domestic workers come from a wide variety of class backgrounds. Some come from poor landless families, but the high costs associated with recruitment agencies also mean that it is not unusual for them to be middle-class professionals. Domestic workers in the European Union

28

include teachers, nurses, university lecturers and lawyers; others are farmers, vendors, mothers, domestic workers or rural/urban unemployed. Reasons for leaving their countries of origin vary too, but the overriding reason for emigration, even among professionals, is poverty. Women want to earn money for their children, parents, or extended family, and often describe migration in terms of bare survival, although Bertha from Peru contrasted the expectations of life abroad with the reality:

> There is a lot of disinformation. Many people say that you go to Spain, you earn a thousand dollars, you pay back your debt in one year ... and finally you get here, and it's not like that. It takes you six months to find work, your debt is increasing because of interest. You don't earn a thousand dollars ... and you spend rent, food and all this and your stay, which was going to be one year, becomes two, three, and you are still here....

Several of the people I spoke to stated a clear link between politics and economics:

> In the first place you have to recognise the economic conditions of countries, and since I for example am from a South American country the political and economic situation is very poor, and gives rise to a situation which still exists even today in countries of ... what we could call dictatorship, because there is only one political party and each day the situation is getting more and more precarious.
> (Magnolia from Dominican Republic in Barcelona)

Although not legally recognised as such, some fell under the definition of refugees under the Geneva Convention:

> I came in 1988. Mengistu was in power then. You were forced to be a member of the party. Unless you were a member of the party you couldn't work or talk. I was told I would be fined and jailed unless I joined the party so I was running around bribing and fixing my passport to get out – very fast. My father was imprisoned and my brother was killed ... at the time I just wanted to save my life.... I had a tourist visa for 15 days. The UN would not accept my claim. I cannot leave. I work as a domestic.
> (Ilsa, Ethiopian in Athens)

It is interesting to note, in the light of current debates over whether states should grant refugee status to women on the grounds that they are persecuted as a 'particular social group' within the terms of the 1951 Geneva Convention, that in one survey of 175 Moroccan women in Barcelona, more than half were either divorced or had left their husband in order to obtain a divorce. Women who are divorced by their husbands must leave their homes to stay with their parents or brothers who often refuse to accept them and:

There are large numbers of women who do not accept their marriage and ask for divorce but are not able to get it. Some decide to escape, but as the police can chase them if the husband reports it some of these women decide to emigrate from Morocco, to Spain for example, because it is the nearest country ... and so because they are outside their country Muslim law has no validity, and they cannot pursue them.
(Sayd 1993: 7)

Escaping unhappy or forced marriages is not confined to Moroccan women. Domestic workers often give personal problems, escaping abusive relationships, family breakdown or the need to join husbands as reasons for migration, while some women were forced to leave to break up relationships – one Filipina, for example, described to me how she had been sent abroad by her family because she was in love with someone of the 'wrong' religion.

The distinction between 'economic migrant' and 'political refugee' becomes even more blurred when one looks at the case of Eritreans in Athens. They had been given a 'blue card' from the United Nations High Commission for Refugees in Greece. This card, recognising them as refugees, was withdrawn in 1991. Many yearned to return to the new, independent Eritrea but were unable to go: because they had been confined to extremely low paid, undocumented work, they had barely managed to survive in Greece and did not have the money to return to Eritrea, one of the world's poorest countries. So they had to remain in Greece, thereby running up ever-increasing fines as overstayers, and making return to Eritrea even less likely. So, although once 'political refugees' they are now 'economic migrants', trapped in Greece because of economic circumstances.

While there are a variety of reasons for migrating, some nationalities tend to head for specific European countries, while others work in a particular city by chance. For some migrants (Albanians to Greece; Polish to Germany; Moroccans to Spain) geography is a factor in their presence in a particular European state. For others it is colonialism (Peruvians to Spain; Algerians to France) or the immigration policy of receiving states (Turkish to Germany). To some extent the networks that facilitate immigration are initiated, intentionally or not, by the European state: 'It's not our fault that we've emigrated. The Spanish came over to our country first, and they bring us to Spain. They're the ones responsible for the immigration, not us' (Bertha, Peruvian working in Barcelona).

There are currently four basic routes by which international migrants enter employment as domestic workers in private households.

1 Individuals with no contacts
Women may come without work permits, either as tourists or evading

immigration controls, seeking work yet without a fixed position or even occupation in mind, and no contacts in their city of destination. On arrival, women find that they must choose between domestic work in private households or prostitution. They are often extremely vulnerable, with nowhere to stay and no money, and at risk of deportation. These women are those who in Europe seek employment through organisations such as Caritas (in Athens and Barcelona).

2 Informal networks

Women may be sent for by specific employers through personal contacts: so an employer will ask a worker for a recommendation of someone from her country. Where networks and support systems are strong – in Hong Kong for example – this method is often preferred to using agencies, as the worker has more information on her future employer. In Europe, too, these networks are an important means of arranging entry. So, for example,

> My sister said, 'If you want to come to Barcelona, come to Spain and I have got a job for you.' So, I came and the next day I was working…. I came with a friend as well…. Then came the sister of my friend and then came my husband, her husband and her mother, … and we had another house, a bigger one. Then I called everybody and my sister and my cousin she was a secretary and we found her some job – it was easy to find work very quickly – then my son came and then my other sister and so the same with others. In nine months everybody was here.
> (Edita, Peruvian working in Barcelona)

The migrant's relative/friend may lend her the airfare and offer help with employment and accommodation, or simply offer to help support her while she is looking for work, enabling the worker to take out a loan to cover the initial expenses of the flight. In Barcelona it was not unusual for contacts to arrange false employers for their friends: asking Spaniards to offer a job to a friend back home to enable them to get a visa, but with both parties understanding that, on entry to Spain, the migrant will look for work elsewhere. There is considerable scope for misunderstanding here, but it has become much more unusual since the Spanish state now checks the bank balances and tax returns of potential employers to ensure that they can afford the worker they are proposing to employ.

Even when women are entering Europe to work for specific employers, they work illegally. They are often told that their employers will arrange their papers, only to be let down after they arrive – though, given the difficulty if not impossibility of arranging work permits, employers may have intended to do so originally, but found the bureaucracy too much.

Irene was told to come as a tourist to Athens and her papers would be arranged later. Having been maltreated by her first employer she left after one year, and spent years trying to regularise her status.

> The employers there took my passport and my papers and they said they were going to make me a nursing aide. My salary was low 60,000 [drachmas = £170] plus 15,000 [drachmas = £42] allowance for food, but even though it was low, because they said they were going to sort out my papers I was happy. But after two years they still hadn't sorted my papers and I said, 'Well, it's enough'.... Since then I was searching for someone to process my papers, but now it's hopeless.
> (Irene, Filipina in Athens)

3 Agencies

The migration recruitment industry is now extremely sophisticated and powerful – the Philippines government's attempt to impose a general ban on Filipinas working as entertainers in Japan in 1991 was successfully opposed by recruiters, promoters, employers and talent managers (an estimated 80 per cent of the entertainment industry in Japan is controlled by the Yakuza). Recruiters range from one-person operations, ferrying people across the Malacca Straits, to huge criminal syndicates. Private recruitment agencies are responsible for nine out of every ten foreign placements in most of the major labour-sending countries of Asia. The migrant is often totally dependent on the agent, who may be the only access she has to employment, her only contact in the receiving country, and the person who arranges her travel documents and keeps her passport. Crucially the agent may also act as a money lender, charging extortionate rates of interest for the fee and expenses the migrant must pay in order to migrate. Debt-financed migration is a serious problem and combines with the legislation of receiving countries to tie migrants to their employers.

Governments of sending countries have made some efforts to control the proliferation of recruitment operators by registering agencies – there are more than 700 licensed recruitment agencies in the Philippines alone. Although male migrants from the Philippines make good use of these licensed agencies, there is some evidence that they are less likely to be used by women, particularly domestic workers and entertainers. Moreover, licensed agents do not necessarily mean legal recruitment, and it is often easy for migrants, employers and agencies to circumvent legislation. For example, the majority of Filipino domestic workers in Singapore, although recruited by licensed agencies, leave the Philippines on tourist visas and apply for work permits only on arrival in Singapore.

There are agencies which specialise in arranging for workers to enter Europe. Sometimes a particular job is in prospect, but more often than not the agency simply brings the woman to a particular city and leaves her. Such agencies were referred to by workers in Paris, Athens, Barcelona and Berlin, but the most detailed information was given by Peruvian workers in Barcelona. They described how different agencies have different means of operation: some obtain false documents such as passports and visas, or a false offer of employment signed by a Spanish citizen. Such assurances cost approximately $3,000 when there is in fact no job at all – sometimes to the worker's surprise. Some agencies arrange bribes for consular officials to give visas – apparently the going rate was $3,000. A group of Peruvian women describe how agencies work:

> In Trujillo there are international travel agencies, and some of the people who work there know the ways out of Peru, they know the levels of need and that many people are taking this as an option ... and what he does is offer tickets to Europe, specifically Spain, which is where he knows most people want to go. Then he says, 'Look, I'll take you to Spain in a roundabout way'.... Then you give him the money ... but if you can't get in, and the police deport you, you can't get your money back.... They charge between $3,500 and $3,800, or up to $5,000 in many cases. Then you go to an EU country, you take a tour, then they pass you to some smugglers who bring you by land to Spain. So what they do more or less is give you a sort of orientation and take all your money.... If you don't have money they'll accept that once you've arrived you'll repay them, because to enter any European country you have to have travel money that you can use to justify your stay there as a tourist.... And what happens, when you arrive in Europe they don't accept you for x reasons. Nobody is master of the world and I think that people should be free to live where they want, there shouldn't be borders, we have needs and they ought to give us our chance to be able to earn enough to live.... But they return you, simply and purely because they don't want you to stay.

> – Yes the majority of agencies are like she says but there are also clandestine agencies. These agencies also charge you huge amounts and then they dump you.

> – They get you a map and say to you, go to here, arrive here, here here, and finally here you are....

> – For example they said they could get me a tourist visa to other countries, so I could be a tourist travelling to different places. But I was refused a visa, so in the end he said, 'I won't send you to that country, because this country doesn't need a visa', so they sent me to the back of beyond....

> – We Latin Americans are very watched, considered very suspicious, and when we showed our Peruvian passports they looked at us from head to toe

... [W]e were three. Then we had to show everything in our suitcase. And when we had got out of all that we had to look to see how to get here spending as little money as possible or none at all ... they told us that for $500 you can go to the furthest part of Spain. But the reality was very different.

Informal networks may also mask unlicensed agents working for financial gain: for example, Filipino women married to Yakuza who paint a rosy picture of life in Japan; or Burmese sex workers, released from brothels in Thailand on condition that they recruit a number of other young women from their village to replace them.

4 Accompanying employer

In Europe and the USA workers may also accompany their employers. Although quite clearly they are entering to work, it is the practice in Europe to give them a tourist visa, or a visa forbidding them to take up employment except with the employer they are accompanying, who may even be named on their passport. This practice has been most thoroughly exposed in the UK through the work of Kalayaan, but it is also operating in Spain, Germany and France.

Like me, like my situation, they take their chance and they run away. People come here for their holidays. [They bring with them] not only Filipinas, Sri Lanka, Marruecos. Because usually tourist places ... because in Malaga it's all Arabic people there, they all have big houses there, it all belongs to Arabic people. It's a tourist visa not a working visa you get when you come here with a family here. Me I have only working visa in Kuwait, otherwise I have only tourist visa, in Germany and in Spain.
(Aida, Filipina in Barcelona)

A compatriot who was working for a female employer's family in Germany had to run away: 'She cannot do anything because she does not have her passport and her employers say that she is a visitor with them. For two years a visitor! It doesn't go.'

How to find work in Europe

Once arrived, migrants may use several means to find employers. In Europe these do not vary according to their legal status (except for some agencies and organisations who demand to see passports). Advertisements in newspapers, for example, are just as likely to be placed by undocumented as by documented workers. Migrants may use their personal networks, taking up additional work offered by employers' friends for example, or by friends' employers. This has advantages for workers, who do not have to pay for the service, and for the employers since, unlike agencies, tapping into relatives and friends of domestic workers employed by acquaintances is free and there is some guarantee that they are trust-worthy. One employment agency in Barcelona admitted: 'you have to realise that employers only go to agencies when it is difficult to get a girl any other way'. In general 'direct hire', as it is known, seems to operate very efficiently. There are problems with this kind of networking, though, particularly for women who are relying on contacts they have made by chance. Of course in some cases these are reliable and provide real support and assistance, but there are other examples of downright exploitation and abuse. Moreover, these networks do not give any real guarantee to the worker that conditions and work will be satisfactory. While the employer often has the added insurance of a reference from a previous employer, the worker must simply take it on trust that the friend of her friend's employer will not abuse or exploit her. Furthermore, use of these networks can shade into commercial transactions with individuals charging for their contacts.

Churches and NGOs can be extremely important as informal place-ment agencies. In Barcelona the Catholic Church mission of La Bonanova coordinates employment placement for Peruvian domestic workers. Angeles Escrivà has analysed some of its records and found that an average of ten new people a day used its work placement services in 1995, 80 per cent of them women:

Table 3.1 *Legal status of Peruvian women looking for employment as domestic workers*

Legal status	1990	Pre-1990	1991	1992	1993	1994	Up to September 1995	Total
Documented	–	60	100	33	23	15	20	251
Undocumented	–	3	32	31	58	114	104	342
Prepar*	–	–	16	15	16	23	9	79
Asylum	–	–	5	8	4	4	–	21
Total	35	65	155	87	102	164	141	765

Source: Table 7 in Escrivá, A. (1996).
* This abbreviation is not explained in the original. I assume that it means those whose legal status is in transition.

Moroccans, too, will call churches and church agencies for work (though not those mentioned above, which clearly work with particular national groups). The women workers in Bayt Al Taqafa said that their being Muslim did not make them reluctant to use Christian networks:

> In North Africa the church is very present, and people go to it to find work and support even if they're not Christians, so they're used to that form of

work and support. In fact many of the women who come to Spain have learnt to read and to sew through church organisations in Morocco so that isn't a problem.

Caritas Barcelona does some placement work, often for Moroccans. It is often the refuge of the most desperate:

> Basically our problem is that, of course the people who come to us are the most marginalised. Because the others can go to the town hall or use other services.... So people who come to us are those who don't have documents, some because they have only just arrived or who have been here a while but have lost their jobs and haven't been able to renew and find themselves in this situation.

Although they do not offer any formal placement service, they do have employers contacting them with offers of employment – but often this work is very poorly paid, or even not paid at all, simply an offer of accommodation in exchange for looking after an old person, for example. Caritas refuses these employers, only passing on offers where the salary is 'decent' which means that they often turn away potential employers. This is not the practice in Caritas Athens, whose main focus is on placing workers with employers. It is regarded by migrants as offering very low-paid jobs, and only to be visited if desperate. For new arrivals, however, and people with no network of friends to pass on jobs, it is clearly an important employment clearing house and it deals with a wide range of nationalities. More informally, women of all nationalities and religions attend Mass in large Catholic churches in downtown Athens as a way of meeting each other and potential employers. Protestant evangelical churches, too, are important access points for workers and employers. In 1995 the Missionaries of Charity in Athens were beginning to work with Sri Lankan women, one of the most marginalised of migrant groups in Athens and were already being contacted by potential employers. As one of the sisters told me: 'I have three jobs at the moment. They might not pay more, but at least there is some connection and they won't maltreat them ... the people are related to us so we know they will not abuse.' Migrants' organisations may also be important points of contact for employers and domestic workers, though it is rarely the associations' priority. So in Barcelona the Filipino Centre had stopped responding to these requests as they found that it took up too much time and not to any good end, since 'the real relationship was between the women and their employers'. They still do this work, though not in an organised way, and estimate that one or two potential employers contact the Centre every day looking for Filipino workers.

Among the EU states France is unique in that it has a government-promoted system for putting prospective workers and employers in touch with one another. The promotion of *associations intermédiares* began in 1987. These are voluntary associations, often locally based, which liaise between unemployed people and those needing household workers, not just putting them in touch with each other, but acting as the employer. So the individual employer pays not the worker but the association. In 1994 the government estimated such agencies dealt with 27 per cent of all employers and 41 per cent of those employers aged over 70, disposing of 35–40 million working hours.

Placement agencies

As well as informal networks and contacts, there are also employment agencies for domestic work. These are a broad grouping ranging from the upmarket and professionalised to the downright illegal. There is considerable resentment among domestic workers at the cost of agencies. In Spain, for example, they typically charge the worker 1,000 pesetas (£5.50) for registration every three months, but there are also those that take a cut of the workers' wages every month:

> and she told me with this condition, that I had to pay the agency 10 per cent of what I earned ... then I went to the interview and the senora paid me 100,000 (£550) then I had to pay the girl from the agency 10,000 (£55) each month ... at first I refused to do this, then my cousin, because it was my cousin who arranged all this, my cousin knew her and she said this is what happens with agencies, they take this and if you get into problems with them then they don't give you any more work.
> (Delia, from the Dominican Republic working in Barcelona)

Workers were extremely hostile towards agencies. Their registration fee did not guarantee a job, and to increase chances of work women had to register with three or four agencies, a significant outgoing when a worker is unemployed. Of all the cities visited, agencies were most common in Barcelona. In Athens they were given a wide berth by those workers interviewed, who felt that they were fronts for the sex industry, while in Paris they tended to be very up-market and for professionalised domestic workers.

Advertisements

Responding to or placing a small ad in local newspapers is an important means of finding work. Personal advertisements tend to be used by people who have been working in the city for some time. There are always far more requests for work in these columns than there are jobs offered, and the migrant domestic workers interviewed had used personal advertisements with varying success. Edita, who arrived in Spain from Peru in 1991, had considerable success with personal advertisements, though admittedly that was at a time when jobs were more easily available:

> I found a job as an *interina*, and I was working for one man on his own and then I was working for a very rich couple. I have got all at those jobs by put a job in *Primavera (Primerama)*, the foreigners here use that a lot and it's good to put an advert in there, because then they call you. They called me and at the time you could take your choice. There were so many who called, more than you would want and you just ask and you listen to them, and then you decided which job you wanted to go for.

Bertha, also from Peru, was less sanguine: 'I put in an advertisement looking for work in a magazine called *Primerama*, but I didn't have any luck, in fact people kept calling me making indecent propositions.' When Magnolia from the Dominican Republic related her experience of responding to an advertisement in the *Vanguardia* and discovering that the employer was only ever taking on employees for a probationary period of one month with no contract and then sacking them, thereby avoiding paying them a salary, her description of the job was immediately recognised by Bianca from Brazil: 'I know him, he was always looking for somebody. I always saw his advertisement in the newspaper, "Señor solo con niña en Fiches...". I never went for an interview with him because I wanted to know why he was always looking for a chica....' The difficulty of personal advertisements is clearly that they are unregulated, and while this makes them useful, particularly for undocumented workers, they offer no guarantees or safeguards. In Berlin it is particularly noticeable that domestic workers advertising in newspapers stipulate 'No Sex', suggesting that those who place them believe that an offer of 'housework' could be misinterpreted.

Although domestic work is atomised and workers are very isolated, networks (of kin, friendship, nationality, religion) are extremely important for placement. Agencies and advertisements are not about to replace 'direct hire', which saves both workers and employers the agency fee. Employers tap into their female friendship networks to find a worker, workers use their female friendship networks to find employers. This is true for both live-in and live-out work. When the arrangement is not commercialised, belonging to a network/community can be an important reference for an employer who is looking, not simply for a worker, but more often than not for a certain type of person. It may operate the other way round in ensuring a community check on employer abuse: as the worker is an equal member of the church community, so the community will reprimand another member who abuses her. I have no proof, however, that workers are regarded as equal within the church communities, and was offered no example of such sanctions being used. Indeed, in general it seems that networks are used to the employers' advantage, but instances where workers have used networks to attempt to sanction employers suggest that it can work. In Kalayaan, for example, a note is made in the employment request book against the names of employers who do not pay workers or mistreat them, and this means that other workers – or at least those workers who are organised – can avoid them. This process may also work more informally when workers come together on their days off and exchange information.

Live-in work

Newly arrived migrants are often under particular pressure to find work in order to repay the debt owed, either to agencies or to family and friends, for assistance in gaining entry. In Hong Kong, for example, Filipinas are usually in debt on arrival according to the '5/6 rule' – borrow 5 and pay 6 on a weekly rate. The debt is high – agency fees in 1992 were HK\$12,000–15,000 (US\$1,500–2,000) – so it is a priority for women to refinance their debt at lower rates of interest. Overseas domestic workers account for 10 per cent of finance company JCG Holdings' business, and they keep five out of their 24 offices open on Sunday specifically to cater for them. Many women surrender their passports to credit agencies as a guarantee of payment: should their contract be terminated they are forced into illegality because they cannot return until they have repaid the debt. Domestic workers may add to their debt incurred on arrival in their efforts to obtain residence and working permits. Repayment of debt is a priority and the strain that it places on new arrivals in considerable:

> Many come with debts from their country because they have borrowed for the ticket, and that's money you have to pay back, if you know what I mean ... a majority come from my country with money they have borrowed, relatives have mortgaged their house or sold them.... Then you arrive in a country with a debt hanging over you, in an illegal situation ... so that if you go to the police they can put you in prison. You don't know anyone who can get you out of there, they can deport you to your country, which is where you have the debt ... and they can put you in prison there as well.
> (Bertha, a Peruvian working in Barcelona)

Pressure to repay this debt forces workers into live-in domestic work, and can make them very vulnerable.

At first sight, live-in domestic work may seem a reasonable option for a newly arrived migrant. Problems of accommodation and employment are solved in one, the worker minimises her expenses and can acclimatise herself to a new language and culture. The Caritas volunteer in Athens explained:

> It's easy to find live-in if you don't ask too much. Fifty thousand a month, and you can find work, maybe an old lady, she just wants small work and the company. So you don't have to work hard, and that is good money, it is money in your pocket. You don't have to spend, the lady will give you your clothes, will take you to the hospital, give you good food. You don't have to spend money.... The foreigners don't think about it. Rent, electricity, food, that can easily be 90,000 [£253] a month.

Live-in work minimises expenses and provides urgently needed shelter. Accommodation is more than a place to live, it is shelter from the police, and many new arrivals and long-term migrants alike are undocumented and terrified of deportation. Workers in Athens described how a police crackdown on undocumented migrants in 1993 meant that they worked unpaid on their days off because they did not want to go outside and risk being caught by the police.

Live-in work is not a good financial arrangement for the worker in the medium term, however. While she seems to incur no expenses, employers will often excuse paying her a low wage because she is being paid 'in kind'. The Caritas volunteer again: 'I heard one Ethiopian say she left because there was no food in the house. Of course, if you ask 130,000 [*drachmas* = £366] you will not get food, but if you get 30,000 [£85] then you will get food'. If rent, electricity and food come to 90,000 [£253] drachmas a month as she claimed, then it seems 'the foreigners' have made excellent calculations in preferring live-out work! Paying in kind makes no allowance for the fact that migrants have come to earn money, usually to send back to families in their countries of origin. As one woman put it:

> You go to work, you need the money to feed your children, and in place to pay you they give you old clothes. 'I give you this, I give you this.' They give you the things, but me, I need the money. Why come? I am a human being. (Maggie, a Zaïrean working in Athens)

These sorts of 'payments' are much more common among live-in than live-out workers.

One of the greatest problems for live-in workers is lack of control over hours: they are usually on call twenty-four hours a day. This is the most common complaint among live-in domestic workers, whatever city they live in, whether they work for 'good' or 'bad' employers:

[Y]ou're working the minute you open your eyes and the minute you close your eyes. You keep your strength and your body going so that you will finish work ... you will keep on waiting to your employer till they get sleep because although you finish your work, example you finish ironing, everything, putting the children to bed or the elder person in bed, even you put them in bed at ten o'clock still there are other members of the family. So you keep on observing, 'Oh, can I sleep or maybe they will call me to give them food or to give them a yoghurt'.... And even if you are sleeping if you are already sleeping still you can feel that you are still on duty, isn't it.
(Nona, a Filipina in Athens)

Workers commonly complain of having to be available at both ends of the day, early in the morning for children and late at night for entertaining guests. It is not simply a question of long hours, as the above quotation makes clear, but of permanent availability. This is particularly arduous when the work involves babies or elderly people who can be demanding at night, as Bertha working in Barcelona put it:

I think that they can never pay you enough for working twenty-four hours a day ... for a job involving such sacrifice as living twenty-four hours a day with a person who has Alzheimer's, who has senile dementia, that work is very demanding.

This is compounded by some employers' apparent dislike of seeing their worker rest: live-in workers complained that if their employer caught them sitting down, they would immediately find them a task to do. Clearly this is particularly difficult when workers are spending not just a few hours, but all their time in their employers' houses and, unlike those in live-out work, cannot control their time and make their own breaks.

The daily exploitation of live-in domestic workers is illustrated by a diary kept for six days by Sally, a Filipina working in Paris for a family with two school-age children whose parents both work full-time. Although paid to work 45 hours a week, in fact she worked for 69 hours and 25 minutes. She worked between 10 hours 10 minutes and 17 hours 30 minutes a day. On Thursday and Friday she finished at 12.30 a.m. and 1.30 a.m. having been at work since 8am with no break even for lunch. After finishing preparation of dinner she routinely travelled for one hour to an elderly relative of the employers, gave him a meal, cleaned and made his bed. Scarcely surprising that she complains about her hours:

Too much hours and unfortunately God knows if she's going to pay me for that, even if she's the one who said she will pay extra hours I never receive the right price for the hours I had for them ... well for how many years that's life working – few hours for yourself. Anyway, got used to them. They're better than what I had before. So wait for Monday and the ball rolls again with the same routine.

41

Live-in workers in Europe do usually (though not always) have one day off a week. The day off is the only time when the worker can 'be herself', quite literally. It is her chance to meet friends and compatriots. Remedios, a Filipina working in Athens, expressed how important this is.

> Sunday is the day all the Filipinos meet and they have basket-ball, they eat Filipino food and it's so nice, it's all I ask, once a month, Saturday and Sunday and the basket-ball court. I am very, very lonely because I live far from Athens, and I want to have Sunday off and my employer just said, 'we'll see'.... Because they out on the boat at the weekend and the house is lonely so I am in the house and maybe somebody will break in or something like that, so I just have to be there and it's so quiet. And all the time I'm thinking, 'Oh now they're in the basket-ball, they're talking', and I have to put on the television or the radio, because it's quite as if I'm going mad.

Domestic work is isolating even when it is the responsibility of a person who is living with family and friends nearby. How much more so when the worker is in a foreign country with such limited access to those with whom she can enjoy an equal relationship!

'Day off swapping', when employers unilaterally decide to change the worker's day off to suit their own convenience, is common. Workers' free time is also often restricted unreasonably – for example, an employer may require that the worker give breakfast to the children before she leaves and be back in time to give them their tea. In Athens and Barcelona it is usual for workers to spend one night away from the employing household as part of their day off. This can be at the worker's initiative, to ensure that she is not available to her employers, or at the employers' insistence, on the grounds that they should not have to provide accommodation for a worker when she is not available to them. No thought is given by the employers as to how the worker is to provide for herself in this 'time off' – usually workers shared flats with large groups of compatriots as an insurance against sudden unemployment and for days off.

Hours, therefore, are a serious problem for live-in domestic workers. Nina in Athens put the employers' point of view:

> She kept asking me, 'How many hours must I do my housework?' I explained that in a house there are no hours ... so I told her, until 2 p.m. just to keep her quiet. One day, she was with a dustpan and brush. She heard the clock, two o'clock, she put the brush down.. and then said, 'It's time for our lunch.' I asked her, 'Why did you leave the brush?' 'Because at two o'clock I finish.' That girl had a problem with her mind.

'In a house there are no hours' may be true for the household manager. It is particularly true of caring for young children and older people, nor would anyone deny the importance of breaks from caring work, whether it is performed by relatives or by paid carers. The problem for the worker is that her work is not definable in terms of tasks performed, nor is there any objective standard – of cleanliness and tidiness, for example – that she must meet; the standard is imposed by the household manager, and the standard can always be raised. It is one thing to be employed to do specific tasks, or to be paid for a set number of hours to do an ill-defined job, but to have to work twenty-four hours at an ill-defined job risks serious exploitation. The difficulty for the worker is that, as 'domestic worker' is a role, living in she has no rest from that role, but is living it twenty-four hours a day. It is as if the employer is buying, not just her time, but her very self.

Another common complaint among live-in domestic workers is lack of privacy. Sometimes they are not even given their own bedrooms, or they must sleep with open doors:

> They told me my door must always be open because the children might cry, but the children were fifteen, and the visitors' bathroom was next to my bedroom, and I am afraid, and I said, 'Please, this is my privacy'.
> (Maria, a Filipina in Athens)

This lack of privacy means that the worker has literally no time to herself, and, as indicated above, leaves her vulnerable to sexual abuse and rape:

> she drove me away because I quarrelled with her son because her son entered my room at 12.30 at night … He entered, but when the door squeaked I woke up and then I saw the door open … and he was there, standing there by my bed looking at me.
> (Tess, a Filipina in Barcelona)

A live-in domestic worker may have no private life, except for those hours snatched on her day off. This has profound consequences for her as a human being. I have already mentioned the problems faced by domestic workers who have children but who cannot care for them. Also devastating is the realisation that when you are working live-in you cannot have children: 'My biggest sacrifice is that I cannot have children, if I did I would have to leave my job. You can't have anyone to stay with you – relatives or friends' (Marie, from Côte d'Ivoire working in Parma). Workers are generally in the prime reproductive years, between twenty and forty, but there was no worker I met who thought that pregnancy would end anywhere else but on the streets, and for those workers who did fall pregnant, this was borne out:

> My wife she was here 15 years, she come for a Greek woman, brought her here 15 years ago.… She sacked her away from the home because she was pregnant. So after she deliver she don't want her again. To work for

somebody for 15 years you become family, but she do nothing for us. Nothing. Nothing she gave to her.
(Emanuel, Ghanaian man in Athens)

Thus the employer can control all aspects of the domestic worker's life, not just her work, and also enjoys almost total control over her time. The clearest example of this is the many arguments live-in workers have with employers over food, surely one of the most basic of human requirements. Baths, sleeping arrangements, letters from home, clothes worn – there is no aspect of the live-in worker's life that cannot be scrutinised by the employer.

Live-out work

Live-out work is almost universally preferred to living in. Employment placement agencies interviewed were clear that while demand from employers was for live-in workers, the demand from workers was for live-out placements (Table 3.2).

Living out usually means working for several different employers, though it is not unusual in London, Paris and Barcelona to work for only one family full-time while living out. In Spain, where it is most common, this arrangement is called *interina*. In France, too, there is some considerable demand, particularly from people with young children, for workers to live out but work full time for a family. The long hours this entails were confirmed by two interviews with French employers of foreign workers: Brigitte described her worker as doing 'everything: she looks after the children, does the ironing, the cleaning and the shopping'. Her hours were 8.15 a.m.–7.30 p.m. daily. Celine's worker works from 9 a.m. to 9 p.m. daily: 'She basically takes care of the children: feeds them, helps them with their clothes, washes them. She also does the ironing and the cleaning of the house. She sometimes does the cooking and the shopping.'

Some 'full-time' workers who live out combine their full-time job with extra part-time work. Lira, an undocumented worker employed full-time by a family of four in Paris, is paid for 40 hours a week, 1.30 p.m.–9.30 p.m. daily. Like Sally, she kept a diary for one week, and this showed that in that week she worked a total of 44 hours and 40 minutes. This unpaid overtime is clearly not as excessive as Sally's – it takes her between forty-five minutes and one hour to travel to her employer's house, however, and so she spends one and a half to two unpaid hours a day travelling. Moreover she has only one chance to eat – the fifteen minutes while they are eating their dessert. She earns 1,500 francs (£206) a week, roughly the French minimum wage, but with no taxation or

Table 3.2   Requests for live-in and live-out work in Barcelona

Agency	Employer requests		Worker requests		Comments
	Live-in	Live-out	Live-in	Live-out	
MBS	75%	25%	20 %	80 %	
PO	90 %	10%	No details		'All foreigners work live-in, all Spanish work live-out'
GS	70 %	30%	No details		'Filipinas compete with Spanish for hourly work'
J					Foreigners live in Spaniards live out
SOS	10 %	90%	Foreigners want live-in		Mainly deals with Spanish workers
PS	90 %	10 %	30 %	70 %	
E	50 %	50 %	No details		'New girls who do not speak Spanish work live-in'
R	85 %	15 %	15 %	85 %	
BS	25 %	75 %	25 %	75 %	'Spanish women do not want to work live-in'

Note: This table is drawn up from responses to questions to agencies: 'What is the proportion of employer demand for live-in vs live-out domestic workers?' and 'What is the proportion of employee supply for live-in vs live-out?'. 'Comments' are drawn from other relevant responses.

benefits since she is undocumented. She also works for two mornings a week cleaning a business premises, where her work includes washing by hand the clothes of the company president. Lira lives in the same apartment block as a former employer, and in the six days recorded in her diary she visits them twice.

> Monday 15 January 1996, 9.30 a.m.: Went down to my former employer in the same building and cooked/prepared for them lasagne for their dinner with some invited visitors free of charge because they're my very first employer and as if I'm part of their family already....
> Saturday 20 January 1996, 6.00 p.m.: I have to visit my former employer with the three kids, which the eldest was the first took care here in Paris ...

I had to cook for the children and play for them afterwards. This is free of charge.

Unlike Lira, most of the live-out workers that I know have three or more employers. In this case time management becomes particularly important. Margie, an undocumented Filipina in Paris, is married and lives with her husband. She works for five employers. Her most regular employer employs her for 22.5 hours (mornings Monday–Saturday, except Wednesday). She worked 52 hours and 5 minutes during the Monday–Saturday that she kept her diary. If one adds the time spent travelling to work and between jobs (13.45 hours), however, this becomes 65 hours and 50 minutes – nearly as long as Sally, who is live-in. Travel time (amounting to nearly one and a half days a week) is not paid. Margie eats with her husband in the evening and prepares lunch for both of them to take to work in the morning. It is noticeable that she spends far more time on her and her husband's domestic chores than the other two diarists, even though she has no children. Her husband is also available to help her at her fifth employers on Saturday afternoon, which means that this job is completed in two rather than four hours. In general the tasks she performs are similar to those outlined by Sally and Lira, including taking children to school, ironing, preparing food and washing. Her time is far more tightly managed than the other workers – principally because efficient time management is clearly crucial to her work:

> Monday 15 January 1996, 1.20–1.30 p.m.: I put the shoes of the little boy and took him down with me to give him to his grandmother waiting at the garden.
> 1.30–1.40 p.m.: I run to my afternoon job....
> Wednesday 17 January 1996, 12.10–1 p.m.: clean the bathroom, toilet, wash 4 pieces of brassiere, clean the salon.
> 1.00–1.05: I run to my semi-full-time job for baby-sitting and cleaning etc.

Live-out work then, makes great demands, including efficient time management, finding work and travelling between jobs.

The advantages of live-out work are clear. Less personal control tends to be exercised by the employer over the worker. The worker is less dependent on the employer, partly because she usually has several employers at any one time and to lose one does not entail the loss of her entire livelihood, and also because she has her own accommodation and is not dependent on her employer for her living space. One must beware of painting too rosy a picture, though, for those who live out are often juggling their own family commitments and domestic responsibilities with those attached to their employers' households. Adgera is a 42-year-old Algerian woman who has lived in France for fifteen years and now has three children, aged eight to thirteen. She works as a domestic worker for four hours every morning, tidying up, hoovering and washing clothes. Her hours are not fixed, which makes it easy for her to combine work with her own responsibilities: 'That is the reason why I can take my children to school in the morning because if I have to start work, I normally start it at 9 a.m. to finish at 1 p.m.; I also have free time to go and collect the kids from school in the evening.' However Adgera is not paid any money. She is cleaning her landlord's flat for a rent reduction – though the rent, at 4,500 francs a month is still expensive. Sara, a Moroccan woman who came to France in 1990, is employed to take a child to school at 8.30 a.m. and to collect her and give her tea in the evening. She earns 40 francs (£5.50) for a six-hour day, considerably below what she could earn if she were declared:

> For taking a kid to school you get 10 francs [£1.35]. For looking after kid work, I earned 40 francs [£5.50] per day. Not much, but I was not complaining because not only was it a job in the 'dark' – in other words without out paper – but it was also easy work in itself.

Hers was 'easy work' because it was possible to combine it with having to collect and feed her own children, aged six, five and four.

The usual pattern among migrant domestic workers in Europe is live-in work on arrival followed by living out after some years. By then the domestic worker has paid off her debts, is more accustomed to the country, and is integrated into networks that can help her find employers. Many of the difficulties experienced by more settled people arise partly as a result of the transition from live-in to live-out work. According to Caritas in Barcelona this was a common source of difficulty:

> Our worker in Rabal district says that of the situations she finds, many domestic workers find work quite quickly, but it's live-in work. Then straight away they bring their family and that causes many problems ... because now she's brought her children she can no longer carry on working live-in because she has to have a flat and to look after her children. She thought because she has found live-in work, she would be able to find live-out, hourly work but she hasn't found it. So the situation deteriorates. And our work in Rabal has found many cases like this.... Because it's not the same as I said before, you can find work as live-in but hourly work is super, super full.

Conclusions

Migrant domestic workers in Europe are an extremely varied group. They come from all continents of the world, from a wide variety of backgrounds and experiences, though where they come from and what their immigration status is depends very much on the policies of the receiving European states. Their experiences in the countries to which they travel vary widely too: while some workers are happy in their work and are well treated by their employers, many feel exploited and demeaned by employers' demands. Speaking very broadly, two factors have a significant impact on the living and working conditions of domestic workers: whether or not they are live-in (their relation to their employer), and whether or not they have papers (their relation to the state). Figure 3.1 offers a diagramatic representation:

Figure 3.1

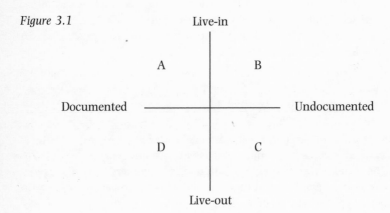

Those workers who are in sector D are likely to be more independent of employers and to enjoy better living and working conditions than those in A, B and C. Those in sector B are particularly vulnerable, since they are dependent on their employers for accommodation, must be permanently available, and, should they come to the attention of the state, are liable to be deported. I posit this only as a rule of thumb since some documented workers, for example, may be dependent on their employers for their immigration status. Each worker brings to her situation her own history, personality and psychobiography, and these can make all the difference in managing the intensely personalised relationship with her employer.

This chapter has provided an overview of the social organisation of domestic work for migrants; in the next, I examine the living and working conditions of migrant domestic workers in the different European cities visited, and give some indication of their variation from city to city.

4

Invisible Women (I)

Migrant Domestic Workers in Southern Europe

Whether workers are documented or undocumented, live-in or live-out depends to a large extent on immigration policy and employers' demands. While there are workers in all cities who fall into each sector of Figure 3.1, patterns stand out. Live-in work predominates in Athens, Barcelona and Bologna; live-out work in Paris and Berlin. There are significant numbers of undocumented workers in Athens, Berlin and Barcelona. Does this model help to explain some of the variation in workers' experiences across Europe?

Greece

One of the crucial factors in appreciating the situation of migrant domestic workers in Athens is that the majority of them are undocumented. Since the late 1970s people have come from Poland and the Third World to work in construction, agriculture and domestic work, usually overstaying tourist or student visas. About half of the migrants working in Greece are Albanians, many of whom stay only temporarily – sometimes for months, sometimes for two or three years – before returning to Albania, and perhaps re-entering Greece some time later. Church and migrant organisations estimate that the largest other single nationalities are the Poles (80,000–100,000) and Filipinos (40,000). In 1995 the Organisation for Economic Cooperation and Development (OECD) claimed that about one in twelve employed persons in Greece is a foreigner, but that the majority are undocumented and earning about half the going rate:

> foreign labour is used by many households for care of small children and older persons, as well as for house maintenance and repairs, where it

provides low-priced and flexible labour. The large size of the informal economy (estimated at 30 per cent of the total) and established networks that assist newcomers with information and accommodation contribute to the continuing flows.
(OECD 1995: 93)

The report goes on to argue that this state of affairs is regarded by many as beneficial to the Greek economy and society. This finding was confirmed when in 1996/7 the government began to consider legalising the migrant population and the Ministry of Labour was sent 62 reports and letters in response to a draft decree. Of these, 57 emphasised the usefulness of migrant labour.

The reason for the continued widespread illegality among migrants in Athens lies in the 1991 'Law for Foreigners'. Under this law priority for employment goes to Greek nationals, 'ethnic Greeks', nationals of other EU countries and foreigners granted refugee status by the Greek government. Only if an employer cannot fill the post with an applicant in one of these categories can they apply for a work permit for a foreigner. This must be renewed annually for a maximum of five years. In 1975, 52.5 per cent of work permits were issued to non-Europeans, and in 1992 this was down to 17 per cent. In 1975, similarly, 16.5 per cent of work permits were issued to non-European women, and in 1992 this was down to 7.1 per cent.

The alleged purpose of the 1991 legislation was to link entry and residence to the needs of the Greek economy; its failure is demonstrated by the continuing demand for migrant labour and the dependence of the Greek economy on undocumented migrants. The adoption of a tough stance on migration by Greece has not meant that it is controlled. I met many people who had entered Greece without passing through immigration controls, though several of their companions had died or otherwise been lost along the way. Many also enter the country as tourists. As well as people continuing to enter the country, the numbers of undocumented workers are swollen by the difficulty in leaving the country. The 1991 Act gave large powers to the Minister of Public Order to pass rules on matters of immigration and asylum. These include passing heavy fines and prison sentences on people who have overstayed or entered the country illegally. Those who enter without documents are subject to imprisonment for a minimum of three months. This resulted in such a large increase in the prison population that the penalty was suspended in 1995, to be implemented only if the person re-entered the country. Those who overstay have to pay a penalty of 500,000 drachmas (£1,400) for every year that they have overstayed. This sum represents a small fortune for migrant workers, and the impossibility of paying means that they have to remain in the country even if they want to return home.

> We are living in a big prison. Nowhere to go. We stay here in this country simply, no recognition. We don't have a chance to go to school, a chance to work, or a chance to have medical care. We are living in a big prison, a big prison.
> (Fira, Ethiopian in Athens)

Even those who do manage to regularise their status are not secure. Josee came in 1974 in response to an advertisement for a babysitter placed in a newspaper in Mauritius. Unbeknown to her, her immigration papers were falsified by her employers, who told her to destroy all documentation on entry: 'I had no knowledge of cheating. I had lived a very neat life until then, so I did what I was told.' So began long years of being an undocumented worker. In 1981 her then employer, a government official, managed to get her a work permit. This enabled her to bring over to Greece her husband and children and it seemed that her situation would end happily. But in 1991 her permit was taken away from her. She did not understand why, other than 'it was because of Maastricht'. Her children could not renew their residence permits:

> My daughter was ten when she came. Then when she was seventeen they took the papers from her. She's twenty-one now and still no papers. My son was trained to be a mechanical engineer. He finished, he got his diploma here in Greece, then lost his papers. He applied to go to Michigan, they accepted him but he could not get a visa to go to USA because he did not have a permit for Greece. I begged them here to give him a visa, just for a month. Because he didn't want to stay here, he wanted to go, but they wouldn't.

Josee, her husband and her children continue to accrue fines of millions of drachmas because they are unable to leave the country. She, like many of the women I spoke to, felt they were trapped in Greece, brought over by unscrupulous employers and agencies, losing any employment opportunities in their home countries and paid such low wages in Greece that they could not afford the fine payable on leaving.

Many domestic workers have never had legal status in Greece other than a tourist visa, although they enter to work for specific employers. One of the women I spoke to had entered with Indian employers, and had been given a tourist visa; another had come in with Lebanese employers on the same basis. There were people who had not passed through immigration controls at all, crossing land borders by foot or in trucks, or swimming from Turkey. One person had spent two days in the sea, much of it underwater, breathing through a tube, to cross the Graeco-Turkish border safely. Some of the Filipinas who had lived in Greece for a while had entered with a 'nursing aide' permit. In the late 1970s and early 1980s this was commonly given to live-in domestic workers as a means of circumventing the problem that employers had in proving that they could not find a Greek worker for the job they wanted to give to a foreigner. They then either did not have their papers renewed by their employer or had stayed longer than the statutory five years and moved to Athens to find work. The 'nursing aide' permit was effectively ended under the 1991 Act.

As in other EU states, domestic work in private households was said to be the only work available to migrant women in Greece apart from prostitution. When I explained to an official from the General Secretariat for Equality that I was interested in the situation of foreign women in Greece, she took it for granted that I meant domestic workers in private households. When I pointed this out, she replied simply that it is the work foreign women do. None of the women I spoke to had had any employment other than domestic work, apart from one woman who worked in a shipping company, and another who was working as a live-out cleaner in the daytime and as a waitress in the evening. This was in a restaurant cooking her national food: 'Because if you are working without papers you have to go under cover.' Many of the women held degrees and skills which they could not use and most spoke extremely good English, often their fourth or fifth language.

The extent to which domestic service in Athens is dominated by non-citizens is striking, and there was a wide range of nationalities working in the sector. I met women from Ghana, Zaire, Philippines, Sri Lanka, India, Mauritius, Eritrea, Albania, Sierra Leone, Chile, Ethiopia and Romania. Many had not intended to stay in Greece, but to use it as a stepping-off point for Canada, the USA or Northern Europe. They had found that it was impossible to get a visa for the country they wanted to enter, so remained in Greece by default. In recording employment requests the volunteer at Caritas listed Poles, Albanians, Romanians, Hungarians, Bulgarians, Yugoslavians, Russians, Czechs and Ethiopians, separately, as well as 'Arabic', 'African' and 'South American'. Her records indicate that certain nationalities predominate at different times. In January–June 1990, for example, 425 Ethiopians requested work from Caritas, but this dropped to 249 in January–June 1991. In June–December 1990, 138 Albanians were listed; one year later, in June–December 1991, this had increased to 456. While one cannot extrapolate from the Caritas figures, they do give some idea of the range of nationalities involved in domestic work.

Almost all the workers I met were living in, often with responsibility for the care of the elderly or children, although this role extended to include a wide variety of household chores such as chopping firewood, gardening, cleaning the garage, ironing, doing the housework of employers' relatives and looking after animals. Hours were commonly a source of grievance: 'we as a live-in are working almost sixteen hours, or twenty hours a day' (Imelda, a Filipina in Athens) Salaries varied between 50,000 (£140) and 150,000 (£420) drachmas a month, with some women earning 300 drachmas (85p) per hour and others over 1,000 (£2.80). Those who had found work through Caritas were earning the lowest wages. All nationalities complained of the widespread problem of non-payment. Some employers bring in a domestic worker for a 'spring clean' and, 'you work hard for one month and at the end of the month they tell you, "No, I can't pay you". Why you come here, you clean their home, and you don't get paid?'

There is also the practice of 'holiday employment', when families employ women for the summer, take them to the islands on holiday for two or three months, and then discharge them without pay. Irene described how she had gone on behalf of a friend to find out about a job she had seen advertised in the paper. The house was in Kifissia, a very exclusive area of Athens, and it was being decorated.

> The woman said, 'I have something to do, if you are free'. So I said, 'Yes, if you will pay me'.... So I cleaned the stairs, I took the paint off, and I put the carpets to wash. It was from 12.30 to 6.00 p.m. I didn't eat because I am ashamed to ask. I didn't even get one glass of water. Then I wanted to leave, and she said, 'I'll drop you at the gate'. Then I asked her for the money – she had promised 2,000 drachmas (£5.60). She said, 'I don't have anything on me now'. But I had seen in her bedroom 12,000 drachmas (£33.80) because sometimes they do that, they leave money out to test, to see if you will steal. She said, 'Call me tomorrow'. Next day I am calling her – she is not in. She is never in. What kind of people are these?

Non-payment is a problem not only in casual employment but also for some workers who enter Greece to work for a particular employer: Moji came believing she had a permit to work in an office, but when she arrived her sponsor made it clear: 'I came to be on the bed.' She refused his advances, so he put her to work in the house, refusing to give her back her passport and return ticket, and not paying her any money. After three months he cashed her return ticket. She continued in this position until she found other work, unable to go home because she had no ticket. Ines came with a Lebanese family who maltreated her until she begged them to give her a return ticket home. They refused to do this, and did not pay her. This forced her into running away, because her children at home, completely dependent on her income, were starving. She found another job, but sent money to her former employers until she had covered the cost of her return ticket to Greece.

Everybody consulted had a regular day off, although obviously this might be because those who had no day off would be unable to attend meetings and interviews. Some complained that in the past they had had no day off: 'For one year I never went out of the house. I had no day off and I worked for nothing' (Irene). Most people had some hours off on Sunday – though they would often be expected to work before they left and to return on Sunday evening. Some had an entire day off, while others – almost all Filipinas – had one and a half days off.

If a worker falls sick or has an accident, she loses her job. The possibility of employers paying for medical care doesn't even arise, it seems. Manwara was seriously injured by a motorcycle in a hit-and-run accident. I interviewed her six months later, when she still could not walk and had her right leg in plaster, with no idea of when she could return to work – 'little by little the doctor says'. Her employers of that time had found another worker, and Manwara was surviving on money collected by her church and contributions from other domestic workers. Neither are employers responsible for accidents at work. One woman, for example, complained of asthma induced by the chemicals she was required to spray on her employers' plants:

> So finally in the morning I went to the doctor and they asked me to make X-rays. There was some problem, they ask me I have to pay, you know. Then they say I didn't pay the X-ray and then they ask me do you have insurance and I said no, he said to me the medicine is very expensive. So I asked him, he was nice, please can you give me a paper for my boss. So my friend called my boss and said I'm sick, really I couldn't breathe, without the pot, I can't breathe until now because of the chemicals, and all those things and the trees and right now she called my boss because I am sick, the next day she was having visitors, you know, for dinner and the next day I went there, I went there and I called her she say that she doesn't want me no more because of that, I get sick because of her stuff and she say stop working.
>
> (Ilsa, Ethiopian working in Athens)

This lack of responsibility is demonstrated with regard to mental as well as physical illness. Mental illness is a serious problem for foreign workers in Greece and one that domestic workers return to again and again:

> *Joy:* Because so many have sickness, mental deteriorated, so many people we know.
>
> *Teresa:* Some Filipinos with problems with their employers also, sometimes they commit suicide. They jump from the fourth floor to the ground.
>
> *Daniel:* There were two Ethiopian girls in the mental hospital. I went to ask

for a doctor so I could pray with them. He told me I could not and I would have to pay for them to leave the hospital. He said, 'If you do not, we will deport her to Ethiopia'. But she was sick and she had no one in Ethiopia. She had worked here for five years, and she had one shirt only.... I told them, the hospital has authority over the police, so they can stop deportation. But the hospital said, that's only for Greeks, and we don't know what happens to her in Ethiopia. It's not our business. So she was sent back to Ethiopia. The other girl was also sent back.

Workers believe that mental problems stem partly from immigration status: constant fear of the police; rejection of claims for asylum; and being trapped by economic circumstances in Greece. These problems are compounded by the drudgery of domestic work, insecurity of employment, physical and sexual abuse, and being cut off from strong community networks. Domestic workers also claim that pregnancy means dismissal, even in cases where the woman is pregnant by her male employer. Shaila was raped by her employer, became pregnant and was thrown out. She delivered her baby on the streets. Some weeks later, while still homeless, the child was taken from her by some officials, she did not know who they were. When I met her she was clearly mentally ill, living on the streets and still unemployed. Women who become pregnant commonly lose their jobs, even when, as with Bose, she had been brought to Greece by her employer fifteen years ago.

In 1997 a regularisation programme was initiated for those migrants who had entered Greece before November of that year. It gave many, on paper at least, the opportunity to legalise their immigration status. But by the end of the registration process in April 1999 only 5,000 workers had received a 'green card', the permit to stay and work, and less than half of those originally registered with the scheme had applied formally. Attaining the 'green card' entailed an immensely bureaucratic process requiring numerous documents, including medical and police certificates which had to be obtained from the authorities. Although the green card was originally available only until 31 October 1998, the authorities were offering appointments for certificates in the summer of 1999. Workers complained of being passed from office to office, with bureaucrats themselves often not understanding the process and treating them abusively.

For example, to get the certificate from the Ministry of Justice that one has not been accused or convicted of a crime, one has to line up for hours, sometimes from 4 in the morning until 12 noon. You see an almost unending line of migrants of different colours, Africans, Albanians and Asians. The police manning the line often get very menacing and impatient. The police would shout at us and treat us very roughly like we are not human beings. There have been cases of migrants being hit with clubs.

(Perlita, Filipina with a green card, speaking at RESPECT conference, Paris, 7–9 May 1999)

There were particular difficulties for domestic workers. Their long hours made it extremely difficult for them to queue outside offices, and employers were reluctant to fulfil their obligation to register the worker, pay tax on her earnings and pay her social security for 40 days. Problems of bureaucracy and delay encouraged corrupt agencies who offered to arrange papers on workers' behalf, but actually simply presented forged documents, resulting in the workers' immediate deportation. By the end of the application period it seemed that the majority of migrant domestic workers were going to remain undocumented and that the half-hearted regularisation exercise would make little difference to their situation.

Spain

In 1991 Colectivo Ioe, a Madrid-based group of sociologists, undertook a study of overseas domestic workers in Madrid which contextualised their living and working conditions within immigration and labour legislation in Spain as a whole (Colectivo Ioe 1991). It found different types of domestic work: *internas* (live-in), increasingly the work of migrant women; *externas fijas/interinas*, workers who live out, but who work for one family only; *asistentas por horas*, often Spanish citizens, who live out, working for several employers and doing a variety of jobs; baby-sitters; and *trabaja-doras familiares* ('family workers'), who are paid for by the social services and who care for older people in their own homes and have attended a recognised course. Colectivo Ioe noted that this last type was becoming more informal; often there are no contracts, with the state payment being made not to the worker but to the person being cared for, while the number of hours worked is often greater than the number paid for. In all four types of domestic work, Colectivo Ioe found that contracts were the exception rather than the rule and that conditions of work were poor, with long hours, isolation, low pay and employer–employee relations characterised by paternalism (*paternalismo*). Workers characterised their situation as 'put up with it so you don't get thrown out'. Similarly, Yakuta Sayd, writing about the lives of Moroccan women in Catalonia (Moroccan women in the province work almost exclusively as domestic workers), found that it was relatively easy to find live-in work, but women, especially new arrivals, were often badly treated, with no contracts, very long hours, low salaries, racism and lack of respect:

The majority of Moroccan women are agreed that they can tolerate the work, but what they cannot tolerate are the employers, for the majority what is difficult is not the work neither is it the fact that employers want to see the employee working day and night, the problem is that they treat them as if they were slaves they do not let them keep their dignity nor do they accept cultural differences.

Those who work live-in do not use the word 'racism', but they speak of the impossibility of watching the television with the employers, of resting on days off. They speak among themselves of plates reserved for 'the servant', of clothes which have to be washed separately from the family's, the majority speak of a kind of disgust that they [the employers] show towards Moroccan domestic workers.
(Sayd 1993: 57, 61)

She also found some women working for Moroccans, either cleaning for a household of single men – with problems of sexual assault, harassment and rape – or taken in by a family following marriage problems or pregnancy. Not only do they have to work without pay in these conditions; they are also closely watched for 'bad morals'.

Migrants working in private households in Barcelona are both documented and undocumented. Undocumented immigration to Spain has occurred on a considerable scale since the 1960s, when it was relatively easy for a non-Spanish citizen to enter Spain and work even if they did not have the necessary papers to do so legally. Moroccan and Portuguese workers, in particular, were encouraged to come and work on large-scale infrastructure projects; many of them obtained work permits but lost them later through unemployment. The tightening of European Community border controls in the 1970s when Spain was still outside the EC meant that many immigrants who had originally thought of Northern Europe as their destination remained in Spain. By the 1980s these were being absorbed by the ever-increasing informal sector which, according to the Ministerio de la Economía, accounted for one third of all jobs by 1985.

The 1985 Ley de Extranjería, enacted in 1986, required foreign workers to have a residence and work permit before they could apply for citizenship. No visa was required for citizens of South America in recognition of Spain's historical ties with the continent, but this was not applicable in the crucial cases of Cuba, the Dominican Republic and Peru – the main sources of female labour migrants. In order to obtain permits a formal work contract was necessary – clearly a potential problem for the many migrants working in the informal sector, but particularly difficult for domestic workers. These restrictions meant that from then on migration to Spain was predominantly undocumented, and that large numbers of people who had lived in the country for many years could not be regularised. By the end of the 1980s the Spanish government was forced to acknowledge the existence of large numbers of undocumented workers in the country, and in 1991 a regularisation process was undertaken with the participation and support of voluntary organisations and trade unions. There were 132,934 applications, and 103,675 workers had been granted a one-year residence permit by March 1992. The continuing demand for migrant labour in certain sectors of the economy, notably agriculture and domestic work, was acknowledged by the introduction of a quota (*cupo* in Castilian) system in 1993. A maximum of 20,000 work permits for non-EU nationals were to be granted annually. Applications far exceed numbers granted. In 1995, for example, the *cupo* limit for Catalonia was set at 1,000 and there were some 5,000 applications. Although the system is directed at ensuring newcomers enter legally many use the *cupo* in order to regularise themselves, taking up approximately 60 per cent of the quota according to 1999 figures. So a worker who has been working for an employer illegally will return to her country of origin in order to present papers – formal offer of employment and so on – to the Spanish Embassy there, and then re-enter Spain legally. There are many undocumented women working as domestic workers, and new arrivals continue to enter this employment. Unlike in Greece, however, where it was highly unusual for a domestic worker to have a work permit, the 1991 regularisation and the continuing *cupo* system have meant that a significant proportion do have documents, and that those who are currently undocumented have a clear means and ambition to regularise their situation in the medium term. In Barcelona there was not the wide range of nationalities working in private households that I found in Athens. The *cupo* system, and the visa requirement for women from certain countries, accounts for the concentration of women from Philippines, Dominican Republic and Peru in domestic work.

Filipina domestic workers

The Filipino community is one of the oldest migrant communities in Barcelona. The Centro Filipino estimates 8–10,000 Filipinos, with up to 40 per cent male since the introduction of the 1991 *cupos*. Migration from the Philippines began in the 1960s, with women coming to work as domestics, predominantly in the homes of the very wealthy. Almost all Filipino women work as domestic workers. The men work in private households too – as gardeners, chauffeurs and cleaners, and often as part of a couple. This is easier for Filipinos than for other groups, partly because they tend to work for wealthier households. There has been some movement from live-in to hourly work by Filipinas, particularly since the

1991 regularisation exercise which has facilitated family reunification. This is generally felt to have stopped, however, not because it is undesirable, but because live-out jobs are so scarce. Live-in work as a couple is one way of resolving this problem. It is also common for Filipinas to rent flats together, where they spend the nights of their time off.

Filipinos tend to be perceived by other nationals as better off than many other migrants: they command higher wages and better conditions, are well organised, comprise a larger proportion of documented workers and are generally thought to be well regarded by Spanish society. 'It is a little bit different situation between Filipinas and other nationalities, firstly because you are a large group, you are a majority, and you have been here for longer than other nationalities. Also you are very united' (Bianca, from Brazil, working in Barcelona). While one should not underestimate the considerable achievements of the group, and their level of organisation, it is as well to remember that they share many of the problems of all domestic workers and many, particularly the undocumented, are badly paid and exploited. Despite their high levels of education it is extremely rare for them to move out of domestic work, and they are one of the communities least likely to undertake any course of study or training, despite the fact that many of them have work and residence papers. This is perhaps partly because language (Castilian or Catalan) is a serious barrier for the Filipino community.

Dominican domestic workers

The Asociación Dominicana estimates there are some 7,000 Dominicans in the Barcelona area, 85 per cent of them women, the majority of these in domestic work. The men work in private households, gardening and chauffeuring, and also in manufacturing and agriculture. The majority come from the provinces bordering Haiti, the poorest and most deprived areas of the Dominican Republic. Their education is often minimal, and many are illiterate. While this is in keeping with general information on Dominican women in Spain, it by no means applies to all Dominican women in Spain:

> lots of people think that they are better than us because we haven't got qualifications or because we're not professionals, but many of us are, and here you can often see a professional scrubbing dishes the same as anyone, because people from here won't give a foreigner a job unless it is in domestic work, and there are many people here with good qualifications, who have no choice but to do this work.
> (Delia, Dominicana working in Barcelona)

The Dominican workers interviewed were very conscious of their image as uneducated, and were keen to challenge the resulting stereotypes:

Speaker 1: The Dominican Republic is a country where, like it or not, women yes they have been oppressed, but women are not silent....
Speaker 2: ... We struggle, we work hard...
Speaker 1: We are not silent....

Peruvian domestic workers

In 1993 there were 7,620 Peruvians officially registered with the Peruvian Consulate in Barcelona, just over 50 per cent of them women (Escrivá 1996). This is likely to be an under-representation, since although undocumented migrants can register with the consulate, people without immigration papers avoid contact with officials. The La Bonanova church mission, which offers a work placement service, registered 80 per cent women, suggesting that there are at least significant proportions of women who are not registering with the consulate. Most Peruvians in Barcelona are in domestic work, and they are particularly concentrated in caring for the elderly, with both women and men in demand. They are a hidden community, partly because they are recent arrivals, because they are not immediately recognisable as ethnically different, and because of their affinity with the 'Spanish cultural heritage'.

Moroccan domestic workers

The Moroccan community, like the Filipino community, began in the 1960s. Unlike the Filipinos, however, this early immigration was predominantly male. Many were attempting to travel to other European countries, but from 1967/8 onwards found the Spanish border with France closed. Spain at this time, and Catalonia in particular, was experiencing economic development and an improvement in infrastructure, and Moroccan men found ready employment in construction and low-paid, low-status jobs abandoned by the Spanish at a time of high employment. It was then relatively easy for Moroccans to travel to Spain and to work without a permit, and coming and going between the two countries on a tourist visa was quite common. The women who entered Spain in the 1960s and 1970s were principally coming to join their husbands, often themselves with no particular desire to live in a foreign country. They rarely entered the labour market but worked in their own homes as wives and mothers. Like their husbands they tended to enter on tourist visas. This group often have very little education. From the mid-1980s onwards young Moroccan women began to enter Spain, not to be with their husbands, but to work, mainly as domestic workers in private households. Like earlier migrants they come predominantly but not exclusively from the North of Morocco and from rural backgrounds. This movement continues to this day, with the women entering on tourist visas. They are more likely to be well-educated, with secondary education and higher. If they have settled for a while they may well share a weekend flat with other young Moroccan women.

Workers of all nationalities were clear that domestic work in private households was the only employment available to them apart from prostitution. Erlinda from Peru put it succinctly: 'Well, all foreign women, or at least the vast majority, end up working as domestic workers because it's the only chance this country gives us.' This was echoed time and time again. Only two out of 29 people interviewed had done work other than domestic in Spain, one as a translator for her compatriots, and one as a secretary. Most had been in Spain for over three years. Once working as a domestic worker, it is almost impossible to leave that sector. According to the Filipino Centre a small number of Filipinos have managed to do so, and they continue to be employed in the personal service area, either as nurses or secretaries.

As in other European cities workers were usually caring for children or an elderly person, but were commonly expected to do all the household chores as well, and they complained that these extended to cleaning the houses of employers' relatives free of charge, cleaning employers' cars, washing clothes by hand even when there was a washing machine, and looking after pets. The following quotations give some idea of the range of work that is expected:

Zenaida: I work from morning to night. She knows that I'm always there.... I just do it if there are things to do ... I do the sewing....

Evelyn: My madam she wants me just to work and work the whole day. In the morning I had to get up at quarter to six I had to start to clean the whole house, until third floor, and then I had to cook, after lunch I had to iron the clothes. Then after ironing I had to prepare the dinner, and then after dinner maybe I will finish until 12 o'clock. My señor always have visitors in the house, they will have dinner at 1 a.m. and then I will finish washing the dishes at 4 a.m. And then I have to get up at 6 a.m. to prepare the breakfast of the children because they are working. And then every day I have to clean their car, they have three cars, and every day I had to clean the cars.

Magnolia: ... In my country an animal is an animal outside in its cage, but here they are much better treated.... I had to make it food which was double work for me, but they didn't pay me for it.... I had to take care of it, give it food, take it for a walk. I think that's work, it's like a child.... And in this cold I had to take it out....

Hours of employment follow a similar pattern to those in other European cities. While live-out workers often have long hours they have some control over their time – though not always, as Magnolia pointed out 'For some jobs 1,000 pesetas [£5.55] per hour is very little. Sometimes they expect you to clean three floors, it takes you three hours and they pay you 1,000 pesetas – and this isn't taken into account.' In general workers with papers who live in can expect 1.5–2 days off a week, though these may not run concurrently. For new, undocumented arrivals there can be no days off at all. Those who work by hours try to arrange for 1.5 days off, usually Saturday afternoon and Sunday.

Wages in Barcelona are very variable. Live-in salaries depend in part on nationality and vary between 50,000 (£277) and 160,000 (£888) pesetas; hourly rates were between 700 (£3.80) and 1,500 (£8.33) pesetas. Agency R stated that: 'a recently arrived Moroccan woman could earn 50,000 [£277]. Like doctors who have just left college don't earn the same as doctors with ten years' experience. Filipinas and Dominicans can earn more.' Hourly wages by agency ranged between 700–800 (£3.80–£4.44) an hour according to Agency B, which deals almost exclusively with Moroccans, and 900–1,500 (£5–£8.33) an hour for Agency S, which deals mainly with Spanish.

One of the key issues affecting the payment of domestic workers who have legal status is that of social security. Although Edita, a Peruvian, was earning a relatively low wage of 70,000 pesetas (£388) a month, she thought this was satisfactory because her employer paid her social security. Ana, a Filipina working in Barcelona for nearly sixteen years, with excellent references and contacts as well as a residence and working permit, describes recent negotiations with an employer which clearly demonstrate the importance of social security, and the extent to which a worker in a position to demand her rights will insist on it:

> They came here to talk to me, they wanted me to look after their mother. The agreement is 110,000 pesetas [£611] per month and I asked them to pay the SSS, and they told me 'Yes'.... They said yes, everything, yes ... and after two weeks, I asked them again, 'Hey señor, you have to send already my security' ... They were liars, I've never seen a man lying like that.... Their mother told me. 'They are earning very little, Ana'. So I understand them also ... so that's why I told them that if they paid me 100,000 pesetas (£555) I will pay my SSS, but they didn't like it, so I said no, for 70,000 pesetas [£388] I will go back to Barcelona and earn more.

Living expenses in Barcelona are heavy. Accommodation is a particular problem, and, as has been seen, while workers may live in to solve this problem, most of the better established will also share a flat with friends as an insurance against unemployment and a place to meet and sleep on off-days, providing a minimum of social contact in an otherwise extremely isolated job. For those who have family or are working in live-out jobs, the bills for household costs and food are high. Bertha expressed succintly the way in which all expenses are felt:

> an immigrant's expenses are very complicated to explain, but I will give my own experience ... live-in has its advantages.... The advantage is that you have hidden expenditures ... you need a room for the weekends, that's not major but it can cost you 12,000, 15,000 pesetas [£66–£83]. Now you don't pay for electricity, water and food for the weekends is minimal. Now if you work live-out ... you have more expenses, you can earn more, but this has its disadvantages.... We can say a room is 15,00–20,000 pesetas, [£83–£111] travel card 15,000 pesetas, [£83] food....

Remittances can account for a substantial amount of income. This was confirmed, in the case of the Filipinos at least, by an interview with SPEED, an agency of the Far East Bank and Trust that arranges for money to be transferred from Barcelona to the Philippines (40 per cent of their clients send to Manila, the other 60 per cent to the provinces). SPEED opened an office in 1990 and sends their clients' money by banker's draft to offices all over the Philippines at a cost of 1,300 pesetas to Manila and 1,600 pesetas to the provinces. Of their 200 clients, most sent $150–300 a month. They are all domestic workers, if one includes men working in household-related jobs such as chauffeurs, drivers and gardeners. Given that the bank sets the exchange rate, and that at the time of interviewing it stood at 125 pesetas to the dollar, their clients are remitting 18,750–37,500 pesetas (£104–£208) a month, a large tranche of the 100,000 (£555) average wage.

Employment agencies play an important role in liasing between employers and workers in Barcelona. I contacted twelve employment agencies through telephone numbers given in small ads. Of these three refused to be interviewed. The information provided by the others is presented in Table 4.1. Apart from MBS agency there seems to be some specialisation in Spaniards or 'foreigners'. But all agencies have a large proportion of foreign workers on their books, even if they do not offer them particular encouragment. There also seems to be some specialisation according to country of origin. Thus Agency BS claimed that it did not attract Filipinas because 'they do other kinds of work, less honourable, massage parlours, prostitution....' In fact there is no independent evidence of any number of Filipinas working in the sex industry in Barcelona and this would seem to be based on plain prejudice. Agency S offered only Filipina workers, and Agency E principally Filipinas. Agency J only included Filipinas as one of the nationalities they placed, remarking (in response to the question, which nationalities are easiest to place) that: 'Beforehand it was the Filipinas because of their character and their elegance, but now they have to compete with other nationalities.' The

Table 4.1 *Employment agencies and migrant domestic workers in Barcelona*

Agency	% Spanish	% non-Spanish	Breakdown of nationalities/regional origins
BS	75	25	Moroccans (75%) Peruvians Colombians El Salvadoreans
R	60 (all live-out)	40	Moroccans (50 %+) Dominicans Peruvians Poles Russians Bulgarians South Americans Filipinas
E	10	90	Filipinas (80 %) Dominicans (5 %) Moroccans Peruvians Africans
PS	2	98	Dominicans (50%+) Peruvians Moroccans Filipinas
SOS	75 %	25 %	South Americans
J	(No details)	(No details)	Dominicans Peruvians Moroccans Filipinas Cubans
S	(No Spanish)	(Filipinas only)	Filipinas only
PO	(No response)	(No response)	no response
MBS	50	50	South Americans (30 %) Moroccans (20 %)

Filipino Centre had been approached by Agency J shortly before the interview, however, and asked if they would send Filipinas who were looking for work to the agency as it could find them some very good jobs.

Of the agencies interviewed, two were run by Filipinas: Agency E and Agency S. The Filipino Centre claims to know of a total of five agencies run by Filipinas (including E and S). Agency S, run by a Filipina and her

German husband, seems to be operating as a *de facto* introduction agency. A German group sent the Filipino Centre a letter circulating in Germany and purporting to come from the Filipina director, saying that she wished to extend to others the happiness she had found in being married to a German, and giving a Barcelona contact number. Agency S refused to give a face-to-face interview and only offered the most cursory information on the telephone. Whether or not connected with this group, there are reports suggesting that Germans are coming to Barcelona to be introduced to Filipinas: one Filipina told me how she and some friends were waiting for a bus when they were approached by a group of male German tourists who were expecting to meet up with a Filipina group at the bus stop for an excursion to Andorra. They informed them that they were the wrong people and later saw the Germans join up with another group of Filipina women and gathered that this must be the party they were supposed to be meeting.

Agency E, the other agency interviewed run by a Filipina director, presents itself as a 'happy family' kind of agency. The interview took place, not in the office, but in a flat shared by a group of Filipina domestic workers and the director had gathered a group of these clients to support her claims to offer a good service. Throughout the interview she was having her nails manicured by one of the domestic workers. The director says that she can recruit workers 'through the informal network – my contacts put recently arrived girls in contact with me' and she will try to iron out any difficulties with the employer. She also worked as an agent for an life insurance company and encouraged her workers to take out loans and make use of her financial help.

Agencies were reluctant to discuss how they operated. Those advertising in newspapers tend to advertise both as agencies and as if they are individuals looking for or offering work. So agency PO advertises in *Los Clasificados* (14–20 February 1996): 'Live-in girl, 60,000 pesetas [£333]' (a very low wage for a worker to be suggesting); agency J: 'Wanted couple for Andorra. Her for the house, him for the garden, vegetable patch and chauffeur. Legal with references. No Moroccans. 180,000 +SS [£1,000]' (*Primerama*, 15 February 1996). The usual rate quoted by workers for registration with agencies is P1,000 (£5.50) for three months, though only one of the agencies (Agency R) quoted this rate. The others claimed that it was the employers who paid the agency or, according to Agency PO, 'there are no norms about who usually pays the agency'. None admitted to taking a regular percentage of the workers' salary, though some workers claimed that they had experience of this. One of those workers present at the interview of Agency E claimed that Agency F takes the first month's salary from the worker. Agency F had refused to be interviewed. Of the nine agencies interviewed, four offered a guarantee of between two months and one year to the employer. There was no mention of any such guarantee to the worker, but this could be covered in the three months registration.

Italy

Domestic work in private households has been an acknowledged area of employment for migrant women in Italy from the late 1970s. Until the 1970s the Catholic association ACLI-COLF promoted 'harmonious' labour relations and the subordination of the domestic worker to the employer as 'part of the family': 'Domestic workers were not selling their labour but collaborating with a family and thus facilitating the implementation of God's plan' (Andall 1996: 6). Nevertheless, the very fact that the association existed meant that paid domestic work could not be ignored, as in other countries, despite the preponderance of migrants in the sector. Andall's historical analysis of the migrant domestic workforce in Italy traces the demand for such workers back to the late 1960s. She argues that Italian domestic workers had become increasingly reluctant to work live-in and were working largely on an hourly basis by the early 1970s: 'This left a specific gap in the market for live-in domestic work which migrant women would be forced (institutionally) and encouraged (informally) to fill' (Andall 1996: 10). Andall's argument is that while the Italian government aimed to discourage the employment of migrant domestics by the late 1970s, its earlier decision to confine migrant domestics to full-time work probably contributed to the attractiveness of non-Italian national workers to the Italian employer (they were not allowed entry to work on an hourly basis unlike Italian nationals). In 1979 their employment situation was limited further by tying their entry to a specific employer. In 1983 an analysis of statistical data from the Ministry of Labour in Italy found that an estimated 90 per cent of employed African and Asian women worked in domestic service (Arena 1983).

  In 1986 the Italian government suspended the issue of labour permits for domestic workers altogether, but provided for a regularisation of undocumented immigrants. During the regularisation period that lasted until 1988, approximately 118,000 non-EU citizens received residence permits. Another amnesty took place in 1990, leading to a further 204,000 non-EU citizens being regularised, the largest numbers being from Morocco, Tunisia, Senegal and the Philippines. Of the Filipinos regularised, the overwhelming majority were female domestic workers. In 1991 a special decree was passed allowing for the hiring of foreign domestic workers on a temporary basis, and in 1993 the majority of the 20,000 non-EU citizens granted an employment permit were domestic workers. The Martelli Act (1990) also eased restrictions on working hours for migrant domestics and tied them to a specific employer.

In November 1995 the caretaker government of Lamberto Dini gave in to pressure from the Northern League and introduced a decree (usually referred to as 'the Dini decree') which allowed for the deportation of 'illegal immigrants' and made employers who hire them liable to a six-year prison sentence. It also introduced provisions for the regularisation of immigrants currently in Italy if their employer declared that they had been in the same job for four months and was prepared to pay social insurance contributions in advance for them. Not surprisingly, by the middle of December the police reported real difficulties in deciphering the decree, and said that few employers were taking the steps to regularise their employees. But, despite the initial confusion, by November 1996 (when the Dini decree could no longer be renewed) it was estimated that 220,000 foreigners had received a residence permit under the decree criteria. The regularisation process indicated that about 25 per cent of Italy's foreign population was undocumented, with Filipinos representing the largest nationality group. Although there are large numbers of domestic workers from the Philippines, Cape Verde and Morocco, these are by no means the only countries of origin. I met women from Somalia, Nigeria, Peru, Côte d'Ivoire and Eritrea.

As in other countries, domestic workers were very unhappy at their enforced dependence on the employer and the hours worked. They also felt that it was becoming more difficult to find work, and that workers had to demand less. Problems they alluded to included: their dependence on their employer for the renewal of their work permits ('that's all right if you have a good employer') and contracts that were not honoured (several women did not even know that they had a contract until informed that it was the paper they had to have when they applied for their work permit). Despite the forty hours set out in the contract, most worked for at least six days a week, some for seven: 'Your employer has visitors, you must stay up until midnight serving them.' Wages were very variable, with some African women I spoke to earning as little as 700,000 lira (£297) a month, while other workers were receiving 1,800,000 (£765). Local informants suggested that 1.500.000 (£638) a month for a six-day week would be the going rate for a migrant domestic worker, but undocumented migrants were paid less. 'One person who phoned me up was offering 800,000 lira [£340] and a free day every Sunday'. For 1,300,000 lire (£553) a month a domestic worker from Côte d'Ivoire described her day:

I do everything. I don't have time to sleep or eat. I do everything in the house. I'm even their carpenter and it's been like this for four years with no pay rise – 1.3 million lire and that's it .... it's not a fair salary, how can they compensate you for your sacrifices?

Other complaints included violence and sexual harassment, and the intense personal relationship with their employers.

Conclusions

Migrant domestic workers are not a new phenomenon in Southern Europe and there is considerable demand for their services. Most of the workers interviewed in Greece, Spain and Italy were living in and working for one family. Yet significant numbers of women still cannot get papers to do this work legally. Almost all workers in Athens were undocumented, as were many in Barcelona, although the latter often were hopeful that they would eventually be able to work with a permit through the *cupo* system. Migrants dominate the live-in sector of domestic work particularly, although live-out work is much preferred by all except the new arrivals, and workers are very quick to point out the many difficulties associated with living and working in the same place. Wages vary immensely, both within the same state and between states, with Greece offering the lowest pay. In general, living and working conditions in Greece seem to be noticeably worse than in Spain and Italy, with larger numbers of people complaining of abuse, degrading work and unreasonable hours.

5

Invisible Women (II)

Migrant Domestic Workers in Northern Europe

Live-in domestic work is far less common in France and Germany than it is in the countries of Southern Europe. Those who do live in are usually undocumented workers, but undocumented workers also undertake live-out work. There have been some attempts to regularise the sector, particularly in France, although Germany is looking to her neighbour for lessons in how to extract tax and national insurance from employers and workers. These attempts have been fraught with difficulties, and do not seem to have improved the conditions of migrant workers, particularly those who live in.

France

In France domestic work is more regulated by the state than in other European countries, perhaps partly because the sector was organised in the early part of the twentieth century through the socialist union, the CFDT. Since 1982 the sector has been regulated officially through the Convention Collective Nationale des Employeurs Particuliers d'Employés de Maison, negotiated between unions and the employers' federation, Féderation Nationale des Groupements d'Employeurs de Personnel Employé de Maison (FEPEM). Although there is some recognition of the need for live-in domestic workers, particularly because of the ageing population, there has been little comment on the racialisation of domestic work. Brigitte Croff's examination of 'emplois familiaux' (1994) is typical:

> We have identified four types of women working in this sector. The first is composed of African women ... the large numbers of foreigners can be explained by the fact that the public sector is not open to them ... they are

69

forced into the private sector, whether it be private households or private retirement homes. These women know the working conditions in these establishments, the underpayment and racism which ensures that they have to do the most menial tasks. This state of affairs reinforces the attraction of the private household which holds the illusion of independence and less heavy tasks, since they have to care for two people maximum.
(Croff 1994: 56–7)

The other three 'types' are: French women with no training who are over 45; students; and women on state-sponsored employment programmes. There is no further exploration of this in the entire book, despite its interest in the 'servitude and oppression' that attaches to being a domestic worker.

Many studies of migrants in France mention the importance of working in private households as an area of employment for migrant women.[1] A 1968 study found that over 35 per cent of female migrants were working as domestic workers, and several surveys after a regularisation exercise in 1981 revealed that this was the most important sector of employment for undocumented women. One study of this data found that 62 per cent of women regularised were in personal service employed by individuals, suggesting that domestic work at that time was an important source of employment for undocumented women, particularly, at least according to the regularisation data, migrants from Portugal, Asia and Morocco.[2] According to both FEPEM and trade unions representing domestic workers, in Paris and other large French cities domestic work is increasingly the province of immigrant workers. Yet, despite the importance of the sector, there is little written on the living and working conditions of migrant women, although there has been some journalistic interest in the plight of women working for non-French families (see, for example, O'Dy 1995).

I focused on the 17th arrondissement, an area of Paris that is home to people with a large spread of incomes, and where there are significant numbers of migrants. I was soon put in touch with two groups with a specific interest in finding workers for private employers: the Emploi Daubigny (ED) and the Association General de Familles (AGF). I also met with Cefia, a voluntary association that runs French classes for migrants and immigrants living in the 17th arrondissement. I found that, as in Athens, migrant domestic workers covered a wide spectrum in nationality and immigration status. There were those who worked part-time as domestic workers because that way they had a flexibility that enabled them to earn money while caring for their own children and doing the reproductive work of their own households. This was particularly true of women with husbands and children who had legal status – although

70

these women were usually working without papers. There were (often undocumented) full-time live-in workers from the Filipino community in particular. There were also people with residence permits who were working full-time, either living in or living out, usually with at least some of their hours declared.

Figures on domestic work in France can be derived with relative ease, although the picture is complicated by the fact that many of the French women registered as searching for this kind of employment are naturalised French citizens but not French *d'origine*. That is, they may well be first-generation migrants and belong to racialised groups, but this is not represented in the official figures, where they are simply listed as French citizens. That this group is significant is apparent in the employment register of the Emploi Daubigny.

The Emploi Daubigny is recognised by the government as an *agence intermédiaire*, an organisation that officially places unemployed people in part-time work. Its statistics are passed on annually to the French national statistics agency and thereby contribute to government figures on paid household work. Its objective is to find work for unemployed people, and the employment it finds is almost all in household work. According to its annual report in 1994 it dealt with 22,215 working hours for 514 *fournisseurs d'ouvrage*, as employers are termed. Eighty per cent of employers (412) were private individuals, the remainder small businesses and associations. The employers were mainly based in the 17th arrondissement, wanting child carers, people to do household tasks or to look after elderly relatives. Sixty per cent of those looking for work were women and 40 per cent men; 56 per cent of those asking for work (273 out of 489) were foreigners and 44 per cent were French (216). This official breakdown followed the French practice of not distinguishing between those who are French *d'origine* and those who have acquired French citizenship. The ED's 1995 employment register, however, an unofficial document with the purely practical purpose of listing who was available for work so they could be placed with employers, indicated that many of the French people who approached them looking for work were not French *d'origine*. Seventy-four of 171 workers registered (43 per cent, as in 1994) were French. But 24 of these 74 workers had a different *pays d'origine* noted, two had years of entry noted against their names, and two were simply *Francaise/etrangère, Francaise/noire*. So a maximum of 46 workers were *French d'origine*, although it is likely to be even less. As the Emploi Daubigny volunteer interviewed revealingly put it when asked about the proportion of those applying to them who were *French d'origine*: 'The real French people? Very small. It's difficult to know, but very very small.' Although I was not allowed to see the Emploi Daubigny

71

employment book, staff members stated quite openly that they asked potential employers 'whether or not they are against employing foreigners in their house'. One volunteer there told me that 'it was really impossible to find work for the really black people' like the Congolese because 'they are too lazy' and 'just sit around all the time'. This process of noting country of origin for at least some of the French citizens in the registration book, but eliminating this information from the annual report, which is used to compile official figures, illustrates that despite the state's anxiety to deny difference between French citizens, it is in reality very important to employers.

Although not an officially recognised as an *agence intermédiaire*, the AGF like the Emploi Daubigny offers a service to residents of the 17th arrondissement in terms of introducing employers and workers. In general, it seems that the AGF deals with more requests for work and employers than the Emploi Daubigny. Between 4 September 1995 and 19 January 1996 AGF registered 408 workers and 257 employers. The employer does not come into the office, but phones in the hours of work and duties required (but not rates of pay) and this information is recorded in an employment book. The worker is then shown the employment book and an attempt to match both demands is made. If this is possible, the worker is given the employer's number, and may have no further contact with the AGF since, unlike the ED system, workers are paid direct by their employers. A further significant difference between the AGF and the ED is that the majority of jobs offered through the AGF are full-time, often including overtime.

Like the ED, the AGF allows discrimination by employers to go unchallenged. The AGF volunteer explained, with some discomfort, that they asked employers whether or not they would be prepared to accept a black person. If they are not, then the employer's details are marked 'PPC', 'Pas Personne de Couleur'. Numbers so marked are alarmingly high. From 4 September 1995 to 19 January 1996, 54 out of a total of 257 employers, or 21 per cent, indicated that they would not accept a particular group, usually black people and/or Maghrebians. Sometimes a string of groups were rejected: 'No blacks, Maghrebians or Asians, prefers English speaker', or a preference was indicated for one group over another: 'Prefer EU or Senegalese. No Maghrebians.' The volunteer knew that this was illegal and the organisation's records are destroyed every year because of this illegal and recorded discrimination.

Unlike the workers registered with the ED, those on the AGF's books are almost exclusively women. Again, there are a surprising number of French citizens registered, but there is a similar confusion over the proportion of those who are French *d'origine*: so in the AGF's employment book from 4 September 1995 to 12 January 1996, 90 of the 347 women were French (25 per cent). Of these 90 French women, 32 had a different *pays d'origine* noted down. Given that different AGF volunteers did not always note the same information, there is no guarantee that the remaining 58 French women (17 per cent of the total number of women) were all French *d'origine* – although there are such women who look for employment as domestic workers through the AGF.

From the employment books of the ED and the AGF it is clear that, while the majority of those looking for domestic work are not French, even in the cities there are significant numbers of French people willing to do this kind of work, although many of these are naturalised French citizens. One must remember, however, that both these associations check that those coming to them have a legal right to work, and are therefore unlikely to attract large numbers of undocumented foreigners. So, for example, although most of the Filipino and Mauritian community work in this sector, not a single Filipina and very few Mauritians figure in the employment books. The effect of informal networks and word of mouth should also be borne in mind – perhaps accounting for some of the concentrations of particular nationalities in each association. For example, 50 of the AGF registered workers were from Côte d'Ivoire and 92 from Morocco, but the ED had only 7 Ivoireans and 18 Moroccans registered. So it is not possible to draw any conclusions about the situation in Paris as a whole from the agency books, other than that domestic work is an extremely important area of employment for migrant women, and that their contribution to the sector is not recognised in the official data.

What is striking about the third country nationals represented in the AGF and ED employment books is the wide range of nationalities, in particular Africans from the Maghreb and French sub-Saharan colonies. The major nationalities on their books were Moroccans, Algerians and Ivoireans, but there were also people from Tunisia, Zaire, Cameroon, Colombia, Congo, Haiti, Mali, Mauritius, Peru, Senegal, Spain, Iran, Egypt, Poland, Bosnia, Togo, Sri Lanka and elsewhere. In this respect Paris was similar to Athens and markedly different from Barcelona. Although immigration to France is far more strictly controlled than immigration to Greece, domestic work in those countries has not been officially recognised, as it is in Spain and Italy, as employment for immigrant women. There has been no permit for domestic work and no governmental control over what nationalities work in this sector. It is not clear if any nationalities predominate. The employers' federation, FEPEM, confirmed that Maghrebians formed a significant proportion of Parisian domestic workers, but claimed that domestic workers from other African countries were unusual. According to the AGF, however, not only do other Africans equal the number of Maghrebians but their numbers have been growing over the past seven or eight years, and if trends continue they will outnumber them in the 17th arrondissement. It may be that the discrepancy between the experiences of the AGF and FEPEM arises partly because FEPEM workers are all documented, while those employed through the AGF may well be working off the books, since the AGF takes no responsibility for ensuring compliance to the law beyond checking immigration status.

The AGF and ED employment books indicate that non-French nationals are likely to be younger than French nationals. Age differences are more clearly apparent when one looks at the percentage of people within a certain age range looking for work as domestic workers (Table 5.1).

Table 5.1 Age range of people looking for employment as domestic workers

Age (year)	French nationals ED (%)	French nationals AGF (%)	Non-French nationals ED (%)	Non-French nationals AGF (%)
Up to 20	11	12	2	4
21–39	39	41	61	63
40–49	31	20	29	24
50+	19	27	8	9
	100	100	100	100

French nationals are more concentrated among older and younger workers, while non-French tend to be in their twenties and thirties. To some extent this may be supported by the findings of the Direction de l'Animation de la Recherche des Études et des Statistiques, which in 1995 produced a report on the development of the employment of domestic workers between 1992 and 1994 (DARES 1995). Based on official data, the report found that 99 per cent of employees were women and that their average age was forty. Their pattern of employment is shown in Table 5.2. Crucially, there is no breakdown by nationality, or even by French/non-French citizenship.

Table 5.2 Tasks and age of domestic workers

Task	Average age	Average hrs/wk
Childcare	33	17
Household work	41	5
Care of the elderly	39	19

Source: DARES (1995)

The educational levels of the domestic workers that I met varied considerably. The general impression given by agencies and associations was that the academic qualifications of foreign women working as domestics were very low and that this was why they were working in such numbers in the sector. Of the five women I met at the voluntary association Cefia, only one had been to school, and that had been between the ages of seven and thirteen. She was the only person to have been employed other than as a cleaner/domestic worker, having come to Paris originally to study and work as a dressmaker. Her maths and French were not good enough, however, and this combined with poor health made her leave the company and take up work as a carer for the old, the sick and the disabled. The other four women (from Morocco, Senegal, Gambia and Algeria) had no experience of working outside their own homes. This was in contrast to the nine Filipinas interviewed, who had left education between 17 and 27. All had been employed outside their homes in a wide variety of occupations – Bureau of Internal Revenue, secretary in advertising company, snack bar proprietor, etcetera. None had done anything other than domestic work while in France, however, unless one includes 'sewing' and 'sometimes cooking and cleaning cars'. This is in keeping with findings in other European cities, where generally Filipinas tend to be among the best educated of migrants. Notably few Filipinas spoke any French at all, although generally they spoke English very well, and as elsewhere were prized for it. Employers usually spoke to them in English and stipulated they use English to their children, making it very difficult for them to learn French.

Table 5.3 Educational level of those applying to ED for employment in 1995

Level	1994 (%)	1995 (%)
Illiterate	7	4
Primary	29	25
Secondary	22	22
Technical	18	23
Baccalaureat	12	15
Degree	8	8

This is not to say, however, that the educational level of non-French domestic workers is uniformly low apart from Filipinas. The ED, unlike the AGF, keeps a note of the educational levels of workers registering there. These are not the same as the educational levels of women working as domestic workers, and may be particularly distorted because there is usually no indication as to the gender of the worker, except in the total numbers. It is possible, nevertheless, to make out some useful figures (Table 5.3).

There is no gender breakdown of these figures, but using the grammatical gender of 'previous occupation' one can conclude that the seven people who described themselves as 'illiterate' were all women working in the home. But there were also women with Baccalaureat qualifications who were working as domestics – teachers, accountants and other professions from Congo, Malaysia, Cameroon, Poland and Zaire. At least 66 per cent of the women presenting themselves for employment to the ED had previously been domestic workers in private households.

In Paris live-out work is predominant. Of the many nationalities spoken to, the only group among whom live-in full-time work was relatively common was the Filipino community. This was also, however, the largest group of undocumented workers to whom I had access. It may be that, as in other cities, there is some correlation between immigration status and live-in work. Filipinas brought out many of the employment problems expressed in Athens and Barcelona: excessive working hours, working with animals, working for no extra money in the homes of employers' families, having to provide free 'trial' labour (and often not employed at the end of it), sexual harassment and false accusations of stealing were all mentioned. There were some complaints, too, about the quality of the service rooms offered, often not in the employer's flat, but on the top floor of the apartment block:

> *Filipina:* Though my room is not so nice as you can say. Others they have studios and mine is something just for to sleep, there is no facilities for maintaining a bath or anything, just a little lavabo, that's all.

> *Interviewer:* So where do you take a bath then?

> *Filipina:* I go to her place, I go to their place. If I have time, I have my small babybath there.... I was allowed to use the bath for the children, but the problem is I have no time, because the moment I enter the house I don't know what to touch, I don't have time to take a bath.

It was generally felt that among the Filipino community wages for the undocumented were not significantly lower than for those with papers; indeed, they could even be higher, since neither employer nor worker are making tax or social security payments. But this is not necessarily so for all undocumented workers: Aisha from Morocco worked for eleven francs an hour taking care of two children and doing housework. For the Filipinos, however, the principal problem is that undocumented workers are not protected, receiving neither sick pay nor other social security benefits. This led to a lively discussion between documented and undocumented as to whether undocumented workers were exploited more because of a lack of assertiveness or because they are in an intrinsically weaker position. Several points came out of this discussion, including, importantly, the particular difficulties of those entering France as domestic workers with their employers, who are not given work permits. This situation, in fact, helps to explain the origin of the Filipino community in France, concentrated in Paris and Côte D'Azur, areas where Middle Eastern employers settled following the outbreak of civil war in Lebanon (1975), the fall of the Shah of Iran (1979), and the outbreak of the Iran–Iraq war in 1980. With them these wealthy refugees brought their Filipino domestic workers, often on tourist visas. 'I was not allowed to leave the house. I was only able to get out when my employer brought me to the police Préfecture together with his lawyer. The lawyer took care of all my papers and I didn't know what these papers were' (Quimpo 1994: 3). Other workers accompany their employers on holiday, as they do also to London and Southern Spain. Of course, this is not the only way Filipinos enter France, and as the community has been established so familiar patterns of chain migration have set in, although this continues to be largely clandestine. The employment situation described by these workers has much in common with that outlined by similar workers in other countries of exploitation, impossible demands and brutal treatment. Maria accompanied her Saudi Arabian employers to Paris:

> eighteen hours of work a day, seven days a week; badly fed, badly treated, hurt, beaten.... Maria begged her mistress to let her return to Manila to no avail. After seven months she fled. Alone, undocumented, without money, in a strange city.
>
> (O'Dy 1995)

But the consensus is that difficulties do not disappear once workers leave their original employers. French employers, too, may be cruel, as is well documented by the case of Veronique Akobe, a young woman imprisoned for the murder of her wealthy French employer and the wounding of his son. Medical evidence confirmed that the two men had violently sexually assaulted, raped and sodomised her several times: 'They killed something in me, something of my real self' (quoted in *Liberation*, February 1990, p. 42).

Germany

The most visible area of paid domestic work in Berlin is working as live-out cleaners with some babysitting or other caring work, but only on a part-time basis. Compared with other European cities it seems that there are few migrant women working as live-in child carers. This may be partly because there is some remuneration (although very modest) for mothers who care for their own children, and because privatised childcare is often provided by *tagşmutter* ('day mothers'), much like UK childminders. These women offer day care within their own homes, not in the homes of their employers, and although such work may be – and is – undertaken by non-Germans settled in Germany, it is not suitable for undocumented workers whose living conditions are often extremely poor. From interviews and advertisements it is also clear that in Berlin care of the elderly is not the hugely expanding area of employment that it is for migrants in other European cities, chiefly because it is far more regulated than elsewhere: 'You don't work so much looking after people who are ill, because there is a special law about that and you have to do it officially. Illegals used to do this work, but not any more.' In 1994 compulsory social insurance, already covering unemployment, accidents at work, health and pensions, was extended, after much controversy, to include long-term nursing care costs, whether at home or in a nursing home. This *Pflegeversichening*, or care insurance, means that those who are paid under it need to have documentation.

Live-in domestic workers were less visible in Berlin than in any other city visited. It seems from those who have had recourse to support groups that they are mainly from Eastern Europe and the former Soviet Union, and are extremely vulnerable.

> The problem is when they stay with the families, they are very badly paid and very badly treated. I don't have much contact with them, because the Polish people are mainly livé-out. A lot of people do live-in but it is difficult to contact them. As far as I know this is a closed story, they have no contact with other people, no information, they don't know where to get help for their problems.
> (Volunteer with the Polnischer Socialrat)

Unfortunately there is as yet no means of estimating the number or proportion of live-in domestic workers in Berlin. Advertisements for and from domestic workers appear in many Berlin newspapers, particularly the local papers. In the publications I had access to, 58 out of 254 domestic workers (23 per cent) advertising for employment in the first week of September 1996 stated that they were not German. Although Polish women have been working in small numbers in this sector since 1980, most of those interviewed believed that the practice of hiring a domestic worker to clean one's house was relatively new in Berlin, really beginning only in the early 1990s, but that it is becoming increasingly widespread. Domestic work seems to be concentrated among the Polish and national groups who are more recent arrivals. As elsewhere in Europe, a hierarchy of nationality operates, whereby some national groups can expect to earn more than others. The salary range for domestic workers is DM7–15 (£3.10–£6.70) an hour, with Polish women commonly earning DM15. This is somewhat misleading, of course, as not all workers are paid by the hour, and those who live in might have to be available 24 hours a day. The Polnischer Socialrat put the situation well:

> Pay for domestic workers depends on nationality. Polish get more money than Ukranians and Belorussians. Polish can get fifteen marks an hour, Soviet Union ten marks and under. Or they are paid weekly or monthly which is not so good, because then you can be working for someone more hours but don't get paid as much as fifteen marks, maybe five marks an hour, so people prefer to be paid by the hour.

There are certainly domestic workers who are being abused physically, mentally and sexually, as well as low-level abuse and exploitation. The extent of abuse is extremely difficult to gauge: 'I am shocked at a lot of the women's stories, but the problem is they do not speak out. They are ashamed and afraid' (Volunteer at the Polnischer Socialrat). This is chiefly because there has been no organising around this issue at all. It is a new area for many nationalities, except for the Polish, who often have the support of family in Poland if they run into difficulties:

> Live-out domestic workers have problems too: they live here with no insurance, if they are sick then they get no help. For the Poles they can go back to Poland if they get a problem, but for Ukraine, Bulgarians this is a problem.

One issue for domestic workers that is particularly striking in Berlin, however, is the sexualisation of domestic work. Many domestic workers who advertise their labour stipulate 'no sex', or that they are looking for 'serious work'. This was only rarely observed in any of the advertisements placed by domestic workers in other European city newspapers. This is not to say that sexual abuse and harassment does not occur in those cities, or occurs any more often in Berlin, but that the link between domestic work and sexual exploitation is particularly explicit in Berlin. Ana was brought from Romania as a domestic worker for a couple. She lived in their flat, did all their domestic chores, and was regularly beaten and sexually abused by both the man and the woman. They also forced her to have sexual intercourse with their friends, and finally forced her to work as a prostitute to provide them with money to pay for their apartment. The woman had no documents and was illegal in Berlin. She met a man who offered to help her, and escaped from the couple to live with him. She loved him, kept house for him and slept with him for four years, unmarried and still undocumented. When she returned from shopping one day he presented her with her passport, told her he didn't want her any more, and refused to let her enter the house again, even to collect her clothes. Ana approached an association for help, but then disappeared.

Because the predominance of migrant domestic workers in Berlin is a relatively recent phenomenon, and because recent migrants from Eastern Europe, apart from the Polish, are not organised, one cannot gauge the range of nationalities working in private households, nor the extent to which they live in. It seems, however, that domestic work is an important employment sector for women from Eastern Europe, Poland in particular, and the countries of South America.

Polish domestic workers

Polish migration to the Federal Republic of Germany (FRG) began in the mid-1970s following the official termination of the Gastarbeiter (Guest-worker) policies in 1973, when the federal government signed bilateral treaties with Central and East European countries as part of its new policy with Eastern Europe. An important component of this policy was freedom of exit for *Aussiedler*, who were welcomed to the FRG. *Aussiedler* are 'ethnic Germans' from Eastern Europe, constructed as being German 'by blood'. By 1989 Poland accounted for the largest number of *Aussiedler* (365,234) followed by Romania (147,528) and the Soviet Union, (72,664). There were also significant numbers of Polish refugees from 1980 onwards, reaching 29,023 in 1988. While Polish long-term immigration has declined, there continue to be large numbers of Polish workers in Germany. This is largely because since 1991 Polish citizens with valid documents have been allowed into Germany as tourists for three-month periods without visas. They are not, except in particular circumstances, given a work permit. This has resulted in 'pendular migration', for 'illegal' work for short periods, particularly attractive in Berlin because the distance is so short. There are strong Polish social networks in Germany, and a profitable exchange rate.

The living and working conditions of Polish domestic workers in Berlin should be seen within this context. There are some 27,000 Polish citizens legally resident in Berlin, and 80,000 *Aussiedler*. The main employment for men is in construction; for women it is domestic work in private households. The majority of Polish domestic workers in Berlin are pendular migrants, working in Germany but living in Poland. Because of Berlin's geographical proximity to Poland, women are able to travel to Berlin for a week's work, returning to Poland for the weekend. This arrangement means that Polish women rarely live in, working instead as cleaners on an hourly rate for several different employers, without legal protection or insurance. Because Poland and their families are close by, these difficulties do not loom as large as with other nationalities. Maria came to Berlin in 1981 from Poland. She was 24 and well educated, but without a permit could only find domestic work. Although she feels that most of her employers were polite and she cannot complain about her treatment, she is clear that the work is difficult and demeaning, and that employers' attitudes and demands can put an intolerable strain on their domestic workers. Her first employers were doctors with three children, two dogs and a house of fifteen rooms. The worker had to do the domestic chores and feed, exercise and clean the dogs. 'Although she was very polite, the woman was very finicky' and insisted on sixteen different cleaning cloths, each with its own purpose (one for cupboard edges, one for inside cupboards, and so on). 'She was always watching me which made the work stressful and claustrophobic.' After nine years with this family as her continuous and sole employer she had to take several weeks off because she had hurt her back at work, and her employer telephoned to complain that she had to employ someone else to cover for her. By mutual agreement she left their employment. Her experiences with other employers were no happier, to the extent that Maria feared for her own sanity: 'Some women called me their "good fairy", but in the end I was only ever the cleaner'. She finally managed to move out of domestic work and to get office work: 'I came to life again. I liked going to work. I got my dignity back.'

Maria's description of employment as a domestic worker is typical of the 'lucky' women who escape abuse and gross exploitation, but nevertheless have to endure a stressful and unsatisfactory employer–employee relationship, and demeaning work that sometimes reflects the employer's neurosis.

Non-Polish migrant domestic workers

To judge by the advertisements that I saw offering work in private households, South Americans were the largest group of domestic workers after Polish. Although they usually described themselves as Latin or South American, several were more specific, including Bolivians, Peruvians, Argentians and Brazilians. Six of the 21 were men – unlike the Polish, who were all women. This suggests that in Berlin, as in Barcelona, Latin American men, unlike African or Eastern European men, also work in this sector. There are also increasingly large numbers of undocumented Latin American migrants, particularly women from Brazil. This migration is very heterogeneous, however, and there are also women from Mexico, Chile, Nicaragua, Peru and Bolivia. Many of them are working as domestic workers, but little is known of their hiring and working conditions. Illegal placement agencies for domestic workers from Peru do have contacts in Berlin, however, since undocumented Peruvian women are smuggled to Spain via Berlin by agents operating in the city.

There is a small Filipino community in Germany but – in contrast with the UK, France, Spain and Italy – very few of them are domestic workers. Many are married to German men. In the 1980s there were significant numbers of Filipino women in Berlin, many without documents, employed as domestic workers and nannies in the households of US servicemen. In 1990 the Southeast Asia Information Center estimated there were up to 15,000 Filipinas working illegally in Germany. Recruiters charged between £1,700 and £3,400 for jobs in Germany and promised high wages which never materialised. The employers were largely families of US military personnel, and there was a large demand for Filipinas on the grounds that 'the Filipina was the only thing we could afford'. Wages as low as £17 a month were supplemented by duty-free goods at the super-market. At the time of the US withdrawal there was some media interest in what would become of these women whom their employers had left, and whether they would take on domestic jobs in German households. This does not seem to have been the case. Virtually no Filipinas work as domestics in private households in Berlin today, and those who do work a few hours a week as an extra job. According to the association Ban Ying, those women who stayed on are now working as maids in hotels, in office cleaning agencies, or as secretaries and clerical staff – that is, in the more formalised service economy. Many of them have also married German men.

There are estimated to be some 8,000 Thais in Berlin, approximately half of them undocumented and almost all of them women. The most significant area of employment for Thai women in Berlin is prostitution; many have been trafficked, and owe large debts averaging some 20,000 Marks (£8,968) to the traffickers. As with Filipinas, no Thai women advertised for employment as domestic workers, and Ban Ying does not know of any Thai women who have moved from prostitution into private domestic work – although some have moved to cleaning agencies. This seems to be for two main reasons. The first is economic: in prostitution they can earn DM50 (£22.40) per customer, DM25 (£11.20) for them-selves and DM25 to the pimp, averaging maybe some DM3000 (£1,345) a month though earnings vary according to the area worked, the age and physical appearance of the woman, and what she is prepared to do. This is substantially more than a domestic worker, who can expect to earn DM1000–2000 (£448–£896) a month if she is in 'full' employment. Moreover, Thai women have been trafficked to Germany since the early 1980s, and are now, whatever their employment, closely associated with the sex industry, to an extent that renders them unsuitable for domestic work. As the Ban Ying worker put it: 'Thai women are so sexualised now by Germans that they would not let a Thai woman touch their grand-mother.' Thai women do work as domestic workers, however, as one facet of their exploitation during the trafficking process. This work is unpaid and performed in slave-like conditions. The women who are trafficked often come from rural areas of Thailand. They may be approached by someone well known locally, or a relative whom they trust, and offered the opportunity to work in Germany – in a restaurant, perhaps, with the opportunity to marry a nice German man. They are brought to Germany, indebted to the person who pays their fare and their living expenses. When they arrive in Berlin they are told there is no job, but still there is the debt to be paid off, so young women have little option but to turn to prostitution. Most are on three-month tourist visas and so must work illegally, although prostitution in itself is not illegal in Berlin. Some women are trafficked into enforced marriages, the traffickers advertising them or responding to advertisements in the personal columns of news-papers. While they are waiting they stay in the houses of the traffickers and often must do the household work.

> Physical abuse in these households is common, beating, physical and mental abuse, calling them names, treating them as less than human. This experience is very traumatic, although the women are poor, they have until now had their dignity.
> (Volunteer with the Polnischer Socialrat)

Nu Nu came to Berlin from north-east Thailand. She had a sister in Berlin who had married a German and she hoped to do the same. She started working in the sex industry, but could not cope with it – there is high competition between Thai women working in prostitution in Berlin and women are often in the position that they must take all clients, whatever their demands. Her sister helped her to find a job with a very wealthy Thai-European family, working both in their highly exclusive shop and in the household. By this time Nu Nu had been in the country over three months and was an overstayer. She was treated very badly by the employing family, but was completely dependent on them because of her legal status. After some months she became sick and weak. Her employers were only concerned that she continued working and did not help. She was too frightened to go for help elsewhere. Finally her sister persuaded her she had no choice but to seek medical attention. By then it was too late. She had inoperable cancer and died in hospital in Berlin. Her employer offered no help and did not visit her. Until she died she only wanted to leave hospital so she could work to send money to her family.

Their traffickers may also force them to work in the houses of friends and relatives, again unpaid, without even the opportunity of slightly reducing their debt. Ban Ying also drew attention to the cleaning work undertaken by Thai women who work as prostitutes. Unlike German women, Thais must clean and prepare the brothels where they work as a part of their duties. This enforced domestic labour is clearly only one facet of the gross exploitation and abuse of Thai women, and cannot be taken from this broader context. The broader context, however, does indicate a relationship between sexual exploitation and domestic labour that seems to be closer, or at least more apparent, than in other European cities.

Conclusions

The fieldwork carried out is summarised in Figure 5.1.

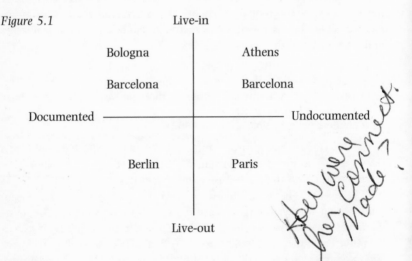

Figure 5.1

Live-in

Bologna   Athens

Barcelona   Barcelona

Documented ——————————————— Undocumented

Berlin   Paris

Live-out

Significant proportions of domestic workers can be found working in each sector in each city. There are undocumented live-in workers in Berlin and Paris. The exception is Athens where, at the time fieldwork was conducted, with only one exception workers were *all* undocumented and living in. Long hours and abuse were particularly prevalent in Athens. This does suggest that immigration status (workers' relation to the state), and living place (workers' relation to the employer) are key variables in the living and working conditions of migrant domestic workers. These axes – relations with the state and relations with the employer – may vary in other ways, as shown in Figure 5.2.

84

Figure 5.2

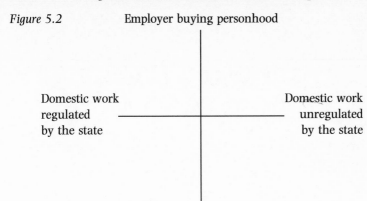

Employer buying personhood

Domestic work regulated by the state ——————— Domestic work unregulated by the state

Employer buying labour power

Such variations all have a combined impact on the workers' living and working conditions which, partly in consequence, also vary widely. Life is not as neat as a diagram! The areas are related, so immigration status and live-in/live-out work are not independent of each other – people may live in because they are undocumented.

Notes

1 Rahal-Sidhoum 1987; European Forum of Left Feminists 1993.
2 Marie 1984; French Ministry of Social Affairs 1984; Wihtol de Wenden and de Ley 1986.
3 On the 4 September 1996 *Berliner Morgenpost* carried 12 advertisements from domestic workers under '*Hauspersonal*'. Four stated their ethnic origin (three Polish and one African). In the *Zweite Hand* of the week beginning 31 August 1996, under '*Hauswirtschaft Reinigung*', there were a total of 148 advertisers. Of these, 12 stated that they were Polish and 6 that they were South American, while 5 indicated that they were foreign (e.g. 'speaks good German') but did not say where they were from. Under 'Baby-sitting' there were 43 advertisers, of which 7 said that they were foreigners. Under '*Sonstige Stellengesuche*' ('other jobs') 3 foreign domestic workers advertised: 1 African man, 1 Brazilian woman, and 1 Portuguese man; and 4 foreign domestic workers (1 Polish, 2 South American and 1 'foreign') advertised under '*Mehrfachgesuche*' (others). The edition of *TIP*, a Berlin weekly arts and culture magazine, for the week beginning 5 September 1996 contained 63 people looking for household work, cleaning and baby-sitting, and 28 mentioned that they were foreigners.

6

Changing the Rules

The Case of the United Kingdom

Young professionals in UK cities spend a good deal of money on domestic help. One agency quotes the example of a 25-year old money broker in London who said he wanted someone to do everything his mother did for him when he lived at home. Once the agency had established that this did not include bathing him or wiping his nose, it was more than happy to provide someone to cook, clean, iron, shop, sign for the post and deliveries, pay the milkman, organise repairs and decorating, and attend to every other practical domestic detail of the young man's life.

(*The Which? Guide to Domestic Help*:18)

Domestic work in private households in the UK is receiving an unprecedented amount of attention. Books, radio and television documentaries, newspapers and magazine articles outline the conflict between work and family life, and the consequent change of culture needed. The particular burdens on women and the continuing unfairness in the division of domestic labour is also receiving attention (though not, as the predominantly female columnists point out, much action). Paid domestic workers, most particularly nannies, regularly feature in the press. News stories describe child murders and abuse. Features deal with the lack of regulation, the dangers, and how to spot a problem: 'Not very nice, but occasionally necessary, is the micro-CC TV technology allowing parents to keep tabs on childminders they may have doubts about' (*The Guardian* 4 February 1999, G2: 15) reads a consumer article on 'Your home safety shopping list'.

In 1998 Which? Books published *The Which? Guide to Domestic Help*, describing it as providing 'Essential advice on employing people in your home, from cleaners to au pairs, nannies and carers'. Citing a 1997 Mintel survey, it claimed that the amount spent on domestic workers in the UK had quadrupled from £1.1 billion in 1987 to £4.3 billion in 1996. Reasons given by *Which?* for the increase include 'working women', the disappearance of extended families and the consequent need to buy in childcare and care for elderly members of the family, early retirement and the 'cash-rich, time-poor market', high earners who feel they do not have the time for household chores. Thus essentially the guide isolates the factors discussed in Chapter 2 that explain the 'need' for reproductive labour, including (though not labelled as such) issues of status and paid reproductive labour. It glosses over the corresponding existence of a 'cash-poor, time-rich' or the 'time-poor, cash-poorer' labour pool to cater for this market. In a paper given to the Royal Geographic Society conference in 1997, Rosie Cox revealed from her survey of Hampstead that many domestic workers were employed, not because people did not have the time to do their own domestic work but because they 'merely wanted to avoid doing the chores themselves and therefore gain the time for extra leisure'. Her work suggests that the cash-rich, time-rich will also employ domestic workers, not just the cash-rich, time-poor. Those who were doing the work, on the other hand, were 'the poorest 10 per cent', often women with heavy childcare responsibilities (scarcely 'time rich' themselves), or with uncertain immigration status. According to Ms Cox's findings, while migrant labour is readily available to do such work in London, outside of the capital domestic workers are more likely to be 'poor English'. Gregson and Lowe have found however, that the UK is unlike many other industrialised countries in that

> no ... close association exists between ethnicity, female migration and waged domestic labour; although anecdotal evidence suggests that in London at least, if not in our study areas, certain households are using migrant women of colour as waged domestic labour.
> (Gregson and Lowe 1994: 123)

They suggest that

> the nanny in contemporary Britain is an occupational category characterised predominantly by young, unmarried women from white collar, intermediate status households, whereas cleaning is the domain of older, married, working-class women.
> (Gregson and Lowe 1994: 124)

Certainly it seems that while in the UK citizens tend to work in the higher-status and better-paid reproductive jobs, in the country as a whole domestic work is not dominated by particular ethnic groups as it is in other EU countries and certain areas of London.

That being said, there are significant numbers of migrants and au pairs employed by middle-class households (this is omitting those who are employed within their own migrant communities) and the *Which? Guide* includes a chapter on 'Employing Foreign Nationals'. This gives advice on the immigration regulations applying to domestic workers entering under different regimes (au pairs, asylum seekers, students) and considers racial discrimination concerns – including reports that some employers view Filipino or Indonesian workers as cheap substitutes for British workers. It exhorts employers to respect customs and 'cultural differences', and asserts that 'no reputable agency will discriminate between races'. It provides no clues as to why employers should choose to employ foreign nationals rather than UK citizens.

The *Which? Guide* also includes a section entitled 'Abuse of overseas domestic workers'. This focuses on a particular group of workers, those brought to the UK accompanying their employers. Their employers are often, though not always, non-UK nationals. These are not the only migrants working as domestic workers in the UK, but I wish to examine their particular situation since it reveals the structural reasons for difficulties faced by domestic workers, and the potential responses to these.

The situation of migrant domestic workers in the UK first began to cause concern in the summer of 1984, when staff at the Commission for Filipino Migrant Workers (CFMW) in West London began to notice a pattern emerging among the Filipinos who were coming to them for advice and support. CFMW had been established in 1979 to serve the needs of the Filipino migrant community in the UK, and it was particularly concerned to act as a facilitator and supporter of groups organised by Filipinos themselves. It had participated in the largely successful campaign against the deportation of Filipino resident domestic workers (mainly working in hospitals and hotels rather than private households) in 1981–2, and had by 1984 already helped set up several Filipino groups. It was at this time that the organisation began to be approached by numbers of women who had left abusive private employers and had subsequently become 'undocumented', living and working 'illegally'. They were coming with similar problems – no passport, unpaid wages, no belongings and disturbing reports of brutal conditions. As the months passed and the numbers increased it was becoming increasingly difficult to respond to their needs on a case by case basis, and in November 1984 CFMW set up a meeting attended by seventeen domestic workers and ten supporters with the purpose of sharing their experiences and discussing a way forward.

Participating in this meeting was a significant step for all present. For the domestic workers, isolated and vulnerable, it meant coming out in front of others, risking being reported to the immigration authorities and subsequent deportation; for the supporters there was concern that they were acting illegally and that, at the very least, the Centre would be closed down should news that they were facilitating such a meeting leak out. Yet once they had come together it was clear that this was a very positive development, and that there was much to be gained from continuing to meet to share information and offer mutual support. Over the next few months it became apparent that abuse and exploitation of domestic workers was widespread, and not restricted to Filipinos but endured by many workers from all over the world. It was decided that CFMW would negotiate with the Home Office, to bring the situation of this group of migrant domestic workers to its attention so that it could rectify what was, to the group at least, an obvious injustice.

'The Concession'

What was the situation of migrant domestic workers, and what did they identify as its root causes? Prior to 1977 resident domestic workers, whether working for hotels, nursing homes, hospitals or private households, entered the UK with a work permit. In 1975, when women's work permits were restricted to 'skilled' workers, resident domestic workers were specifically excluded from the restrictions and a quota for their numbers set. That year 66 per cent of permits issued to resident domestics were issued to Filipinos. Other communities represented included Latin American, Moroccan, Portuguese and Turkish. The quotas were progressively reduced; as from August 1977 only European women were permitted to enter the UK as domestic workers, and at the end of 1979 quotas were phased out altogether.

Yet the government was very aware of a continuing demand for live-in domestic workers in private households.

> Looking at our national interest, if wealthy investors, skilled workers and others with the potential to benefit our economy were unable to be accompanied by their domestic staff they might not come here at all but take their money and skills to other countries only too keen to welcome them.
>
> (Lord Reay, Hansard Col. 1052 28 November 1990, House of Lords Debate on Overseas Domestic Workers)

To allow for this demand, the government devised a concession for wealthy employers that would enable them to continue bringing their domestic workers to the UK. Under the domestic worker concession the employer could bring in workers under one of two categories, as 'visitors' or as 'persons named to work with a specified employer'. Immigration officials were issued with the following guidelines:

89

A person engaged abroad as a domestic servant, who has been in the service of the employer for more than twelve months abroad may accompany the employer to the United Kingdom to continue the employment. The employer must undertake to provide maintenance and accommodation for any dependants and the Immigration Officer must be satisfied that the person intends to continue in the employment. Domestics may be allowed to benefit from this arrangement even if they are outside the normal age limits or have dependent children. Leave to enter should be given on Code 4 for up to twelve months. [Code 4 gives leave to enter on condition that the holder only engages in employment for a particular named person; the holder is required to register with the police].

Domestic servants, chauffeurs, private secretaries and other employees who render personal service may be allowed to enter with their employers if only a visit is intended in which case leave to enter as a visitor on Code 3 for the period of the employer's authorised stay is appropriate. [Code 3 gives leave to enter for a specified period on condition that the holder does not enter employment paid or unpaid; again, the holder has to register with the police.] If the employer is to remain in the United Kingdom other than as a visitor e.g. for settlement or to set up in business, such employees require work permits.

In practice the stamp given was often a matter of chance, and many domestic workers were given a stamp under Code 5N, namely 'Leave to enter, employment prohibited'. Although the Concession appeared to give some structure to the immigration status of domestic workers accompanying their employers, the reality was very different. Not only were those entering with visitors given visitors' visas (Code 3) even though they were entering for employment, but there was a 'concession culture' under which domestic workers accompanying their employers were admitted to the UK with a wide variety of visas. Many women, particularly African women working for African families, entered as family members, thereby opening themselves to accusations of illegal entry because of deception, even though their immigration status was entirely a matter for their employers and the UK immigration authorities. Vivian is typical:

> She (the employer) brought back two pieces of paper and asked me to sign ... so when I did that the driver took the two pieces of paper back and for a week after that the passport was ready. I do not know how they make it or what happen, even my age.... So the passport was ready and it was time now to get the visa.... So she answered the questions, she said, yes she is coming with me and she will look after, she will help me to care for the children when I go out, and she's going to do some studying.... So I really have nothing to do with the visa and the paper.

There were also workers entering the UK who did not come through immigration controls at all. Aodh O'Halpin, who worked at the CFMW in the 1980s, cites the example of two Filipinas who were staying in Europe with a Saudi Princess who decided to come to London for a visit in her private plane. She brought the domestic workers with her and on landing they were simply ushered through the VIP lounge with no passport formalities for either the employer or her workers. Finally the domestic workers accompanying diplomats were not admitted under the concession but under the category of 'permit free employment' listed under the immigration rules. So the workers coming to CFMW had all entered the UK legally – accompanying wealthy employers as their cooks, cleaners, nannies, and carers – but they had not been given an immigration status independent of their employers. As the then Home Office Minister, David Waddington, stated in a letter to Lord Avebury: 'Admission in such cases is on the basis that the employee will be expected to leave the country with the employer, or on prior termination of the employment' (cited in the booklet accompanying Kalayaan's Open Space film *Domestic Slavery*, broadcast on BBC2, 16 November 1987).

Whatever the stamp on the passport, the many descriptions given by domestic workers of their living and working conditions bore an alarming similarity.

> The smallest things which did not please my madam resulted in abuse, shouting and slapping of my face. One dreadful occasion I washed a jumper in too hot water, this caused shrinkage. I was not only hit, but almost choked to death. The combined attack by the husband and wife left me beaten up on the floor. So I decided this is the time I had to save my life, for me, I am a prisoner, I can't go out, no day off, can't talk to anyone, they pay me £120 a month but I don't receive it. Only if I tell them I have to send money to my family, they give me one month, they owe me five months or more then. So I decided I had to run away.

> I had to clean the house, we live in a very big house which is four floors, do the cooking, look after all the family's needs, their children, their friends' children, about five to ten children on my own. I have to look after them all. I had to cook for them, care for them and do all sorts of work in the house. I had to clean the house, do the gardening, clean the car and also do my female employer's office. I have no day off, no time off for me. She held my passport. I was not allowed to see my passport and I was not allowed to speak to anyone else. She hit me.... Most of the time I stayed in the house crying, hoping that something would free me from there.... I couldn't bear to stand the abuse and the shouting, screaming, calling names and stuff. I couldn't stand it any more so I decided to leave the work.

> As soon as I came to London and to her house I feel like she brought me to jail.... I have to sleep on a shelf, which is made to keep all things and the suitcases, everything.... So morning 4.30 to midnight I have to be up. I

have no rest and I have no place to sit. She ask me not to sit on the chair, not to be near the children. Everytime I go to the toilet I have to wash with the dettol and all and not touch anything about the children. She treat me as if I have bad disease. And always she calling my name, and when I say 'Yes madam, I am here', she shouts, 'What are you doing here? Go and do the work' ... and then in September after two and a half months she passed me to her friend. So I have to work to her friend and she asked her friend not to pay me anything and not to let me go out. My madam said not to talk to anybody. She kept me locked in the house and not even to open the window. All the time the curtains are closed.

One of the factors behind this abuse pinpointed by the group in 1984 was immigration status. They could not change employers legally, and if forced to run away (often without their passports) they could not work for anyone else. Although applications for extensions to remain with the original employers were usually granted, applications to change employers were routinely refused on the basis that no work permit was held on entry and once their original visa expired they lost all right to be in the UK. This meant that, having escaped from one abusive situation, workers were very vulnerable to exploitation by secondary employers (usually British), who could take advantage of their immigration status with poor working conditions, low pay and further abuse. For her MA thesis then Kalayaan staff worker Margaret Healy interviewed ten women before and after their change of employer. She found that two months after the first interview, six had left their British employers. Problems included:

[T]he negotiated salary was not adhered to. Likewise with the hours of work. For example when asked to change a day off or to do overtime, if the worker said she had an appointment with the doctor, the employer would say, 'Well I can always call the Home Office'.... The treatment of the employers ranged from shouting at them, insults to their person, passing derogatory comments; constant complaints. One woman said she was treated 'as if I'm nothing'. One of the six had to sleep on the living-room floor and wasn't given any place to put her personal belongings. She had to keep everything in her bag. One of the women experienced overt racism by the employer making personal derogatory remarks about her, not allowing her to sit on the settee in the sitting room.... Another of the women complained that her male employer was constantly sexually harassing her by making suggestive comments and even offering her money for sexual favours.
(Healy 1994: 29)

In her study Margaret Healy points out that the kinds of comments made by employers phoning the centre looking for workers suggest that they are going to make high demands of their workers:

I'm looking for a domestic help.... I have three children, and expect her to begin work at 6.30–7.00 and work as long as is needed;

I want someone to live-in ... she'll work twenty-four hours of course ... a friend of mine told me Filipinos are willing to work 24 hours a day ... they're willing to do anything;

someone to live-in with the family.... I can bring her here as a student – let her study English in my Training College ... in return she'd live with my family.
(Healy 1993: 31)

Interviewed some two years later Margaret Healy said that problems with physical abuse from second employers – while certainly occurring – were greatly outnumbered by cases of mental abuse and the exertion of psychological or emotional control, with the employer using the threat of immigration papers to extract extra babysitting or fewer days off: 'The more they know the more they will exploit you. So workers think that by telling the employer their whole story it will help, but it doesn't.' As elsewhere in Europe, those hiring domestic workers expected them to work for relatives for free, controlled their access to food, and demanded demeaning work:

Like Manjit. She has a huge house, nine bedrooms, and she has to put the dog to bed, in a lovely bed, and wash his paws before she does with talcum powder to make them nice and white. She has to wash and brush him twice a day. And she has to give it vitamin tablets. Manjit is ill, she's the one that needs the tablets.
(Interview with Margaret Healy)

When one British employer was telephoned to tell her that her undocumented worker had terminal cancer and would not be working for her any longer, her response was: 'Well, what about the dogs? They're very sensitive. This will ruin their holidays.'

In 1998 Cecile Divino interviewed 39 workers on their working conditions, accommodation and access to health services after leaving primary employers. She found that 18 per cent of live-in workers were working eight hours or less a day, and that nearly 30 per cent work more than twelve hours a day, many working up to 16 hours a day. Most are 'on call' in the night – that is, they must be permanently available. It is common for employers to deduct room and board from workers wages. In short:

The wages paid and hours worked in secondary employment by the majority of Overseas Domestic Workers in this sample have improved in comparison with the experiences in primary employment recorded in Kalayaan statistics, but only slightly.
(Divino 1998: 17)

History of a campaign

Workers were clearly hampered by their immigration status, both in terms of the first and second employers. It was decided, therefore, to lobby the UK government to change the immigration regulations tying domestic workers to their employers. The initial response seemed positive. CFMW enlisted the support of Cardinal Hume and the local Kensington and Chelsea Conservative MP, Sir Brandon Rhys Williams. This also meant the organisation at least had some protection should they be accused of criminal activity. The domestic workers and their supporters were meeting regularly, with benefits to the workers themselves:

> I went back to normal. Before, when I was alone, I didn't trust anyone. My experience with my employers meant that I couldn't speak up. It makes you silent and not open. When I began to talk to people in similar situations, and I saw that I was not alone, I realised that the problem was not just to do with me, that it was the Philippines and Britain and the government in those countries.
> (Sandy, quoted in Anderson 1993: 59)

Workers supported each other psychologically and also in meeting the immediate needs of women recently escaped from their employers. They shared information and networks on jobs, and gave loans to help those looking for work. They also would accommodate people until they had found their own place or a live-in job. This eventually became formalised in the organisation of Waling Waling – a Tagalog name for a flower that grows in the mountains of the Philippines, to be found under rocks and stones rather than out in the open. As well as being an organisation for mutual support, Waling Waling was concerned to provide a social service, to help its members lead as normal a life as possible, by organising discos, outings and other events. Crucially, members were also encouraged to join the Transport and General Workers Union (TGWU). CFMW already had links with the TGWU from earlier organising work among Filipinos in the hotel and catering industry. Despite the difficulties attached to their immigration status the TGWU welcomed the new members, again helping to mainstream the domestic workers and their concerns.

While the organisation thrived, however, the negotiations with the Home Office stalled. By 1987 it was clear that a full-blown campaign was needed to shame the British government into a change. On 16 June 1987, following the broadcast of a Face the Facts programme on BBC Radio 4, when CFMW was overwhelmed by the public response with hundreds of offers of support, the organisation Kalayaan was founded. Kalayaan, the Tagalog word for 'Freedom', was established to work for the rights of all migrant domestic workers, and specifically to campaign for the right to an immigration status that recognised their standing as workers, their right to change employers, and their right to normal work benefits and health care. It was established by the supporters of Waling Waling to be the public face of unauthorised domestic workers, raising the profile of the issue and helping through referrals to other groups and service agencies. It was also concerned to offer practical support to workers, in particular legal advice. Thus the basic structure of the campaign was established: two organisations, one a self-help group composed of the domestic workers themselves, the other comprising their supporters working to change the immigration guidelines governing the entry of domestic workers into the UK.

These different groups fulfilled different roles. The workers' group was and continues to be crucial for support and networking among the workers themselves. When people run away from their employers having been physically, psychologically and maybe sexually abused, they often have all kinds of needs that can best be met by people who have endured similar situations. Waling Waling (now the United Workers Association) provides practical and emotional support. Through a membership sub-scription service it can help people over their immediate needs when they are recovering from their experiences or looking for work; it can help find jobs and accommodation, and provide someone to talk to. It also has a wider social function, and the importance of the informal networks that it facilitates, in both social and work terms, should not be underestimated. For Kalayaan, too, running an effective support service – providing immediate and concrete help, with solicitors, doctors, counsellors and other inputs, not just future promises – was important to the campaign and to developing relations with domestic workers. Organising, working closely with and being accountable to a strong organisation of migrant domestic workers was crucial to the Kalayaan campaign. Migrant domestic workers were not cast as victims, to be rescued by campaigners: rather, the groups worked together, using their different skills and social positions. From the campaigning point of view one of the main difficulties faced by Waling Waling was the possibility of deportation, bringing with it the justifiable fear of 'going public'. It was an important function of Kalayaan, then, to be the public face of Waling Waling, dealing with the media, the Home Office and other groups. Its members also brought with them valuable campaigning experience and contacts. Waling Waling members were on the management committee of Kalayaan (but not vice versa). This recognised distinction between undocumented workers and their supporters is a means of avoiding the dominance of the middle-class citizens while using their skills, contacts and goodwill.

With the support of Kalayaan, domestic workers began to find the courage to talk openly about their experiences. In November 1987 they participated in a BBC 2 film, and one worker even allowed her face to be shown:

> I decided to appear in this programme because I wanted to tell my story, and I want the British people and the British government to know what is happening to us and how they can help. Not only Filipinos like us, but other people, other nationalities who are in the same kind of situation. How can we be helped? What can they do for us? That is why I decided to appear in front of the camera on this programme.

Since then many women have followed in the speaker's footsteps, risking identification and deportation in the effort to bring public attention to their case.

Campaign strategies

Media and publicity

Following the public sympathy generated by the Face the Facts and Open Space programmes, it was clear that enlisting public support through judicious use of the media would be crucial to strong campaigning. The media in general, however, were and continue to be hostile to 'illegal immigrants' and it was clear that there had to be some control exercised over their access to their 'story'. All media requests were screened and discussed, and, at Waling Waling's request, a Kalayaan committee member was always present at interviews with Waling Waling members to ensure workers were not intimidated into replying to hostile or inappropriate questions. In general the policy worked well, although it gained Kalayaan some enemies (I remember well a Radio Talk Show host, who had been hassling a domestic worker and was told that she would not participate in his live chat show, telling me, 'If you want control of the media, you'd better stop working in a pissy little community organisation'!) In her 1994 analysis of 85 articles and four television documentaries on the issue, Margaret Healy found that:

> the factual information given by both Kalayaan, CFMW and the domestic workers was presented with the highest degree of accuracy. But what I found particularly impressive was the fierce and open criticism by the media towards the government. Many of the articles took a proactive stance, calling for changes in both government policy and law. The factual information in the majority of the articles and documentaries relied heavily on case studies from the women interviewed. This provided a space for the women to tell their own stories, in doing so it jointly depicts them as taking

an active stance in their situation, revealing their strength, courage and resilience.
(Healy 1994: 57–8)

Having the courage to expose their past (often including stories of violent abuse) enabled Waling Waling members to be regarded as people with their own experiences and stories to tell, rather than 'illegals'. It gave campaigning material a very strong human rights focus, taking individual cases of abuse, people's stories, and then drawing out the role of immigration legislation in facilitating this abuse and showing the possibilities for change. This meant that the campaign could appeal to an audience not necessarily sympathetic to undocumented workers. The danger of such an approach, however, was that, since the nature of the immigration concession meant that many of the employers were non-UK nationals, presenting individual experiences risked allowing the interpretation that the abuse was a consequence of bad 'foreign' cultural practices. I am not for a moment suggesting that one should not highlight and condemn the abuse of domestic workers, whatever the nationality of their employer, but rather that one should be aware of the context in which such condemnation takes place, and also, what it leaves out. Kalayaan and Waling Waling were keen to avoid the notion that the living and working conditions of migrant domestic workers was simply a case of individual bad employers importing uncivilised behaviour. In 1990 Kalayaan began to keep statistics detailing the kinds of difficulties faced by workers they interviewed who had escaped from the employers whom they had accompanied to the UK. Kept annually, these figures are more or less constant year to year. In 1996–7 the 195 workers registered at the centre had worked for employers from 30 different countries. Eighty-four per cent reported psychological abuse, 34 per cent physical abuse and 10 per cent sexual abuse. Fifty-four per cent were locked in, 55 per cent did not have their own bed, and 38 per cent had no regular food. Workers coming to Kalayaan do not necessarily constitute a representative sample – they are workers who have run away from abusive employers, so it could be argued that they are in particularly bad situations; although equally one could say that they are workers who have succeeded in running away, that those who are under the harshest regimes or particularly isolated can never come to the group's attention.

Having such statistics available bolstered the media work. It meant that women's experiences could not be passed off as simply due to a bad employer, and encouraged people to look for the structural causes of such abuse. It gave Kalayaan a reputation for having substance to their arguments and research, and helped to indicate the kinds of support that were necessary. In later years, when the government moved to make changes to the concession, it meant that the difference (or not) that such changes made could be monitored.

Building bridges

The campaign did not rely only on public support and media pressure to advance its objectives, but worked to put the issue of migrant domestic workers on the agenda of other groups, both nationally and internationally. Migrant and refugee community organisations, church groups and human rights organisations lent the campaign crucial support and experience. Key to the campaign's work was its close relationship with the TGWU. As noted above, the relationship with the TGWU had its roots in CFMW's earlier organising work with hotel and catering workers. Many Waling Waling members had joined the TGWU and, despite the complications attached to their immigration status, the union encouraged them to join and participate in branch activities, particularly in union education courses. Workers were given advice and support at special meetings to advise them on what few employment rights they had. Membership of the TGWU meant that Waling Waling could bring the issue of migrant domestic workers before grassroots TGWU membership, but also gave them the opportunity to draw comparisons between their situation and that of other members, particularly women. Crucially, the Union facilitated its Waling Waling members in their public participation in the campaign – covering the cost of their travel to Labour Party conferences, for example. At the campaign level, the TGWU were extremely important in using their political experience and contacts in lobbying the Labour Party, then in opposition.

Lobby and Parliamentary Work

The original response of the Home Office to the newly organised campaign and publicity seemed promising:

> I do sympathise with domestic servants admitted under the arrangements ... who nevertheless find their conditions of employment intolerable ... we remain concerned about this problem and I am open to suggestions as to changes we could make in our immigration control to improve the situation.
>
> (Letter from Mr Timothy Renton, Minister of State for the Home Office, to Mr Michael Day, OBE, Commission for Racial Equality, 27 October 1988)

But one year later nothing had changed, and on 15 October 1989 the issue was brought to the wider attention of the House of Commons through an Early Day Motion introduced by Conservative MP David Evenett. This is a means traditionally used by MPs to draw their colleagues' and the government's attention to matters of importance. Early Day Motion 1216 was signed by 104 MPs from all parties. It read:

> That this House notes with concern the plight of some overseas domestic workers brought into the United Kingdom by their employers; and calls upon the Secretary of State for the Home Department to ensure that all domestic workers from overseas are provided with a suitable immigration status which enables them to work legally and change employers whilst in the United Kingdom, and which will help to end the maltreatment and abuse of overseas domestic workers by some employers.

A further 14 MPs signed an addition:

> and therefore urges the Government to include the necessary regulation or legislation needed to bring about such a change in immigration status in the forthcoming Queen's Speech.

In March 1990, Kalayaan and CFMW again met with officials from the Home Office, this time in a meeting sponsored by Lord Hylton. The principal point put at this meeting was that workers should be given the right to change employers within their existing employment category (that is, as long as they continued as domestic workers). Other suggestions included a requirement that a written contract of employment, enforceable in the UK, be signed by employers and employees staying more than a certain period in UK; and that there should be an amnesty for those workers who had escaped from their employer and found other work.

This position was clarified in a forum sponsored by the Commission for Racial Equality on 11 July 1990 and coordinated by Kalayaan. Domestic workers took the platform and spoke of their ordeals before a large audience: Sally told of how she climbed down a drainpipe to escape from a Kensington house after years of abuse. She was discovered by the porter lying in a pool of blood, having fallen from the second floor and broken her arm and her pelvis. Her life when she came out of hospital was still hard: she worked for six days a week from 8 a.m. to 6 p.m. for two different employers every day, and from 7 p.m. to 1.30 a.m. she worked as a garment piece-worker in her room. Confronted by experiences like this, the forum agreed the following resolutions as the basis for discussions with the Home Office:

1 This forum seeks either a change in the Immigration rules or a concession to mirror that already offered to employers; the beneficiaries would be people who came to the United Kingdom in circumstances where it was clear on arrival that they were already recruited as domestics and were coming to the UK to work in that capacity.

2　Such persons should be able to change employers if their employment continues to be within a similar field of occupation.

3　After four years of any such employment, such persons should be able to claim settlement in the UK.

4　Those persons who entered the UK as in point 1 above, and then left their employers and have now overstayed their leave to remain in the UK, should have their position regularised, bringing them within the terms of the concession.

Pressure was maintained on the Home Office in the House of Commons where six Parliamentary Questions were raised on the issue in 1990. The campaign could claim the support of some 250 MPs. There was also mounting international pressure which was being encouraged through the work of Anti-Slavery International. On 24 July 1990 the Home Office announced its regret that cases of abuse and exploitation should have occurred and imposed new controls to minimise abuse. These were:

1　All domestic servants will be required to obtain entry clearance before coming here. The entry clearance officer will carefully consider the individual circumstances of each application and will refuse entry clearance unless he is satisfied about the bona fides of the domestic arrangement and that it comes within the terms of the concession.

2　The domestic servant must have been in continuous, paid employment with the employer abroad for at least the previous 12 months before coming with a visitor, or at least two years in all other cases.

3　The minimum age at which a domestic servant will be granted entry clearance is 17 years.

4　Information leaflets will be issued to both employers and domestics at the entry clearance stage, setting out the legal rights of domestics working here and the protection available to them under United Kingdom law.

But how did such measures address the reality of the situation of the domestic worker? Entry clearance interviews are those held with British representatives abroad to determine whether or not a person can enter the UK, and what kind of visa they are to be given. Typically, interviews with domestic workers were held with the employer or an employer's representative present, so even if the worker were minded to complain, it would be extremely difficult. Moreover, workers typically were in Remy's situation. A widow with two young children, she earned £20 a month from her work as a bookkeeper in the Philippines, and made this up by

100

selling fish in the market at weekends. When her sister agreed to look after her children she applied to an agency for work abroad at a cost of 20,000 pesos, some £500 and one month's salary. She was given work with a Saudi diplomat based in London.

> I worked with them for eleven months. My experiences of this were very horrific.... I became terrified of the husband and wife. One time I was with the family in Egypt in 1989 December. There was a water shortage and I was expected to wash clothes in the minimum of very cold water. I was unable to squeeze all the water out of synthetic fine garments and the water drips. So angered the husband, shouting at me, calling me a liar, that it resulted in threats and hitting of me. I resulted broken skin all over my hands. Their main threat was to send me home immediately. Where was I to find the 20,000 pesos to repay the agency and to provide more money for my children? So I would always beg to stay in spite of the treatment.
> (1995 Slavery Still Alive Conference Report: 10)

Workers in such poor economic circumstances are unlikely to denounce employers to a UK representative in a foreign land. None of these measures tackled the root cause of the problem, which was not the 'bona fides' of the relationship. Nor was the insistence on previous employment by the same employer any help – as has been seen, many of the workers who had come to Britain had been suffering extreme cruelty from their employer for a number of years. Although there had been cases of children being brought to Britain as domestic workers, point 3 above was not adequate to prevent even this, and it was certainly no help in tackling the general problems faced by domestic workers. Although Kalayaan and other supportive parties were consulted on the information leaflet mentioned in point 4 above, its final draft and distribution were heavily criticised by Kalayaan. The leaflet's alleged purpose was to prevent abuses of domestic workers by employers, yet it was aimed, not at the abusers, but at the workers. Indeed, because it laid its principal emphasis on the employee's immigration situation and made it clear that, in law, a domestic worker can work for nobody other than her abusing employer, the campaign felt it could only encourage exploitation.

The Home Office position had obviously hardened. In a debate on Overseas Domestic Workers in the House of Lords on 28 November 1990, Lord Reay, speaking for the government, affirmed:

> The Government do not accept the suggestion that it is the concession itself which in some way creates the problems that have arisen.... The conditions for work permit holders are in line with those for overseas domestic workers who come here under the concession, and there would be no practical advantage at all in bringing domestic workers within the work permit arrangements. Another suggestion which is made is that we should

good review of it.
post it.
X

at least allow domestic workers to change employers. The government cannot accept that. Domestic workers are admitted in this exceptional way in order to safeguard their livelihoods.

This was a far cry from Timothy Renton's 1988 statements. The government's line was reiterated in a letter to Lord Hylton from the Home Office on 5 February 1991 which admitted concern 'about the cases where domestic workers have apparently been abused'. A note of doubt as to whether the cases of abuse and exploitation even take place was thereby introduced into the argument.

Kalayaan's concerns were justified. The monitoring of those workers entering after the Home Office leaflet was introduced demonstrated that in fact the leaflet was given out very arbitrarily. Of 195 workers interviewed by Kalayaan for 1995–6, 148 were interviewed for a visa, and only 25 received the leaflet. Moreover, the incidence of abuse was, if anything, greater among those who entered after the leaflet was introduced than among earlier entrants. For example, of those who entered before May 1991 the incidence of imprisonment went up from 18.6 to 25 per cent, the incidence of passport confiscation went up from 46 to 69 per cent, and the average monthly salary declined from US$195 to US$184.

By 1993 the Kalayaan campaign was in full swing. It had documented 1,600 case studies systematically, demonstrating the extent of abuse, and was offering legal advice sessions, supporting key legal cases, and undertaking publicity and lobbying work. It was also beginning to take the campaign to a European level, and had the support of 41 MEPs for a European Parliament Resolution noting concern at the situation of overseas domestic workers in the UK and other community member states. In a cross-party initiative 170 MPs again signed an Early Day Motion in 1994 noting that the 1991 measures had not resolved the problems and calling for an immigration status which would enable domestic workers to change employers within the same category of work.

In December 1994, under increasing pressure to do something to resolve the problem, the Conservative government announced new regulations. Employers had to give a written undertaking to provide adequate maintenance and accommodation, in particular a separate bedroom. They also had to set out in writing the main terms and conditions of employment in the UK. Domestic workers were to be given a copy of the statement of the main conditions of their employment at the entry clearance interview, and they had to confirm that they agreed to those terms. As Patricia Ready, then chair of Kalayaan, put it:

> The government will have us believe that a domestic worker is in a position to negotiate effective protection, probably through an interpreter, through

102

a contract of employment within the hallowed precincts of a British Embassy abroad. The pressures on the worker are neither recognised nor acknowledged.
(1995 Slavery Still Alive Conference Report: 5)

When the Immigration Minister was asked in Parliament what minimum wage a domestic worker could expect, he replied that 'it is up to her to negotiate with her employer' employment terms which 'will still be a matter only for the parties concerned'.

Again Kalayaan's monitoring of the living and working conditions of overseas domestic workers demonstrated that these changes were making no difference to workers' lives. So, while employers had, under new immigration rules, to undertake to provide a separate bedroom for domestic workers, 112 out of 181 workers interviewed by Kalayaan in 1996–7 did not have their own beds. Their 1996–7 statistics put the figure at 108 out of 195, a very marginal improvement. As civil litigation lawyer Jean Gould put it:

> I've seen many contracts in my office, some of them are brilliant, some say the women will be entitled to one day off a week, receive a reasonable wage, they'll be entitled to medical care and so on. But it doesn't happen, none of these things happen, they are not paid, they are not given time off, they work enormously long hours. Contracts are simply not, in this situation, worth the paper they're written on.
> (1995 Slavery Still Alive Conference: 12)

There was simply no way of enforcing such agreements (see Chapter 9), and this kind of approach was not providing any solutions to some very desperate situations. Work began in earnest on two fronts, first the international level, and, second, the targeting of the Labour Party in opposition to make commitments it would then be held to in government. In 1996 the TGWU organised a fringe meeting at the Labour Party Conference for Kalayaan, where undocumented migrant domestic workers shared a platform with the Shadow Minister for Women and the General Secretary of the TGWU. With support from local constituency labour parties coordinated by the TGWU, the Labour Party officially pledged itself to take action to protect migrant domestic workers and passed conference resolutions to this effect. The Labour Party was in fact very supportive of the campaign, and the future immigration minister Mike O'Brien, chair of the Labour Party Home Affairs Group, in 1996 offered the group his full support.

It was in the summer of 1997, ten years after Kalayaan was established, and twelve years after the establishment of Waling Waling, that the incoming Labour administration indicated that there would be a substantive change in the immigration status of migrant domestic workers and that those who had entered the UK under the concession could have their immigration status regularised. Following intense negotiations, on 23 July 1998 the Home Office announced:

> With effect from to-day, only those domestic workers whose duties exceed those set down in the International Labour Organisation's International Standard Classification of Occupations will be allowed to accompany their employer to the United Kingdom. This means that those whose duties are only cleaning, washing and cooking will not qualify. Once in the United Kingdom they will be allowed to change domestic employment to another employer, provided the nature of their duties meets the above criteria.
>
> These changes, which we shall include in the Immigration Rules at a suitable opportunity, will reduce the number of overseas domestic workers admitted to the United Kingdom. However, once here, they will be able to change to another employer if they suffer abuse from their original employer.
>
> We also propose to regularise the stay of those overseas domestic workers, who, because of the shortcomings of the provisions in the past, find themselves in an irregular position through no fault of their own.
>
> (Reply by Mr Mike O'Brien to parliamentary question for a written answer on changes to the arrangements for overseas domestic workers who accompany their employers to the United Kingdom.)

Success?

There are two elements to this announcement: first, the substantive change, giving domestic workers the right to change employers and putting them within Immigration Rules, and, second, the regularisation of those who entered under the old system. It is worth nothing the spin put on the announcement that is obviously informed by fear that the government will be criticised for 'opening the floodgates'. It reassures the public that this move represents a tightening of immigration regulations while downplaying the regularising of undocumented workers. This strategy seemed to pay off as far as the media were concerned (*Independent*, 25 July 1998, 'Overseas domestics granted basic rights'; *Guardian*, 25 July 1998, 'Government acts to stop abuse of foreign domestic servants'; *Daily Telegraph*, 25 July 1998, 'Rules on overseas staff are tightened'). Far from arousing controversy, the regularisation did not even attract much comment. Indeed there has been some concern that those who might be eligible for regularisation might not even be aware of it. So the *Daily Telegraph* reported, for instance, that:

> Immigration rules were tightened yesterday to reduce the number of

overseas domestic workers allowed into Britain and to prevent their abuse by unscrupulous employers.

Wealthy foreigners will be forbidden to bring cooks, cleaners and laundry staff with them.... These changes will reduce the number of overseas domestic workers, Mr O'Brien said in a written Commons answer. (*Daily Telegraph*, 25 July 98)

Immigration rule changes

The change from being an opponent of the current system to building an alternative is not always easy! Having challenged the government's concession to employers for many years, Kalayaan was now asked to discuss the alternatives. It was clear from the start that a work permit was not an option. In the light of this, should Kalayaan call for the concession allowing domestic workers to enter with their employers to be abandoned altogether? This would remove the risk of abuse (from the UK at least), but also could mean some workers losing their jobs. The alternative was to accept the concession but press for it to be modified in some way. To what extent should Kalayaan, a campaigning organisation, be involved at all in formulating the new immigration rule, which, inevitably, would be aimed at restricting the entrance of workers to the UK? The closer the involvement at this stage, the more difficult to criticise the rule, if necessary, later on. On the other hand, if Kalayaan's involvement in the discussions could help minimise abuse, did it not have a responsibility to do so? It was the latter view that won out, and Kalayaan, in consultation with Waling Waling, negotiated for a modified concession. Under the rules announced in 1998 domestic workers with 'higher skills levels' may accompany non-visitors to the UK. These domestic workers may change employers. Employers who are entering as tourists are not allowed to be accompanied by their domestic workers, and those who are entering for other purposes can be accompanied only by those who offer 'specialised duties' (such as cooks or nannies). In practice it remains to be seen what this kind of skills distinction, which is highly problematic as has been noted, will actually mean.

Regularisation

While the changes in immigration rules proceeded relatively smoothly, however, there were many problems around the regularisation of those already in the UK. One of the roots of the problem was that the Home Office was offering a case-by-case approach rather than a blanket amnesty. This caused three basic and related problems: bureaucracy, eligibility, and procedural difficulties. In terms of bureaucracy, the rules, directions and other matters regarding regularisation took a long time to filter down to the enforcers. So, for example, the Home Office wanted workers to make best efforts to have a valid passport. The Indian Embassy would not issue a passport without a police report that it was missing. When Indian workers, still undocumented of course, reported to the police to say that their passport was missing, they were arrested. This is only one example of the kinds of bureaucratic difficulty that proliferate with the case-by-case approach. Moreover, the bureaucracy also created problems for Kalayaan, which had agreed to assist with the regularisation process. Concretely, that meant running general advice sessions and one-to-one interviews. This was very time-consuming and demanded a lot of resources.

The second difficulty was with eligibility. This question arose when the Home Office moved, on 2 June 1998, from 'criteria will simply be that the worker has left the previous employer and is doing domestic work, broadly interpreted' to stating explicitly that 'This only applies to those who were originally admitted to the UK with the correct entry clearance for employment as a domestic worker.' As noted above, however, there was no single correct entry clearance for domestic workers, and the concession allowed for domestic workers to be given visitors' visas. The exact stamp on their passport was something that was completely out of the workers' control. This difficulty, and the fact that its cause lay within the concession itself, was brought to the attention of the immigration minister, who responded by allowing that those workers with proof that they were working as a domestic worker when they entered the UK would be eligible for regularisation. A case-by-case approach lends itself to this kind of categorisation, however, and there is still the difficulty of those who entered under the 'concession culture'.

The third difficulty with the case-by-case approach was the procedural problems arising from the imposition of a standard immigration application process which pays little regard to the particular situation of those working in private households. Standard documentary requirements such as passports, bank accounts and proof of income were often impossible to meet. One issue which continued to cause many problems was the requirement of confirmation of employment from the current employer. Many workers found it impossible to obtain this from their employers and were faced with the option of remaining unauthorised or seeking alternative employment in the hope that the new employer would oblige. This requirement for regularisation thus reinforced the dependence of domestic workers on their employers.

These problems are problems for individuals, but they were also problems for the Kalayaan and Waling Waling organisations because of their divisiveness. The negotiations encouraged trade-offs, some workers against others. People were desperate to regularise their status, and as waiting lists for reputable solicitors increased workers became vulnerable to the depredations of immigration vultures who promised to sort out their papers immediately on payment of a large fee.

There are clear similarities in the problems experienced by workers attempting to regularise their status in the UK and Greece, suggesting the need to undertake some serious comparative work in order to avoid such difficulties in the future. Expectations among migrant domestic workers in the UK nevertheless continued to be high. By ending dependence on employers it was felt that a major source of abuse would be eliminated. I have no doubt that this is so, but there continue to be problems around the nature of the transaction when domestic work is paid for, and within the employer/worker relationship, as is evident from the experiences of documented workers in Spain and Italy. How domestic workers in the UK negotiate these problems remains to be seen, but I intend to unpack some of these difficulties in the hope that this will help in finding solutions.

7

Selling the Self

Commodification, Migration and Domestic Work

[handwritten annotation: labor power vs personhood]

Issues of immigration status and employer/worker relations may be related and addressed in the discussion of contract. First, however, one must deal with the question of what is being contracted *for*. Specifically, what is being commodified when employers pay migrant domestic workers? I have argued that the domestic worker is not just doing a set of tasks but is fulfilling a role. This already suggests that it is not simply her labour power that is being commodified. The worker who had to stand by the door when her employers left for the evening and remain in the same position until they came home could not really be constructed as selling her labour power.

The migrant worker is framed by immigration legislation as a unit of labour, without connection to family or friends, a unit whose production costs (food, education, shelter) were met elsewhere, and whose reproduction costs are of no concern to employer or state. In this respect, the worker who moves across continents may seem the logical result of capitalism's individual subject, the juridical person, torn from all social contexts, selling her labour power in the global market place. But while states and capitalists want workers, what they get is people.[1] This tension between 'labour power' and 'personhood' is particularly striking with reference to migrant domestic workers, and I believe it has broader repercussions for migrants and for women (see O'Connell Davidson 1998; Pateman 1988).

Who profits from migrant domestic workers?

As well as individual capitalists, the receiving state might be said to profit from migrant workers, since their labour power has been produced without

108

any outlay from this state and, theoretically at least, they are to return to their countries of origin one day, thereby saving the receiving state any expenses associated with their old age. Again, theoretically, they do not bring their children with them, saving the host state associated health and education costs. In practice immigrants are less likely to draw on social provisions than citizens, and yet they do pay taxes: a US Federal Department of Labor study of undocumented workers in the early 1980s found that 73 per cent had income tax deducted from their pay, 77 per cent paid social security, and 0.5 per cent received benefits (cited Harris 1995: 206).

Migrant domestic workers and state provisions

But what of the migrant domestic worker? Like most domestic workers in private households, whether migrants or citizens, she and her employers are unlikely to be paying tax. In this respect, then, migrant domestic workers differ from Harris's general picture of undocumented migrants – although of course, like all inhabitants of a state, they must pay indirect taxes on food, clothes and other goods. Moreover, the migrant domestic worker, in common with other migrants, makes few demands on the state – other than those spent in searching and deporting 'illegal immigrants'.[2] Indeed, increasingly the provision of those very social benefits that are the right of citizens rests on the labour of migrant domestic workers, and without a radical overhaul of the organisation of European economies and welfare systems, this is set to continue. While women's participation in the labour force is rising, provisions for childcare and care of the elderly remain extremely limited. All European Union countries have demonstrated a feminisation of their labour force over the past twenty years. So in France, for example, female participation in the labour force in 1996 was at 60 per cent, up from 51 per cent in 1975. In France, Italy, Greece and Germany, women's employment patterns are increasingly masculinised, remaining in the labour market after marriage and returning to it soon after the birth of children, rather than dropping out of the labour market after the first birth and returning, if at all, when the children have left home. In Spain it is married women, even those with young children at home, whose participation in employment rates has increased the most.[3] Yet there is a desperate shortage in publicly funded service for children. France is the only EU state which makes any accommodation for children of three and under, and even there only 20 per cent of those children will find a publicly funded place. In Greece, Spain, Italy and Germany publicly funded services are available to between 2 and 5 per cent of three-year-olds and under. Childcare is not simply an issue that stops being a problem when children go to school. Short school days and school holidays make it difficult for both parents to be employed full-time, and school-age childcare has been identified as a growing need by the European Commission Network on Childcare. Given the lack of public provision for childcare many of those women remaining in the labour market following the birth of their first child are having to make private provision, often paying for childcare out of taxed income.

But it is not only children who need to be supported. The population of Europe is ageing and as people live longer and are more often living alone there is a 'caring gap'. Even when relatives live nearby and visit regularly, they do not or cannot undertake basic domestic chores or provide the necessary physical assistance. This gap will widen: according to a report published by the European Commission in March 1996, Europe is set to experience a massive demographic shift, with a 50 per cent increase in the number of people over sixty in the next thirty years and an 11 per cent decrease in the under twenties. At the same time as this demographic change, European states are pursuing policies of decarceration and 'care in the community', not just for older people but for others with special needs such as the mentally ill. The reduction in residential care has not resulted in expansion of domiciliary care; and personal social services, like public expenditure in general throughout Europe, has been subject to fiscal retrenchment. According to a 1992 Eurobarometer survey, a relatively small proportion of older people (60+) are receiving regular help with personal care and household tasks (excluding those people in institutions), and this is a smaller number than those suffering some form of incapacity, an indicator of the need for care. The survey found that spouses were important care providers, and that when a spouse died the public sector did not fully compensate for this loss of care. This finding pointed to a consequent care gap, particularly since women were more likely to provide care for husbands and to outlive their partners (Walker and Maltby 1997). Long-term care continues to be predominantly family-orientated – that is, dependent on women in private households:

> This raises a dilemma for policy makers, since declining birth rates combined with the rise in labour force participation of women and higher incidence of divorce has led to a reduced potential source of care for older people in poor health. A new system of long-term care is urgently required in many countries of the Union, since the predominant forms of care based largely upon filial obligation may soon be impracticable.
> (Walker and Maltby 1997: 93)

There is thus an increasing need for care services to be provided for the elderly, partly because of an ageing population, and partly because of social welfare policies which are cutting available public services. This is at a time when, as noted with childcare, there are fewer women at home, and when marriage breakdown and geographical mobility are making kinship obligations, in so far as they ever existed, more and more difficult to enforce. Changing family structures and the withdrawal of state support mean that families and, more specifically, women within families are finding it more difficult to carry out the basic reproductive work of the family. This is in part to do with women's entry into the labour market, but it is also part of other profound changes to intergenerational contracts – not only are grandparents less likely to be near children to be cared for, but often they are simply not available for caring for grandchildren.

As women citizens are unable or unwilling to provide unpaid care for the elderly, the young and the disabled, it is individual migrant women, rather than the welfare state, who are filling in the gap.

[T]he foundations are apparently being laid for the effective demand for unregulated caring labour. This will not only affect women, but also, particularly in the context of an EU-wide international labour market and the great migrations of labour and refugees arising out of the break-up of the old Communist regimes, 'outsiders' will inevitably be brought into this pool of unregularised workers. Hence there are issues of race and nationality embedded in these developments as well as gender.
(Ungerson 1995: 48)

The demand for 'caring' work is recognised by formal and informal placement agencies. Five out of the eight employment agencies I interviewed in Barcelona mentioned care of children and/or elderly people as offering the principal employment for migrants. One of the remaining three agencies was called SOS – Hombres Solteros (SOS – Single Men), and catered specifically for single men 'unable to cope' with household responsibilities. Providing services to older people was felt to be the growth area. In Paris the AGF dealt with 40 requests for childcare workers in the period 4–19 January 1996, out of a total of 42 employers. Part of the reason for this heavy preponderance is clearly the nature of the AGF, which is specifically set up to help local families. However, the age breakdown of the children requiring care is illuminating. In France some 95 per cent of pre-school children aged 3–5 attend publicly funded *écoles maternelles*, but the available provision for under that age and for after-school care, although significantly better than most EU states, is still limited. So, of the 40 employers requesting childcare through the AGF, 23 were requiring care for at least one child under three, and eight for children when they came home from school: in other words, 78 per cent of requests were specifically to fill those acknowledged gaps in provision, and, of the remainder, six were unclear about the age of the children to be cared for, and only two were for childcare for children aged three to five.

Workers themselves were clear that privatised caring constituted an important part of their work:

Filipina: We can be a nurse, inside job with old ladies, caring the old ladies, pampering the old ladies (general agreement and laughter).

Zairean: Why can't we go work in the hospital? The hospitals are looking for these people?

Ethiopian: They wouldn't allow you to go and work in the hospital, even if they didn't allow you to work in the household.
(Athens consultation)

In some instances European families may be said to be profiting from the low value accorded domestic labour: if a female barrister pays the going rate – say £4 an hour – for childcare, and is herself earning £250 an hour, she/the family is profiting from a discrepancy in the low cost of reproduction and the high cost of the bar. The household income is greater than it would be if the female employer were to do the childcare herself. But not all employment situations fit this model so neatly, and I have already discussed the difficulties around the valuation of domestic work. To ask which individuals profit financially from domestic labour is not the real issue, there is a broader question: what exactly is being commodified in the case of paid domestic labour? And what is the employer buying?

Commodification and domestic workers

According to Marxist theory, workers sell their commodified 'labour power' (that is, their property in the person). Marx's theory of surplus value claimed that capitalists profit from this exchange: the value of labour power is determined by the value of the labour time socially necessary to produce it and

If their working day or week exceeds the labour-time embodied in their wage, they are creating surplus value: a value over and above the variable capital investment, for which they will receive no recompense.... Profit can thus arise.... Its premise is exploitation of labour.
(Sayer 1991: 3)

However, as Pateman (along with Marx) has pointed out, labour power is a political fiction:

Labour power, capacities or services, cannot be separated from the person of the worker like pieces of property. The worker's capacities are developed over time and they form an integral part of his self and self-identity.... Moreover, capacities or labour power cannot be used without the worker using his will, his understanding and experience, to put them into effect....

> The use of labour power requires the presence of its 'owner', and it remains as mere potential until he acts in the manner necessary to put it into use.... The fiction 'labour power' cannot be used; what is required is that the worker labours as demanded.
> (Pateman 1988: 150–1)

This might be said to be a reworking of the Lockean tension around property in the person: a person does not stand in the same relation to the property in their own person as they do to other types of property, because that property is sacred and integral to personhood. 'Contracts about property in the person inevitably create subordination' (Pateman 1988: 153). What the employer is really buying is not labour power but the 'power to command', apparently limited by, in the case of the worker, the employment contract. But the fiction of labour power is useful to distinguish between those functions/aspects of the self that can be bought and are allegedly not integral to personhood, and those that are integral to personhood and cannot be sold without volunteering oneself for slavery. Labour power can be commodified, exchanged for money, and the two parties, worker and capitalist, are, like their products, apparently socially equated in the act of exchange, both being equal subjects of exchange:

> Living labour capacity belongs to itself, and has disposition over the expenditure of its forces, through exchange. Both sides confront each other as persons. Formally, their relation has the equality and freedom of exchange as such. As far as concerns the legal relation, the fact that this form is a mere semblance, and a deceptive semblance, appears as an external matter.
> (Marx, *The Foundations of the Critique of Political Economy* 1939–41, in Robert Tucker, (ed.) 1978: 255)

Labour power is, in this fiction, not integral to the person and can be traded in the marketplace with buyer and seller constructed as equals.

Are migrant domestic workers selling their 'labour power'? I have already explored the question of what domestic work produces and broadly concluded that it is concerned with the physical, cultural and ideological reproduction of human beings. Paid domestic workers reproduce people and social relations, not just in what they do (polishing silver, ironing clothes), but also in the very doing of it (the foil to the household manager). In this respect the paid domestic worker is herself, in her very essence, a means of reproduction. It is not just her labour power that is being harnessed to the cause of her employer's physical and social reproduction, but it is the very fact that *she*, the domestic worker, and not her employers, is doing this work, much of which seems invented especially for her to do. The employer is buying the power to command, not the property in the person, but the whole person. It is this power to command

113

that is manifest in ordering a worker to stand in the same position all day, in calling a person 'dog' and 'donkey' (Anderson 1993: 3), in making her clean the floor three times a day with a toothbrush. So, while domestic workers are usually attempting to sell their labour power (itself a political fiction) within an employment relation, they find themselves frustrated:

> because you are a black, because you are doing domestic work, therefore, you are nothing. Always they look down upon us as a hungry people. We are not here to put our hand into their pockets, we are not here to do any bad thing to them, but rather to help them to clean their houses. But they don't give that respect to us.
>
> (Joy, Ghanaian woman in Athens)

> You need the money to feed your children, and in place to pay you they give you old clothes. 'I give you this, I give you this'. They give you things, but me, I need the money. Why come? I am a human being.
>
> (Maggie, Zaïrean working in Athens)

Employers want more than labour power. They often openly stipulate that they want a particular type of person (Gregson and Lowe 1994: 3) justifying this demand on the grounds that they will be working in the home. So employer Anne Marie was emphatic that she would not accept an employee who 'smells too strong', because 'I cannot stand strong body smells'. Or if the worker is to have responsibility for caring work she should be 'affectionate', 'like old people' or 'be good with children'. The worker wants to earn as much money as she can with reasonable conditions, but the employer's wants are rather more complicated. This is an oversimplification of the differences between what is being bought and sold by employer and worker, but I think it is an adequate description of how many employment situations begin before more complex interpersonal relations develop.

Can money buy love?

The contradictions and tensions involved in paying for domestic labour are most clearly apparent when the function of that labour includes care. The political fiction of labour power is strained to breaking point – can one pay a care worker for her labour power and be unconcerned with whether she is a 'caring person'? Can one pay a person to 'be' caring? Can money really buy love?

Women and care

It is widely accepted that there are two meanings conflated in the term 'care': care as labour and care as emotion, and it can be very difficult to disentangle the two. Finch and Groves (1983), in the introduction to their edited volume, write that caring cannot be reduced to 'a kind of domestic labour performed on people', but that it always includes emotional bonds. In her contribution to the volume, Graham states that affection and service 'can't be disentangled', and Waerness (1984) argues that caring is about labour and feelings, about relations, and that we all need to be cared for. Much of the labour of care is devoted to basic domestic chores. It would be difficult to care for a child and not include cooking her food, washing up her dishes, wiping her face and the table, changing and throwing away her nappy, tidying up her toys and washing her clothes. But once one allows that caring does include some measure of domestic work it is difficult to draw the line – how much of the domestic work is part of caring for one's charge, and when does it become general servicing of the household? And could not domestic work in general be seen as 'caring', as looking after one's loved ones and making sure they are comfortable and at ease? As Rose puts it: 'It has been both a theoretical and an empirical problem that even where we tried to separate housework from peoplework, they continually merged' (Rose 1986: 168). Indeed, much female-directed advertising is encouraging us in this perception – show your husband how much you love him by buying our brand of powder and washing his shirts *really* white.

The problem is that while X doing something for Y may demonstrate X's love for Y, it may also demonstrate Y's power over X – and these two are not mutually exclusive. And of course, this is heavily gendered. The labour of care for men is usually manifest in the labour involved in 'providing for' the family – few are primary carers either of their children, or of their parents. Eighteen per cent of older women are cared for by their spouse, as compared with 53 per cent of men. As for household chores, in Europe there has been no significant change in men's participation in domestic work despite female employment rates. The labour of care, whatever proportion of it is domestic chores, is chiefly women's work.

This gendered relationship between care, labour and power in the private sphere, and its relation to status and the public sphere, can be seen in 'The good wife's guide', taken from a women's magazine in the 1950s. This is advice on how to prepare for your husband's homecoming:

- Have dinner ready. Plan ahead, even the night before, to have a delicious meal ready, on time for his return. This is a way of letting him know that you have been thinking about him and are concerned about his needs.
- Prepare yourself. Take 15 minutes to rest so you'll be refreshed when he arrives ... .
- Be a little gay and a little more interesting for him. His boring day may

need a lift and one of your duties is to provide it....

- [Y]ou should prepare and light a fire for him to unwind by. Your husband will feel he has reached a haven of rest and order, and it will give you a lift too. After all, catering for his comfort will provide you with immense personal satisfaction.
- Take a few minutes to wash the children's hands and faces (if they are small), comb their hair and, if necessary, change their clothes. They are little treasures and he would like to see them playing the part. Minimise all noise. At the time of his arrival, eliminate all noise of the washer, dryer or vacuum. Try to encourage the children to be quiet....
- Listen to him. You may have a dozen important things to tell him, but the moment of his arrival is not the time. Let him talk first – remember, his topics of conversation are more important than yours....
- Your goal: Try to make sure your home is a place of peace, order and tranquillity where your husband can renew himself in body and spirit.
- Don't ask him questions about his actions or question his judgement or integrity. Remember, he is the master of the house and as such will always exercise his will with fairness and truthfulness. You have no right to question him.
- A good wife always knows her place.

(*Housekeeping Monthly*, 13 May 1955, cited in *The Independent*, 13 May 1998)

Such advice should serve as a warning for an uncritical acceptance of the care as labour/care as emotion conflation. The particular danger of viewing care as labour and care as emotion as indistinguishable is that it can lead to an argument that care is not exploitative because women want to do it ('After all, catering for his comfort will provide you with immense personal satisfaction') and because they are doing it of their own free will. It also can lead to an argument that informal care is necessarily better care because it is guided by love, which, as Ungerson has pointed out (1995), has serious implications for unpaid women carers.

The negotiating of labour and emotion poses particular problems for women. Much of the literature on care in the 1980s focused on this, and in particular on women's experiences as unpaid carers in the home.[4] Issues around paid care in the home and its relation to gender remain unexplored. One of the most influential recent works on care is Bubeck's *Care, Gender and Justice* (1995) which examines how and why caring work is exploitative of women, and renders women peculiarly and structurally vulnerable to exploitation. Bubeck's definition of 'care' emphasises the difference between doing something for someone who cannot do it, and doing something for someone who will not do it (which she calls 'servicing'), rather than distinguishing caring from other types of domestic work in terms of tasks performed. So cooking a meal for a bedridden person is 'caring', cooking a meal for a husband/able-bodied employer is 'servicing'. No matter that they have not got time to cook, it is possible for them to cook in a way in which it is not possible for someone who is bedridden. Her definition also seeks to elucidate both why caring work is necessary and its peculiarly human quality:

> Caring for is the meeting of the needs of one person by another person where face-to-face interaction between carer and cared for is a crucial element of the overall activity and where the need is of such a nature that it cannot possibly be met by the person in need herself.
> (Bubeck 1995: 129)

Even if it were possible for the need to be met by machine, without face-to-face interaction, it is unlikely that this would be deemed desirable – the prospect of totally mechanised old people's homes is a nightmare rather than a utopia. The definition does seem to miss the point, though, that it is only human to show one cares through meeting such needs – whether or not the objects of our affections can meet those needs themselves – and, from time to time at least, to meet them in an 'excessive' way. This is evident from Bubeck's own example of 'care' according to her definition, 'cooking her favourite dish for a sick child' (Bubeck 1995: 130). But why 'favourite'? Cooking food for a sick child is caring according to her own definition, but cooking her favourite dish suggests labour beyond the strictly necessary. And if one's only consideration is the most suitable, easy and economical dish for the sick child, and what she likes to eat doesn't enter into it, is that really showing 'care'? The central difficulty around care as labour/care as emotion has not been resolved. Human beings can labour to demonstrate affection – for the able-bodied and powerful as well as for the weak and vulnerable. Community and human relations, with their ties of power and of affection, are lived and are created through care. To offer totally mechanised old people's homes is literally inhuman.

Care as labour/care as emotion and paid domestic work

What implications does this have for the relationship in which one woman pays another to do caring work? While Bubeck states that caring in the sense of providing for the family is 'peculiarly male', this is not so. In fact, when a woman is working, the salary for a paid carer is often taken out of the woman employer's wages. Migrant women are themselves usually 'providers for' their families, often 'providing for' their children back home, who are themselves cared for, paid or unpaid, by another:

> you have to look at it from the point of view of necessity, because what they were paying you there (in the Dominican Republic) for doing a job was not even enough to pay for your children's upkeep, let alone pay for someone to look after them for you. On the other hand, when you emigrate

to a country, they give you double what you were earning there, you have enough to send back money to your children there, to pay someone else to care for them, and on top of that to live yourself.
(Magnolia, Dominicana working in Barcelona)

The problem in our country is that before men emigrated. Men were going to the US, but the women were staying in the house. Then what happened was that the man emigrated and did not send anything back, he sent back no money. So the woman was a single mother with children, so if she got the chance to emigrate, she emigrated too ... because she didn't have any other option to find a better future for her children. So it's terrible for her, very difficult, because they are here, they can only send money back home and their children are being brought up and cared for by another, by their relatives....
(Gisela, Dominicana in Barcelona)

While most of the migrant domestic workers I met relied on unpaid care by female family members, it is not unusual for domestic workers themselves to employ carers, often rural migrants. Polish women working as domestic workers in Berlin, for example, reportedly often employ Ukrainians to care for their children in Poland. Yet for the majority of migrants interviewed, being a 'provider for' rather than carer of their immediate family was not experienced as a liberation, as it is for European female employers, but as another level of exploitation. While the female European employer may continue in her emotional and supportive role, migrant women can have little emotional and moral input into the upbringing of their children. They do not enjoy care as emotion freed from physical labour. Instead the opposite applies: their care for their children is demonstrated in the fruits of hard labour, in remittances, rather than in the cuddles and 'quality time' that provide so much of the satisfaction of care.

It's terrible for us, because we are far from our children, but we are giving them food, education, we are giving them everything, although staying here you are dying because everything depends on you ... for this I am saying, I'm spending three more years here, then I'm going back to my children, whatever happens, because like it or not I am keeping my children going, even though it is with this pain and lack of love.
(Berta, Peruvian in Barcelona)

It would seem at first glance that in the case of female European employers, the hiring of a carer reflects those distinctions highlighted by Davidoff (1974) of mutually interdependent female stereotypes being worked out in the domestic worker/employer relationship. In this case the stereotypes are the work of servants (the physical labour of care) and the work of wives/ mothers (the emotional labour of care). Could it be argued, then, that the hiring of carers facilitates some privileged women buying into Rose's 'care-giving myth' (1986), that care involves only emotion and no labour, and like men, enjoying care as emotion freed from labour? In this case, to take up a point mentioned above, it would be possible for someone to care emotionally for a child and do no physical caring work. Female employers therefore are, like men, divesting themselves of the physical labour of care, but are still the 'mother' in terms of their responsibility for and involvement in the emotional and moral development of the child. As Rothman (1989) has pointed out, the exultation of genetic links which has its roots in patriarchy and which has now been 'modified' to allow for the equal importance of 'male and female seed' has led to a downgrading of nurturing, which includes the labour of care. The privileging of the genetic link, and of care as emotion over care as labour, has rendered the importance of the labour of care invisible and un-acknowledged. The labour of care is work that anyone can do, as opposed to care as emotion, which is ultimately dependent on some genetic relationship.

This constructs paid domestic labour, then, as simply that: labour. It sometimes seems as if employers are adopting this model, particularly those who hire and fire easily (the carer is 'just' a labourer, and the relationship between the carer and the cared-for is of no consequence). It is also made use of when the worker oversteps the mark and gets 'too close' to the cared-for. Very occasionally workers, too, attempt this emotion/labour divide:

> I'm telling you, on top of what they are paying you for, the physical work, there is also psychological work, that's double work ... double pay. Some-times, when they say to me for example, that I should give her lots of love, I feel like saying, well, for my family I give love free, and I'm not discriminating, but if it's a job you'll have to pay me....
> (Magnolia, Dominicana working in Barcelona)

Those who were more experienced and who had a greater choice of jobs sometimes refused to work as carers or limited themselves to a par-ticular period with any one family. But it was often a hard lesson to learn:

> I cared for a baby for his first year ... the child loves you as a mother, but the mother was jealous and I was sent away. I was so depressed then, seriously depressed. All I wanted was to go back and see him ... I will never care for a baby again, it hurts too much.
> (Juliette, from Côte d'Ivoire, working in Parma)

But in practice this separation is not maintained. Employers are not only looking for a labourer when they are looking for a carer; they want somebody 'affectionate', 'loving', 'good with children'. Sometimes employers attempt to keep workers by appealing to their 'finer feelings' (rather than offering an increase in salary):

> [I]t's too much. I said, 'Madam I am very sorry, I cannot stay here, I have to find another.... 'Why Lina, you cannot leave me like this.' I said, 'Yes, I can, I don't like.' 'Where is your heart, you will leave me like this? I have no worker.' I said, 'I'm very sorry. I have to leave you.' I cannot stand it. Otherwise maybe I will kill her!
> (Lina, a Filipina in Paris)

Sometimes an employer seeks out a domestic worker for a private household precisely because she offers one-to-one care and a 'special' relationship, something perceived as lacking in, for example, a nursery or an old people's home. Gregson and Lowe (1994) found that the reason that middle-class English families chose nannies rather than childminders was because they offered a 'mother substitute':

> In a sense, then, whilst the employment of the nanny form of waged domestic labour enables middle-class households with both partners in full-time service class occupations to combine paid work and parenthood, such employment is, at the same time, reproductive of very traditional ideas about the care of young, pre-school-age children.
> (Gregson and Lowe 1994: 120)

When necessary, however, employers can make use of the labour power fiction, so that any relationship between carer and cared for is not 'real' or, if it threatens to be, it can be disrupted immediately without responsibility to the worker. When money does buy care – that is, when care is explicitly commodified – then it is not real care, because real care cannot be commodified: 'Money can't buy love', so workers' feelings for their charges are not important. For workers, on the other hand, it can prove impossible to disentangle care as emotion from care as labour: 'What they say at the beginning of the job and then what happens, are very different things ... with old people like it or not it is a job where you have to get to know this old person and take care of them' (Magnolia, Dominicana in Barcelona). For not only may affection be expressed through labour, as has been discussed in the literature, but labour may engender care, and this is particularly true in the case of childcare. As anyone who has been intimately involved with a child can tell, it is often through interaction on the level of basic physical chores – nappy changing, feeding, cleaning, that one develops a relationship with a young child. Workers who are involved in such a relationship and who are deprived of their 'own' children may love the child intensely. The difficulty for the worker is that, as Bubeck allows, caring requires 'face-to-face interaction' – that is, at the very least, relating. If this face-to-face

120

interaction is repeated on a daily basis in the kinds of conditions experienced by many domestic workers, particularly those who live in, it almost inevitably develops into a relationship. The paid worker loves the child, the child loves the worker, and jealousy and family friction result. And it is even worse when the relationship is between a worker and an old person, and financial settlements are involved!

Care involves the whole person. It is bound up with who we are. A worker is not only a worker, she is a woman, a human being, and caring is, as Bubeck puts it, a 'deeply human practise', with a particular resonance for women since 'Caring as an activity, disposition, and attitude forms a central part of probably all cultural conceptions of femininity' (Bubeck 1995: 160). Employers of domestic workers take advantage of the fiction of labour power but they also acknowledge that care involves the whole person in the personal requirements. The domestic worker is not equated socially with her employer in the act of exchange because the fiction of labour power cannot be maintained: it is 'personhood' that is being commodified. Moreover, the worker's caring function, her performance of tasks constructed as degrading, demonstrates the employer's power to command her *self*. Having allegedly sold her personhood, the domestic worker is both person and non-person. She is, like the prostitute, a person who is not a person, someone for whom all obligations can be discharged in cash (O'Connell Davidson 1998). So, particularly for those jobs which necessarily demand some human interaction, an employer can purchase the services of a human being who is yet not a real human being – with likes and hates, relations of her own, a history and ambitions of her own – but a human being who is socially dead (O'Connell Davidson, 1998; Patterson 1982). Such an exchange further dishonours her before her employer: 'I can say that they think about themselves, how to take more money, better conditions for them. They offer because they have to, not because they feel sympathy. Love is silly for them' (Nina, employer in Athens).

The contradictions in the concept of property in the person, apparent from Locke onwards, trap the worker between being a labourer without emotions, selling commodified labour power, on the one hand, and a dishonoured person on the other. The resulting tensions are experienced by workers and employers as part of E. P. Thompson's 'experience', a sense of these contradictions, even if not explicitly articulated. So Bertha expressed the contradictions implicit in the attempt to commodify that which cannot be commodified fully:

> Live-in, what are they paying for? Freedom. It's emotional work, and physically you have to be there twenty-four hours, you have to give them your liberty. That is what they are paying for. To be there all the time. Even

if they pay you, give you free time, I think a young person is worth more than the money. There is no amount that they can pay you that can justify you being imprisoned.

'"Member of our family" – oh really?'

In order to negotiate the contradictions inherent in the attempted commodification of domestic work, and the tension between the affective relations of the private and the instrumental relations of employment, many employers and some workers made use of the notion of the family.

> We are treated as a servant ... like my employer, they say, 'Ah Teresita, we used to treat you as a member of our family.' Oh really? But try to observe ... they will introduce you to their friends as a member of the family, and then they are sitting down, eating with crossed legs, and you will be the one who is running for their needs. Is that, can you consider that a member of the family? It's very easy to say, but it's not being felt inside the house.
> (Teresita, Filipina in Athens)

'Part of the family'. This phrase appears time and again in the literature of domestic work, as it did in my own discussions with domestic workers. This is in part precisely because of the intertwining of domestic work and caring work that I have attempted to tease out (but which employers clearly have no interest in unravelling!) which allows for what Bubeck would count as 'servicing' to be portrayed as 'care'. For employers can argue that domestic workers 'love' their employers and show it through action. So while they hire a labourer, gradually the labourer becomes incorporated into the family and has the same kinds of relationship with family members as the kin do.

But which part of the family are they, one is tempted to ask? It is true that some workers may actually become part of the family, by marrying a male employer and becoming wives and mothers. Until the 1960s white European women were preferred as domestic workers in Canadian policy, because they were also potential Canadian wives and mothers. The idea that domestic workers may really become 'part of the family' and reproductive workers in all senses of the word is confirmed by the immigration policies of some countries such as Singapore and Malaysia, which explicitly forbid domestic workers from marrying their employers. In some European countries, notably Italy and Spain, this move from domestic worker to wife is not unusual.

But generally this is not what is meant by becoming part of the employer's family. Rather the phrase suggests a special relationship beyond the simple bond of employment, in which the worker will be loved and cared for, entering into a network of rights and obligations. For the employer there are clear advantages to the obfuscation of the employment relationship, since it seriously weakens the worker's negotiating position in terms of wages and conditions – any attempt to improve these are an insult to the 'family' and evidence of the worker's moneygrubbing attitude. The worker risks forfeiting 'good' relations with her employers by making too many demands. It must be remembered that in these highly individualised work situations, good interpersonal relations can be extremely important, to the extent that a worker will often consider a lower-paying job if she feels happier with the family, since this will have a significant impact on her living and working conditions.

For employers of carers, describing a worker as part of the family facilitates the myth that caring is untainted by the market place. They can imagine that the worker is fulfilled by a 'real' relationship with the person cared for – while retaining the possibility of terminating the relationship because it was contracted on the labour market and, therefore, can be deemed unreal if necessary. Workers who described themselves as part of the family tended to use the term to emphasise that their employers were 'good' employers, not like those being described by other workers – though some were more sanguine:

> the problem is, they don't treat me as a slave or anything. The problem is they treat me as a family. I think being a family, you stay in the family, I say, if you in the family you are there from morning to night, doing the same as they are.
> (Jacki, Filipina in Paris)

What the 'part of the family' rhetoric obscures is that relations in paid care are, to use Waerness's (1984) term, 'asymmetrical'. While the worker is expected to have familial interest in the employing family, this is not reciprocated. Cock (1989) found in South Africa that employers were simply unwilling to consider their workers' private lives, and similarly very few employers I spoke to had any idea about the lives of their domestic workers – indeed they resented it if their worker 'talked too much'. Relations within the family are typically asymmetrical, with women doing more 'caring' than men. But paid workers, unlike 'wives', 'mothers' and 'daughters', are not part of a network of obligations and responsibilities (however unequally distributed): all obligations are discharged in cash. 'Caring' work requires human beings to do it and cannot be mechanised, but when care is paid for, the person who is paying can avoid acknowledging that the worker is expressing and forming human relationships and community (which is not to say that unpaid care may not be expressing and forming oppressive human relations); her caring brings with it no mutual obligations, no entry into a community, no 'real' human relations, only money. So a worker who has cared for a child over many years, who has spent many more hours with her than her 'natural' mother, has no right to see the child should the employer decide to terminate the relationship, because the worker is paid. Money expresses the full extent of any obligations.

This reduction of human relations to cash is rendered easier because the emotional relationship is typically not between the carer and the person who is paying her wages (who is, in the final analysis, her employer) but between the carer and the cared-for, and both are relatively powerless before the financier of the care. The growth of this emotional relationship renders the carer vulnerable to exploitation, and the cared for vulnerable to the whims of the person holding the purse strings. As Bubeck points out, some unpaid carers may find themselves empowered by care, their self-esteem enhanced by making others happy and well: 'it is this sense of power that underlies the peculiar logic of care, whereby the more one gives the more one is given in return' (Bubeck 1995: 148). This is strikingly inappropriate for paid carers, where even on the level of the individual relationship between carer and cared-for, a genuine affectionate relationship does not bring empowerment but rather its opposite. The care financier is able to manipulate the relationship between the carer and the cared-for to her own ends – to extract more labour from the carer for lower wages for example – safe in the knowledge that the carer will want to do her best for the cared-for. So, in Paris, live-in carer Sally, worked on her day off: 'Exceptionally today I will take C with me ... for a birthday party – no one is available and for a child it's a pity to miss the party, his old friends – so I did it.'

Becoming 'part of the family' is not only a means of maximising labour extracted from the worker. It is an attempt to manage contradictions. For the employer it helps to manage the contradictions of intimacy and status that attach to the role of the domestic worker, who is at once privy to many of the intimate details of family life, yet is also their status giver, their myth maker. It emphasises the common humanity of employers and workers, and explicitly rejects the commodification of human relations while sustaining an illusion of affective relations, and, in some instances, encouraging their formation. The situation of Zenaida, a Moroccan woman working in Barcelona, reveals the vulnerability of carers and the problems for them in being regarded as part of the family. She had cared for an old woman for five years, doing domestic chores as well as caring work. She lived in, was 'part of the family', and felt she was treated with respect by her employing family. She was paid by the woman's sons, who even took a holiday in her house in Morocco. Yet she could spend only one night a week with her five children, who lived in Barcelona, and the rest of the time had to leave them to fend for themselves because she lived in. Although he could have obtained a residence permit for Spain, the father of her children remained in Morocco because the first two children were too old to be admitted to Spain under family reunification. The youngest child was six, and she had left her when she was only a baby for six days a week in order to be the old woman's carer. There was no question of her being allowed to sleep with the baby: 'You can't do these things. No. Everyone thinks, I don't know, about themselves. You can't do that.'

Zenaida's terrible situation points to one of the greatest advantages to the employer of regarding the worker as part of the family, which is the erasure of the worker's own family. While being part of the family may be perceived by the employer as a great favour, for the worker it may be experienced as a denial of their humanity, a deep depersonalisation, as being perceived only in their occupational role, as a 'domestic' rather than as a person with her own needs, her own life, and her own family outside of the employers' home.[5] By incorporating the worker as 'part of the family' employers can not only ignore the worker's other relationships, but feel good about doing so – for it is an honour to be part of the family.

I have highlighted the caring function of domestic work because it brings out the contradictions and tensions in paid domestic labour. But the slippage between labour power and personhood, and the employer's power to command the whole person of the domestic worker, applies whatever function of domestic work the person is hired to perform. It is this slippage that can help us begin to understand what Bubeck sets out to explain, but never fully accounts for: how it is that some women exploit others within a general theory of care as women's work.

Notes

1 This comment has stuck in my mind for years, but I can find no reference to it. I only know that I did not originate it.
2 The cost of enforcement and the bureaucracies it sustains should not be underestimated. For asylum seekers in the OECD receiving countries alone the total cost of determining their legal status in 1990 was an estimated $7 billion – twelve times the total UN budget for refugee assistance worldwide and one seventh of the OECD's development budget for the Third World (Collinson 1994: 21).
3 France: Bernard Brunhoes Consultants 1997; Italy: Fondazione Giacomo Brodolini 1996; Greece: Athens University of Economics and Business 1996; Germany: ifo Institute for Economic Research 1997; Spain: Toharia *et al.* 1997.
4 See, for example, Stacey 1981; Waerness 1984; Dalley 1988.
5 Palmer 1992.

8

The Legacy of Slavery

The American South and Contemporary Domestic Workers

In May 1998 the US Attorney General, Janet Reno, announced that she was setting up a joint task force between the Justice and Labor Departments to investigate 'domestic servitude', the 'serious problem of modern day slavery' in the USA.[1] Thousands of migrant domestic workers are, it was alleged, being abused by employers who themselves work for embassies and international organisations such as the United Nations, the IMF and the World Bank. Tied by immigration laws to their employers, they cannot leave the sponsor of their special visa and endure abusive treatment, no free time and sometime no wages at all. 'Slavery' is a term commonly used to describe domestic work, past and present, all over the world. In the UK and the USA it is often used of migrant domestic workers in particular: 'Five years for a couple with a slave nanny' (*Evening Standard*, 1 November 1991); 'Slavery in Britain: servant makes midnight run to freedom' (*The Independent*, 16 December 1991); 'Slavery flourishes as never before, even in Britain' (*Woman's Journal*, May 1991); 'The slave state of Britain' (*Times Magazine*, 12 November 1994). Is it simply shorthand for the appalling living and working conditions some of them face, or does it point to more profound issues around the employer/worker relationship? What is the 'social consciousness' that leads copywriters, campaigners and the workers themselves to find 'slavery' such an appropriate term to describe the plight of migrant domestic workers?

When one analyses some of these articles it does indeed seem that 'slavery' is often short for long hours, low or no pay, and imprisonment. Thus:

> Although her former employer would no doubt be indignant at the title Slave Master, if obliging her to work 17 hours a day; denying her liberty of movement and refusing to hand over her wages constitutes slavery, then

Celine was a slave in England of the 1990s.
('Girls in the slave trade', *The Guardian*, 26 February 1996).

The kind of work that has to be done, and in particular the intimate bodily work, also seem to invite the notion of slavery – 'Jane's day started at 6 a.m. Like a slave, she would run a bath for her employer and then soap his entire body' ('Secret shame of our poshest addresses', *Daily Mirror*, 29 February 1996). The power exercised over the worker, and her corresponding lack of control over all aspects of herself, also provoke comparisons with slavery: 'She told how the woman treated her like a slave, banning her from talking to other domestic staff, locking her passport away and intercepting her private mail' ('Woman wins victory in British "slavery" case', *The Big Issue*, 1–7 February 1999, No. 320). Power and lack of control are manifested in many different ways: in physical, psychological and sexual violence; and in being tied to employers: 'The domestic's visa is linked exclusively to the employer which makes her a bonded employee or, given the conditions, often a bonded slave' (*The Guardian*, 26 February 1996).

The use and exploration of the term by campaigning groups, academics and others interested in paid domestic labour suggests that it is more than a sensationalist rhetorical flourish. Kalayaan claimed that fourteen out of thirty Articles in the United Nations Declaration of Human Rights were directly contravened as a result of the UK Home Office's policy on Overseas Domestic Workers, including Article 4 against slavery. Anti-Slavery International (ASI) has also taken on campaigns for the rights of domestic workers who are migrants and/or children. Using the three main international conventions on slavery – the United Nations Convention on Slavery 1926; the International Labour Organisation Convention Concerning Forced Labour No. 29; and the Supplementary Convention on the Abolition of Slavery, the Slave Trade and Institutions and Practices Similar to Slavery 1956 – ASI defines masters/ employers as having three kinds of power. These are: the power to buy and sell, thus exercising the right of ownership over another human being; the power of control over the most basic freedoms of another person; and the power to command.[2] ASI argues that migrant domestic workers fall under their remit, even if not 'owned' by their employers, because they are often unable to refuse work (power to command) and subject to their employers' control over such choices as where they sleep, or what they eat and drink (power of control), as well as having their liberty severely restricted.

As seen in the previous chapter, the application of this definition has proved extremely useful for campaigning purposes in the UK in particular, but it is worth drawing attention to two (related) problems with the use of the term 'slavery' as applied to migrant domestic workers. First, as ASI's sources demonstrate, there is an elision between slavery on the one hand, and unfree/forced labour on the other. The distinction, if one wishes to make it, can be extremely complicated, but perhaps the key point to make is that slavery and wage labour ('wage slavery') are not diametrically opposed. Second, contemporary domestic workers' experiences vary widely, even within the same state, so while some might seem to be formally 'enslaved', others quite clearly are not. Many feel that their employers treat them with respect and are very concerned to emphasise that they are happy with their conditions, that they are pleased to be working as domestic workers and choose to continue in this employment: 'Since the beginning we find employers who are kind, who are nice, who treat us as somebody they know, not like slaves. So we are happy. That's why we stayed' (Joanna, Filipina in Paris). The individual employment situation depends on a multitude of factors. I have already argued that the worker's formal relation to the state and to the employer are crucial. More generally, migrant domestic workers are working in different political, economic, social and ideological environments: the power invested in the employer, the working out of the management of boundaries by the employer, are very specific. It is also worth considering the extent to which the treatment of domestic workers, including the use of violence, reflects the position of women in general within different states, how domestic work is constructed, the position of racialised groups, and so on.

Female slavery in the antebellum South, USA

Slave systems are and have been many and varied, and slaves have been used for household labour all over the world since earliest times. Latin for 'slave' was *famuli*, and the original *familia* a group of slaves living under one roof under the authority of the man. In what is now India, the Middle East, South America and Africa, domestic labour in private households was at different times the work of slaves. Slavery, then, has long been associated with reproductive labour, and reproductive labour with women. Slavery, equally, has also been associated with difference, with people from other tribes or language groups. The very word 'slave' comes from the Latin *sclavus* – the ethnic name of the Slav people, popularised in Germany in the tenth century. The association between 'foreigners', domestic work and slavery has a long history. For many people today the paradigmatic case of slavery is the slave system of America in the eighteenth and nineteenth centuries. As Kevin Bales, author of *Disposable People: New Slavery in the Global Economy*, writes: 'People think about

128

slavery in terms that are narrow and historical – concentrating on the slave trade of the sixteenth to nineteenth centuries' ('Thai girl, 14, good teeth ... $2K', *Times Higher Educational Supplement*, 7 May 1999). If more formal definitions of slavery are problematic in their application to migrant domestic workers, there are nevertheless lessons to be learned from a comparison, at the experiential level and in particular the relationships between slaves and mistresses, of the lives of slaves in the American South, and those of contemporary migrant domestic workers.

I must first emphasise again the diversity of women's experiences of slavery even at a specific historical period and geographical location. One of the most common distinctions drawn is between the field hand and the household slave, with the household slave generally held to enjoy the better living and working conditions – though writers such as bell hooks and Angela Davis have disputed this. Indeed, within a single woman's life, depending on her master or mistress, she might have very different experiences. Sojourner Truth compared her experiences under her second master, Charles Ardinburgh – 'comparatively speaking a kind master to his slaves' (Gilbert 1991: 13) – to John Nealy: 'Oh! My God! ... what a way is this of treating human beings' (Gilbert 1991: 27). What such variety indicates is precisely the lack of control that the slave had over her life, and the power of her owners – whether for good or ill was up to them. The experiences of slaves also depended on the economic conditions of the household to which they were attached. Large plantations supported households of specialised slaves, and there could operate a hierarchy, with cooks and senior nurses at the top and general maids of all work, washers, ironers, etcetera, below them. The slave owners might even enforce marks of deference shown by some slaves to others – curtseying to the cook, for example (Fox-Genovese 1988: 162). Of course, this does not alter the fact that all were slaves, that favour was within the power of the owner to withold or deny, that even treasured nannies were likely to be dumped in their old age, left to die in poverty and loneliness, abandoned ('freed') by their former charges. Small farms, on the other hand, might have one slave who worked alongside the woman of the house doing the hardest of the gendered chores and household production. In general household slaves had no control over their living and working conditions. Should their owners require it they must sleep in the same bed with themselves or their children. Their time was, quite literally, not their own. Not all owners enforced this rigidly, but this was not an expression of the slave's rights, but of her owner's kindness.

Until the first third of the eighteenth century the system of slavery generally relied on black males and black women were cheaper than black men. Between about 1730 and 1750, however, women became more valuable: not only was their capacity for fieldwork recognised, but also their importance in reproducing the slave labour force. Thus the sexual exploitation and manipulation of slave women became a part of the slave system (White 1985: 66ff). Slavery, unlike citizenship, was passed on through the mother – so all children born to slave women were slaves, whoever the father. While masters could be held legally accountable for the deliberate murder of slaves, the rape of a slave woman was not a crime. Slave women could be used to augment their master's capital, and could save the cost of replacement slaves, and their childbearing capacity became particularly important after the overseas slave trade was outlawed in 1807. While some women became pregnant following rape by masters and overseers, others were induced by policies favouring pregnant women, and by rewards for women who had many children: 'Missus, tho' we no able to work, we make little niggars for massa' (White 1985: 100).

Having had children, a woman had no hold over them, whoever the father, for they were the property of her master. They could be, and were, put to work as he demanded, and could be sold away from her at any time. While Angela Davis has argued that reproductive labour in the slave dwelling was the only meaningful labour available to slave women, as it could not be claimed immediately by the slave owner, the fact that their children could be ruthlessly taken from them argues a lack of control over their reproductive labour in any sense. There are many terrible descriptions of enforced partings and children torn from their parents. In 'A slave auction described by a slave', the attempts of Eliza to stay with her young son Randall are described. She begged his purchaser to buy herself and her daughter Emily too so they could all stay together, promising to be the best worker he had ever had. She wept and begged to the extent that she was threatened with a whipping, but it was to no avail: 'Then Eliza ran to him; embraced him passionately; kissed him again and again; told him to remember her – all the while her tears falling in the boy's face like rain' (Aptheker 1951: 208).

The physical, sexual, emotional and spiritual violence that characterises accounts of slavery in the antebellum South is incaulculable. As far as household slaves are concerned, violence is both casual, unpredictable, and a feature of punishment and control. hooks graphically describes a white slave-owning mother and daughter witnessing the particularly brutal flogging of a black slave-woman by the husband/father and hypothesises:

> Incidents of this nature exposed to white women the cruelty of their husbands, fathers, and brothers and served as a warning of what might be their fate should they not maintain a passive stance. Surely, it must have

occurred to white women that were enslaved black women not available to bear the brunt of such intense anti-women male aggression, they themselves might have been the victims.
(hooks 1981: 38)

Physical violence, however, was not the province of the master of the house alone. Slaves and those who have documented their experiences have been clear about the violence of female slave owners. While this often was manifest simply in observing and not intervening in the brutality exhibited by male owners and overseers, it was also perpetrated by slave-owning women themselves. Beatings, starvation and all manner of cruelties could be imposed by the mistress of the house: 'As slaves would have been the first to insist, and as both male and female slaveholders well knew, mistresses could be the very devil. A mean mistress stood second to no master in her cruelty.' Anna Dorsey did not hear her mistress call her, and was attacked with a large butcher's knife; Hannah Plummer's mother was stripped to the waist and whipped with a carriage whip; while Mary Armstrong's sister was beaten to death by her mistress (Fox Genovese 1988: 309 ff). The daily proximity and intimacy between household slaves and their mistresses resulted in intense personal relations that might at any time flare into violence. Indeed, there seems to have been great tolerance of physical violence within the home despite its construction as haven of domesticity. Mrs Flint may have been deficient in energy – weak and having difficulty in managing the house, 'but her nerves were so strong, that she could sit in her easy chair and see a woman whipped till the blood trickled from every stroke of the lash' (Jacobs 1988). Grimke, a woman abolitionist who wrote much on the evils of slavery, described the condition of a woman slave owned by a devout Christian family. She had tried to run away several times and been severely punished, marked by having a front tooth torn out and forced to wear an iron collar. The contradictions and tensions inherent in domesticity are borne by this woman:

> this suffering slave, who was the seamstress of the family, was continually in their presence, sitting in the chamber to sew, or engaging in ... other household work with her lacerated and bleeding back, her mutilated mouth and heavy iron collar without, so far as appeared, exciting any feeling of compassion. (Davis 1984)

Sexual abuse and rape by white masters of black women was a flashpoint for relations between slaveholding women and slave women. Rather than protecting women against a husband's depredations slaveholding women often regarded the slave women as a threat: 'I would rather drudge out my life on a cotton plantation, till the grave opened to give me rest, than to live with an unprincipled master and a jealous mistress' (Jacobs 1988: 49). One mistress was so tormented by her knowledge that a slave's baby had been fathered by her husband, that she stole into the slaves' quarters and murdered the child – much to her husband's fury. Sexual abuse and rape were much cited by northern female abolitionists as a manifestation of the evils of slavery, and by male pro-slavers as bene-fiting white women by keeping their men 'regular'. White has argued that the enslavement of black women and the racist stereotypes and justifica-tions arising from this further 'benefited' white women by enabling them to be distanced from their reproductive functions and associated promis-cuity and lasciviousness. While respectable white women were covered, their arms and legs hidden, black women were exposed and handled on the auction block, and could be thoroughly inspected by potential purchasers with a view to reproductive ability. Black women's bodies were exposed through the exigencies of their physical labour, skirts pinned up, sleeves rolled up, and were exposed during punishment – descriptions of women being whipped often refer to their nakedness (White 1985: 31–3). So once again we have women divided into clean/dirty, moral/physical, virtuous/sexual, white/black. Mistress and slave, both women, are driven yet further apart.

> She felt that her marriage vows were desecrated, her dignity insulted; but she had no compassion for the poor victim of her husband's perfidy. She pitied herself as a martyr; but she was incapable of feeling for the condition of shame and misery in which her unfortunate, helpless slave was placed. (Jacobs 1988: 53)

Sexual jealousy indicates only the most extreme source of tension between mistresses and slave women. From slaveholder women's accounts it is clear that many felt guilt at leaving their children to the care of others, blaming themselves for instance if a child died, and becoming jealous of the relation between slave nurses and their charges. There was tension also between their managerial role and their ignorance of how to actually do the housework, and a failure to acknowledge the expertise of slaves or even acknowledge their labour as work. To this extent sexual jealousy may be only the most extreme example of jealousy and con-fusion over the respective gendered roles of black slave woman and white mistress. Moreover, it was often observed that the white wives of plantat-ion owners fell easily under the influence of slaves, and adopted their lazy vulgarity, for of course women are always prone to the promptings of their baser nature (hooks 1981: 32–3). White women had to make con-scious efforts to distance themselves from black women, to reinforce the distinctions between them. Linda Brent describes how one mistress was present during the difficult birth of a master's baby by a slave woman: 'In her agony she cried out, "O Lord, come and take me!". Her mistress stood by, and mocked at her like an incarnate fiend. "You suffer, do you?" she exclaimed. "I am glad of it. You deserve it all, and more too."' (Jacobs 1988: 24) It is difficult to envision a more extreme distancing than that of one woman rejoicing in another's pain during childbirth.

Contemporary 'slavery'?

When the horrific experiences endured by household slaves have been fully acknowledged, is their comparison with the lot of migrant domestic workers in the twentieth century an unpardonable exaggeration? There are workers whose experiences are similar: Nay Zar-Htun, a 15-year-old from Moulmein in Burma, was sold by her parents and taken to Bangkok. A Thai woman took her on as a domestic worker. She worked 18-hour days, cooking, cleaning, doing the laundry, massaging her employers and sleeping on the floor in a store room. When she asked for her salary, 'The woman said that she had bought me for 5,000 baht and that I would have to work five months without pay.'[3] When she escaped she was brought back at gunpoint. Roseline from Southern Nigeria was bought for £2 from her impoverished father, who was led to believe he would be paid that sum regularly every month to help feed his other five children. Roseline, he was told by the couple, was to stay as their guest and be taught domestic science. They brought her to Sheffield, where the husband worked as a doctor. She was not allowed out, had to sleep on the floor, and was made to kneel on the floor for two hours if she fell asleep before being allowed to go to bed. Her working day started at 5.30 a.m. and lasted 18 hours. She cleaned and washed for her employers and their five children. She was beaten and starved. On one occasion, in desperation, she wrote a note intended for the next-door neighbour offering sex for a sandwich.

These experiences seem close to those endured by some of the chattel slaves of the American South. Rosaline, Nay Zar-Htun and many others are physically confined, and work unlimited hours with wages (if any) going not to them but to third parties. Neither Rosaline nor Nay Zar-Htun were voluntarily contracting for their labour power, and while they were in extreme situations it is not unusual for domestic workers to be expected to labour in the businesses and houses of employers' families and friends for no extra payment. In Hong Kong one survey found that 25 per cent of respondents claimed they had to work for other households, 18 per cent had to do additional work in the employer's factory, shop or office; and 18 per cent were passed to others by their employers or recruitment agencies in Hong Kong.[4] One employer remarked, when her actions were questioned: 'I bought her. I am her employer. I can do anything I want with her.' Workers said they felt degraded at being handed from one employer to another, by 'the humiliation of being bought and sold and treated literally like slaves and commodities'. Alice, for example, a Filipina who went to Taiwan as a domestic worker, was told on arrival that she had to work in her boss's furniture factory as well as doing the housework. She asked for extra pay for doing two jobs, but this was refused. In Malaysia and in the UK it is not unusual for domestic workers to be 'sold' – passed on for a fee between employers. It should be noted, however, that in general such practices are not, as under slavery, legally sanctioned.

Unlike the children of slave women on Southern plantations, the children of domestic workers are not the property of her employers. They serve not to increase the employer's capital but to provide an unwelcome distraction from the domestic worker's main responsibility, which is the employing family rather than her own children. Migrant domestic workers, unlike slave women, are positively discouraged from having children. This may be overt and state policy, as in Singapore where domestic workers must have a pregnancy test every six months and return to their country of origin should they be pregnant and not consent to a termination. Generally, workers are concerned not to get pregnant because they would lose their jobs, yet they are also conscious that in many instances they are forfeiting their own chance to have children by remaining as migrant domestic workers for their crucial reproductive years. As with slaves in the USA, parents' relations with their own children receive neither recognition nor support, and this is so even for those whose children are present in the same country with them.

In Greece the community groups Kasapi and Pan-African Association have established crèches to try to address some of the difficulties they faced. When I visited it, Kasapi's crèche had been running for two months with its maximum of 24 children. Many of the children there were clearly disturbed. The crèche workers explained that they did not know how to play or to relate to other children. One five-year-old girl sat silently on a chair throughout the visit. Her mother had not been able to take her to work with her and had left her with a neighbour. She had been told to sit on a chair and not make a noise, and had sat on a chair not making a noise for six days a week for three years. Another child of three and a half screamed as soon as he woke up from his nap. The crèche worker explained that he had been kept locked in a room since he was a baby, and now suffered from claustrophobia. Although obviously desperately needed, the crèche was proving extremely difficult to finance because most of the mothers had no surplus income with which to finance childcare. But by 1999 it had grown to accommodate over one hundred children, and had developed into a centre that also provided primary education.

The fact that they do not benefit economically from rape does not mean that male employers do not rape and sexually abuse migrant domestic workers. They undoubtedly do. Teblez's employer raped her and when she became pregnant she was thrown out onto the streets of Athens. Homeless and unemployed, she delivered her baby in the street. She survived by begging, but after some two weeks, the baby was taken from her by some officials – she did not know who they were or what they represented. I met her some four weeks later; she was still on the streets, and clearly mentally disturbed. The extent of this violent abuse is not clear. In their report, 'Punishing the Victim: Rape and Mistreatment of Asian Maids in Kuwait' (1992), Middle East Watch Women's Rights Project found that one third of the sixty cases they investigated involved rape or sexual assault by employers. 'We found that while not all domestic servants in Kuwait suffer at the hands of their employers, there exists a significant and pervasive pattern of rape, physical assault and mistreatment of Asian maids that takes place largely with impunity' (Middle East Watch: 4). In the EU male employers commonly expect the domestic worker to be sexually available to them: 'Sometimes when some girls want to go to work, especially when his wife is not around, he will come for you naked, expecting you to take to bed. That's the way they treat you' (Alem, Ethiopian in Athens). Advertisements in European newspapers are often associated with men allegedly in search of a domestic worker, but actually looking for sex and workers advertising often stipulate 'No sex'. Domestic work and sex work are elided by those who looked to the worker to do the cleaning with no clothes on, or wearing certain types of clothes. Workers in both Athens and Paris have described going for interviews with potential male employers and finding that their employer had no clothes on: 'A friend of mine went for a job, and he opened the door and he was totally naked. She didn't want to show how she felt, so she said, "Do you want me to clean your house or watch your body?" He said, "What's wrong? It's only natural"' (Alem, Ethiopian in Athens). One worker in Paris was furious when her friend passed on a male employer who liked to watch her clean when he had no clothes on. When she complained, her friend told her that she had worked for him for years under these conditions.

One of the most striking aspects of workers' experiences of sexual abuse is that, if it is discovered, the female employer almost invariably sides with the male offender. Female employers blame their workers for 'stealing' their husbands, when they are raped by them. In Barcelona Teresa was sacked when she complained about her employer's son coming into her room at night, on the grounds that she was 'interfering in the mother/son relationship'! Issues of sex serve to further divide domestic workers and female employers, rather than unite them – even when it is the employer who is objectified: 'The Greek men have a big problem with sex. I found a fourteen-year-old watching his mum through the keyhole in the bathroom. I didn't tell her because she wouldn't believe me' (Joy, Ghanaian in Athens).

It is perhaps in the area of mistress/employer–slave/worker relations that the comparison with slavery proves most useful. Grimke's example of the seamstress, cited above, reminded me forcibly of Laxmi Swami, a woman from India who worked in London, whose two female employers yanked out two of her teeth and damaged her eyes when they threw a bunch of keys at her face, as well as regularly beating her with a horsewhip and knotted electric flex. Of course workers and slaves throughout the world and over generations have been beaten and had their teeth torn out by their masters and their owners, but as with the experiences of household slaves in the American South, routine physical violence perpetrated by the female employer is characteristic of many of the narratives of migrant domestic workers. T, an eighteen-year-old Ethiopian woman, had been in Greece for two months. She worked looking after a six-year-old boy and cleaning the house. The female employer had beaten her from the outset, and she had burns on her arm that she said had been inflicted with an iron by the six-year-old. Her face was swollen from a beating several days before which forced her to flee the house and leave all her belongings, including her passport. At the time she was penniless and relying on an uncle for a home. In the UK, workers have reported broken bones, beatings and an almost ritualised violence used overtly to demonstrate the employer's control over the worker, similar to the degradation expressed through work: 'We were three Filipinas, she brought us into the room where her guests were, she made us kneel down and slapped each one of us across the face' (domestic worker interviewed at the Commission for Filipino Migrant Workers and quoted in Healy 1994: 42).

Nor is such abuse restricted to Europe. NG, for example, is a 25-year-old Bangladeshi woman who was working for a relative of the Emir of Kuwait. Every morning she had to start work at exactly 5.30 a.m.: 'If I was one second late, [the employer] would slap me on the left side of my face. She has a slightly paralyzed left hand so she always hit us with her right hand on our left cheeks'. As a consequence of these beatings she is scarred on her stomach, arms and legs, is deaf in her left ear and has pain in the left side of her jaw. Another Bangladeshi worker described how:

> They shouted all the time and the Madame pinched my cheek or back with her long finger nails, sometimes drawing blood, almost every day. She would also catch my hair and bang my head on the floor. When the baby cried she got angry; if the baby broke a glass, she would say 'You broke it' and slap me in the face.
>
> (*Human Rights Watch* 1992: 21)

Janet Reno's team in the USA are uncovering examples of serious abuses:

> She told local social workers that she sometimes had to beg neighbors for food and clothing and was regularly beaten by the wife. She said the couple told her that if she fled their home, she would be arrested immediately because she is black.
>
> (*Washington Post*, 5 January 1999)

This particular worker had endured these conditions for over nineteen years.

There are many current examples throughout the world, therefore, where the experiences of migrant domestic workers parallel those of household slaves in the American South. It remains important to point out that the legal limitations on the power held over migrant domestic workers are generally greater than those held over those slaves – although this may have little impact in practice. So, for example, unlike the rape of slaves in the American South, the rape of domestic workers in Kuwait and in the European Union does constitute a crime; it is not socially sanctioned. Yet in Kuwait Middle East Watch found that, even when cases are reported, police are reluctant to credit such allegations, and fail to follow up and investigate even the most serious of cases. Singala, a 20-year-old Sri Lankan, was raped by her employer with such violence that her bladder and rectum were both torn, and then thrown off the balcony, breaking bones after falling several floors. She was catatonic and unresponsive for several weeks following her admission to hospital. Her employer visited her while in hospital and stated that she should return to his house upon her discharge. Some weeks previously another domestic worker, a Filipina, admitted to the same hospital after she had jumped from a fourth-floor window with her hands tied behind her back and a gag in her mouth after her employer had raped her, had been returned to the same employer's home following her discharge. In France, a wealthy French employer and his son were not dissuaded by the possibility of criminal charges from their regular rape and sodomising of Veronique Akobe, an undocumented domestic worker from Côte d'Ivoire. Terrified of deportation should she report it to the police, Veronique endured the abuse for some months until she could bear it no more. She stabbed both abusers, wounding one and killing the other. Her lawyer in court (now the National Front member for Nice) defended her on the grounds that her illegality had led her to 'fantasise' about rape. So, while the rape of a migrant domestic worker by her employer does constitute a crime, her right to control over access to her body may in practice be very limited.

Power

This suggests that while some workers' experiences may be similar to those of slaves, the mechanisms of power exercised over them are different. Workers are given legal rights (although for non-citizens these will be less extensive than those enjoyed by citizens), but it may be difficult, if not impossible, to exercise them. So, in the examples given above, it is illegal for employers to pass their workers to other employers, but nevertheless it is the practice. Similarly, it is illegal for employers to withhold payments from their workers, or to abuse them physically, but nevertheless it is the practice. It is particularly difficult for a person who is undocumented to exercise her rights, because she may be deported if she comes to the attention of the authorities. Rights given with one hand are effectively taken away with the other. This is most clearly revealed in the practice of dependent immigration status prevalent in the USA and in Europe. While employers do not 'own' their workers and cannot legally do so, in the USA, for example, the visas given to domestic workers require them to work only for the employers who sponsor them. If they leave those employers they are liable for deportation. Effectively, then, the actual experience of the worker may be similar to that of a slave. The 'civilised' state both limits and reinforces the power of the employers, who may take advantage of this to the extent they choose. Not all of the 30,000 domestic workers brought to the USA under special work visas are abused but, according to Bill Lann Lee, acting assistant attorney general for civil rights and co-chairman of Reno's task force, some abuses are 'so severe they rise to a level of involuntary servitude' ('Modern-Day Slavery? Imported Servants Allege Abuse by Foreign Host Families in US', *Washington Post*, 5 January 1999). So the abuses are privatised, no longer the responsibility of anyone but the employer – and the state can point to its protective mechanisms if necessary. In a debate in the UK Houses of Parliament in 1990, for example, when confronted with evidence of abuse and exploitation of migrant domestic workers, the Department of Employment retorted that workers should have recourse to industrial tribunals and the courts, prompting Lord Hylton to reply that such a position is:

138

totally unrealistic. Few resident domestics will dare to use those procedures while they are still in employment. If they leave or are sacked, they immediately breach their conditions of entry and become liable to deportation.... Rights are a pure illusion unless they can in practice be fully exercised.

Yet at the same time the employers themselves are also absolved of certain responsibilities. Take the example cited above of the removal of slave children from their mothers. Maria is from a landless peasant family in the Southern Philippines who left for Saudi Arabia:

> The worst thing was to leave my child. He was just 13 months old and I was still breastfeeding him. I wanted to feed him until he slept, so it would be peaceful goodbye for him. But I fed him for one hour, and still he did not let go of me. He didn't want me to go. So in the end I took the breast from him, and he cried, he didn't want me to go, and I just gave him to my mother and said, take him to his father. I cannot stop thinking about that, and I shouldn't have left my baby.

As she described that parting, thirteen years ago, Maria was crying. Unlike Eliza, she clearly feels that she had some choice in leaving her baby – although the kind of 'choice' allowed to a young woman from an impoverished family in a war zone, when confronted with a recruiter offering waged work, is clearly limited. Her current employers, moreover, cannot be held responsible for this distant, traumatic event. They are, however, reaping the benefit of their relative poverty and wealth, of wider social and economic circumstances that impinge on both differently.

It is useful in this context to return to Patterson's distinction between personalistic and materialistic idioms of power, if only to illustrate that, although relations of dependence may be disguised as power over money rather than power over persons, the *experiences* it gives rise to on the part of the worker/slave may amount to the same thing. While this is not confined to domestic workers, what is particular about their situation is how this combines with the blatant personalistic power exercised by employers even over workers' most basic physical needs, such as water, accommodation or communication. This is common to both ASI's definition (power to control) and press coverage of domestic workers. On this level the parallels with Southern slavery are noticeable. In the American South the management of food and its distribution to slaves was the responsibility of the slaveholding woman, and it was often complained that she measured out food to the last crumb, and ruined leftovers to ensure that the cook and other household servants were not able to eat them. One cook was ordered to make some food for the dog: 'He refused to eat, and when his head was held over it, the froth flowed from his

139

mouth into the basin. He died a few minutes after' (Jacobs 1988: 23). Whereupon the cook was compelled to eat the food. This particular woman was also compelled to eat food she had cooked for her master if he did not like it: 'The poor hungry creature might not have objected to eating it; but she did object to having her master cram it down her throat till she choked' (Jacobs 1988: 22). Among contemporary domestic workers I have spoken to, one of the most common problems faced is control of food. Food consumption is a measure of common humanity, and eating arrangements are an important means of enforcing distinctions between workers and family. Workers are typically expected to eat on their own in the kitchen, separate from the family. This separation is often extended to the utensils used by the worker. This is a particular complaint of African workers, that they are given separate crockery and cutlery to use. Sometimes a person's need to eat is denied completely: one woman described how she was given no food at all, but stole bread and ate it in the toilet, while another had to beg food from a neighbour. More usually workers are allowed to eat leftovers from their employers' plates. Other food is often closely monitored and marked to ensure it is not stolen by the domestic workers. Indeed, employers' attitudes towards food verge on the neurotic. 'They say, "Don't throw anything away, and when the girl comes to clean we will give it to her". And when I say "Give this to the dog", she says, "No, no it is reserved for you"' (Elsa, Filipina in Athens).

Employers and slaveholders alike can control access to other essentials of life such as water, clothing and bathing facilities.

> We are not happy. How can you tell somebody in wintertime, in wintertime, if you use my hot water I will be very annoyed with you. Meaning, you should always use cold water, even in winter. We all need good health. How can you clean balcony when it's cold, when she's not going to use the balcony.... It is not fair. You wouldn't tell your fellow human to do something you would not be happy to do. But they don't respect.
> (Joy, Ghanaian in Athens)

Personalistic power may be demonstrated in demanding particular services in an unnecessary way: Linda Bent's mistress was irritated by the creaking noise of her shoes and demanded that she take them off or they would be thrown into the fire:

> I took them off, and my stockings also. She then sent me a long distance, on an errand. As I went through the snow, my bare feet tingled. That night I was very hoarse; and I went to bed thinking the next day would find me sick, perhaps dead. What was my grief on waking to find myself quite well! (Jacobs 1988: 32)

Migrant domestic workers in Europe today are similarly required to do totally unnecessary work, or to work under such unreasonable conditions that their health is threatened. One of the most frequent complaints by domestic workers is that they are not allowed to rest, that they are treated 'like machines': 'and what is it that makes us similar to machines? You can kick it if it doesn't work properly, you can use it and use it, and when it is broken you can throw it away' (Workshop Report, Migrant Domestic Workers in Europe Conference held by RESPECT network, Paris, 7–9 May 1999).

Some aspects of this personalistic power are masked by money. Employers defend unreasonable behaviour by alleging financial constraints:

> I worked with a woman who used to order me out to buy an egg, half for her and half for me.... I wasn't allowed to sit on the bed for a moment, because it would use up the mattress and make it soft ... and at ten o'clock the lights went out and you had to walk like this, feeling your way. It was ridiculous!
> (Flora, Brazilian woman in Barcelona)

Thus while workers are responsible for their employers' reproductive needs and demands, some employers resent any cost associated with their worker other than their wage and sometimes, it seems, they resent even that. It is striking that these costs may be for amounts of money that are likely to mean very little to a middle-class European family – the cost of a hot shower, for example. Money is not really the issue; rather, it is an expression of the attempt to commodify all human relations, and human beings:

> If you don't remove your shoes or slippers they will use embarrassing words, and it's no good saying 'sorry'. They just say, 'In what bank are we going to deposit your sorry? We are spending money. We are paying you to do a job. Why are you not working properly?'
> (Filipina domestic worker cited in Anderson 1993: 14)

It is similar to arguments over the cost of workers under slavery: there is the need on the one hand to sustain the labour, but on the other hand the desire to minimise costs of reproduction. The person has been bought, the capital outlay made, now the owner must profit from her.

Dishonour

Patterson has famously defined slavery on the level of personal relations as: 'the permanent, violent domination of natally alienated and generally dishonoured persons' (Patterson 1982: 13). This concept of 'honour' and 'dishonour' is worth examining further since it can point us to similarities between paradigmatic slavery and migrant domestic workers that lie

141

beyond the simply experiential. I have argued that the commodification of personhood results in the paid domestic worker being dishonoured. But domestic work, paid or unpaid, is dishonourable work because it is constructed as dirty and is associated with the body, with physicality. The nineteenth century was obsessed with the elimination of dirt and disorder which represented the transgression of social boundaries and was associated with nature, with being out of control. It led to the sense that the body is dirty (Davidoff 1974). The privileged are disembodied to the extent of feigning alienation even from their own bodily functions – though of course this is really impossible. The 'Others' are trapped within their bodies, defined and cast out by the privileged. So women and certain 'races' are closely associated with bodily functions, while bourgeois, white men are disembodied, and rarely have to deal with their bodily detritus. Spelman (1981) critiques those feminists who have identified women's bodies as the source of oppression and who consequently attempt to disassociate women from bodies as failing to challenge somatophobia, 'fear of and disdain for the body'. Somatophobia is one of the mechanisms which oppresses women, and black people, and in particular, black women. It denies dignity to the work of the body, much of which is repro-ductive work. Those who would disassociate themselves from the body and its work inevitably leave the work to be done by somebody else: 'For example, if feminists decide that women are not going to be relegated to doing such work, who do we think is going to do it? Have we attended to the role that racism (and classism) historically has played in settling that question?' (Spelman 1981: 53). So, the relationship between hatred of women (misogyny), hatred of the body (somatophobia) and hatred of racialised groups (racism) is played out in the use of racialised female labour to do the work of servicing the body, and in the treatment of domestic workers by their employers.

Patterson argues that it is in the nature of slavery that the master gains honour through the slave's dishonour. Female slave owners and employers of domestic workers also gain honour through dishonour, as well as a workload significantly decreased:

> The position held by the women of a tribe determines to some extent whether or not slaves are wanted. Where all the drudgery is performed, and can be performed by the women, and men do not want to relieve them of it, there is not great use for slave labour. But where women enjoy high consideration, the men are more likely to procure slaves who are to assist the women in their work.
> (Neiboer 1971, cited in Rollins 1985: 21)

Pro-slavery apologists cited the improved situation of white women as

142

one of the great benefits of slavery. Thomas Dew, for example, argued that slavery signified human development and progress from barbarism by substituting 'the labor of the slave ... for that of the women'. White women could thereby cease being beasts of burden and become 'the cheerful and animating center of the family circle'. This is not so far removed from contemporary explanations of the necessity of having a (working-class) cleaner to be able to spend quality time with children and husband. Although one might baulk at calling it 'progress', several historians have argued that slavery did ostensibly benefit some white women by raising their status and giving them power over black slaves (hooks 1981, Fox-Genovese 1988, White 1985) while leaving patriarchy intact. With the black woman taking the role of the doer of female dirty work, including the reproduction of workers (though not the repro- duction of heirs), white women were free to take up their proper function as moral centre of the home. So white women were portrayed as noble, innocent and non-physical, the home their sphere of influence, and 'The figure of the lady, especially the plantation mistress, dominated southern ideals of womanhood' (Fox-Genovese 1988: 47). The plantation mistress must have slaves, but more than that, as hooks has argued, the only way for the mistress to maintain her superiority was through asserting herself over black women and men: 'since the white woman's privileged social status could only exist if a group of women were present to assume the lowly position she had abdicated, it follows that black and white women would be at odds with one another' (hooks 1981: 154).

Like the plantation mistress, the contemporary employer of a migrant domestic worker must assert herself over her worker to maintain her superiority, but more than that, she must assert her difference. Like the slave mistress she needs to show to herself and others that she is a woman, but a different type of woman from the dirty woman who does the dirty work. The dirty worker/slave provides the labour through which the employer/mistress demonstrates her skill. Domestic workers some- times express their sense that female employers are in some way 'jealous' of their worker, that they don't want to do the domestic work, but then they don't want anybody else to do it either. One can see that, for those female employers for whom 'home making' is very bound up with their gender identity, this would result in precisely the kind of jealousy described by the workers. It is the female employer who must establish difference, superiority and inferiority. It is the female employer who relates directly to the worker; the male employer is at one remove. It is important for the female employer to police boundaries. If she does not, she may lose her privileges (or she might find the domestic worker usurping 'her' place in the affections of her children and the sexual attention of her husband). To this extent the employer must overcome their common gender and shared experiences as women. Violence may be one mechanism for doing so.

'Kindness' and power

O'Connell Davidson has pointed out, with reference to prostitute users, that honour and power are linked, citing Hobbes: 'to obey, is to Honour: because no man obeyes them, who they think have no power to help, or hurt them' (Hobbes 1968: 152, cited in O'Connell Davidson 1998: 170). Power may be manifested over others, then, by helping them as well as hurting them. This is particularly relevant to female employers/slave owners, for through kindness and charity the powerful woman asserts her 'feminine' (clean woman) qualities of morality and pity over the helpless recipient. Take Nina, for example. She had employed dozens of migrant domestic workers to care for her mother. She offered, she said, exceptional conditions and a loving household, only to find that her employees were gold-diggers. According to Nina she responds to the lamentable situation of other nationalities by employing them. She was genuinely hurt by the ingratitude of her employees:

> But there is no feeling for what I offer. I give you an example of the last woman from Bulgaria ... I had a bright thought, 'she needs to see her friends'. Because I was tired of all the girls changing so many times I gave her Sunday off. Now, every morning, including Sundays the girl wakes, helps grandmother to the toilet and changes her pamper.... Then she goes, but she must be back for seven pm.... Then, after all I do for her, the girl says every Sunday she would like to be back at midnight and not to do any work – that is not to change pamper in the morning.

So, she employs workers because she pities them, she treats them kindly, but in return is simply taken for granted.

Nina exemplifies Rollins's notion of 'maternalism', the attitude that she believes characterises the relationship between domestic workers and their employers. Maternalism is based on the superordinate-subordinate relationship, with the female employer caring for the worker as she would for a child or a pet, thereby expressing, in a feminised way, her lack of respect for the domestic worker as an adult worker. It is encapsulated in the use of the term 'girl' to describe the adult woman. It is an over-personalisation of employment relations and a refusal to properly acknowledge the employment relation, but presenting this overpersonalisation as a benefit, as friendship. It is clearly an important component in the 'part of the family' stance previously discussed. Unlike Rollins I would not characterise maternalistic relations as fundamentally different from paternalism, for like paternalism, maternalism ultimately serves to reinforce patriarchy, although it does so indirectly, by reinforcing differences between women. As paternalism offers protection in exchange for work and obedience, so too does maternalism. Domestic workers, now as in the past, are often offered employment as a kindness or in exchange for a room and board. Maternalism is particularly insidious because it seems to offer some kind of equality between domestic workers and employers as women, whereas in fact it is precisely that commonality which it works to deny, reinforcing superiority and inferiority. So rather than giving the domestic worker a day off as a worker's right, Nina does it as a consequence of her 'bright thought', thereby actively demonstrating her kindness. The worker's insistence on a full day off is presented as a rejection of this kindness, proof of her heartlessness and emotional inferiority.

Maternalism manifests itself in many ways. The domestic worker may be a confidante, an emotional release, since employers can be safe in the knowledge that their social worlds do not touch, that the worker will not pass on information to her (the employer's) friends. She may be a 'window to exotica', as Rollins terms it. Since a domestic worker may well be the employer's only contact with a 'Third World' lifestyle, she may elicit details of her worker's personal life, not from interest in the same, but in a verbal voyeurism, using it to confirm racist stereotypes and assert her own superiority and kindness:

> I have a good personal relationship with her. When she was in hospital she phoned me to say how grateful she was because the symptoms she had had, I had had, because I'd lost a baby and the experience was very similar.... I made her feel much better. She tells me her problems and I've also told her of experiences that I've had with the baby ... she told me about the woman she lives with who's desperate for work, and she told me about her mother-in-law who practises voodoo and puts pins in dolls. She's got some strange ideas.
> (Jean, employer in Paris)

Here is maternalism as described by Rollins, a friendly relationship between women that works to confirm the employer's kindness (her female 'honour') and the worker's childlike inferiority (her 'dishonour'). Maternalism is also expressed through gifts, giving domestic workers cast-off household goods, often unwanted. The meaning of such gifts is loaded, and becomes clear when one tries to imagine a domestic worker giving her cast-offs to an employer! For maternalism is an asymmetrical relationship in which the domestic worker can never be equal to the employer. Although ostensibly bringing the 'female' characteristics of nurturing and kindness to the employment relationship, this nurturing does not facilitate development, but sets the domestic worker in permanent inferiority, to be pitied, helped, but never viewed as an equal.

Maternalism was also a feature of some relations between slaves and their mistresses. Fox-Genovese describes how slaveholder Sarah Gayle nursed and mourned the death of her beloved nurse, Rose:

> For one single such sense of intimacy, affection, and love for a slave would be enough to confirm the mistress, psychologically and ideologically, in her own vision of herself as bound by ties of human fellowship to those whom she not only governed but owned – a confirmation achieved without necessarily betraying a trace of hypocrisy.
> (Fox-Genovese 1988: 131)

Once again the slave is bolstering the mistress's sense of self and her place in the world. Slave women and domestic workers may be perceived as part of the affective universe of the mistress and employer – at least by the mistress/employer: one slave woman said of her mistress who was mourning the death of a slave woman that it was because 'she don't have no one to whup no more'. I suspect that one of the functions of maternalism in the contemporary world can be for the mistress to prove that she is not racist, that she can enjoy excellent human relations with her black domestic worker. Similarly, the maternalism of slavery never questioned the existence of slavery, the ownership of black by white. Maternalism of its nature cannot be reciprocated. Harriet Jacobs described how her grandmother, a slave, by dint of baking crackers, with her mistress's kind permission, late at night, managed to lay up some savings to buy her own children back: eventually she managed to save $300, but her mistress begged it from her as a loan, promising to repay her:

> The reader probably knows that no promise or writing given to a slave is legally binding; for, according to Southern laws, a slave, being property, can hold no property. When my grandmother lent her hard earnings to her mistress, she trusted solely to her honor. The honor of a slaveholder to a slave! (Jacobs 1988: 13)

Needless to say she was never repaid, and on her mistress's death was told that she could not reclaim the money from her estate.

Power/subjugation and honour/dishonour at the level of personal relations seem to be key to our understanding of 'slavery' and what is being appealed to by comparing migrant domestic workers with slaves. But there is another reference that underlies the headlines: racism. Slavery has for centuries been associated with foreignness, with being an outsider and, as the paradigmatic case of slavery is that of the American South, and that was the enslavement of black people by white, so slavery and racism are intertwined in contemporary consciousness.

Racism

In the manufacturing of difference between female employer and female worker 'race' can be very important. The fact is that women, though classed as the embodied Other, may themselves make other women into objects. To rid themselves of the hated characteristics of pollution and embodiment, they load them on to another/an Other group of women. While 'Other' women may be appropriate to do servicing work, there is often an overt fear of contamination from the bodies of these 'Others'. So typically workers' clothes have to be washed separately while black African workers in Athens had to take an Aids test (at their own expense) every time they changed employer. In the UK employers have specified that they do not want African workers because 'I'm sick so the girl will have to touch me'; or 'I have young children and Aids is such a problem in Africa'. The domestic worker is embodied by virtue of her gender, her 'race' and by her enforced association with (the employer's) dirt, and the employer's reaction is one of disgust: 'the daughter was very rude to the extent that she wouldn't even accept water from my hand simply because I am black, and it intimidated me a lot' (Rose, Ghanaian woman in Athens). 'Race' is not the only means of managing this complicated relationship, but it can play an extremely important role. I do not mean to suggest that the employer consciously sets out to employ a worker from a racialised group in order to manage such tensions, but that she draws on Thompson's 'social consciousness' to do so, and that this is an important factor behind the racialisation of paid domestic work. 'Race' also intersects with notions of citizenship and nationality, and to help unpack notions of slavery/foreignness/racism it is useful to examine classical notions of slavery and the Aristotelian distinction between natural and legal slavery. This gives us some means of disentangling a complex and multilayered relationship. What follows is only the beginning of an attempt to do this.

Aristotle justified slavery as long as master and slave are such by nature, that is, by the different degrees of rational control over themselves of which they are capable – just as male rule over female is justified by superior male rationality:

> Where then there is such a difference as that between soul and body, or between men and animals (as in the case of those whose business is to use their body, and who can do nothing better), the lower sort are by nature slaves, and it is better for them as for all inferiors that they should be under the rule of a master. For he who can be, and therefore is, another's, and he who participates in rational principle enough to apprehend, but not to

have, such a principle, is a slave by nature.... And indeed the use made of
slaves and of tame animals is not very different; for both with their bodies
minister to the needs of life.... It is clear, then, that some men are by
nature free, and others slaves, and that for these latter slavery is both
expedient and right.
(Aristotle: 1255)

Legal slaves, on the other hand, are those taken in war, by conquest, and
in this instance justifying slavery is more problematic:

But this right many jurists impeach.... They detest the notion that, because
one man has the power of doing violence and is superior in brute strength,
another shall be his slave and subject.
(Aristotle: 1255)

This distinction, between those who are 'natural' slaves and those who
are 'legal' slaves by conquest, proves useful since it is a distinction that
underlies our 'social consciousness' of slavery. For the contemporary
reader, despite squeamishness over slave systems (institutionalised slavery),
it may seem on the surface easier to justify arguments for 'legal slavery'
than those for 'natural slavery'. Lack of citizenship or not having legal
status certainly means that it is acceptable to be denied basic human
rights and employment protection, while it is not acceptable to be denied
human rights on the basis of 'race' alone (that is, natural slavery). In
practice, however, the two ('illegality' and having a racialised identity)
often coincide, and the denial of rights to 'illegal immigrants', for example,
is made more palatable by the fact that the majority of people to whom
these rights are being denied have a racialised identity. Thousands of
Australians and New Zealanders work without work permits in London,
but they are not those who come to mind when one uses the phrase
'illegal immigrants'. Natural and legal slavery came together in the case
of slavery in the American South, people were natural slaves by 'race'
and also slaves under the law. The end of slavery as an institution did not
mean the end of racism, and in particular the notion that black people are
naturally suited to certain kinds of physical labour, and black women to
domestic work. There is a surprising consensus that slavery continued
despite its formal abolition – particularly for domestic workers. According
to the 1890 census, in the Southern USA domestic work was exclusively
performed by black women, and nationally it was the largest occupation
in 32 out of 48 states. With the exception of the Southern States, where
black women also worked in agriculture, domestic work was the only
occupation open to black women – in Philadelphia 91 per cent of black
women working were in domestic work in private households. In her
interviews with black domestic workers in Philadelphia in 1899 Isabel

Eaton found women were anxious to leave domestic work 'partly because they consider that service savors of slavery and that they are degraded by it ... partly also because they hope for higher wages' (Eaton 1899: 465). The fact that these comparisons with slavery are drawn by black women themselves, many of whom had themselves endured chattel slavery (48 per cent of domestic workers in the ward came from Virginia or West Virginia) is important. In 1912 an unnamed black woman living in Georgia, who had been working for more than thirty years as a domestic worker, had her thoughts published. 'I will say, also, that the condition of this vast host of poor colored people is just as bad as, if not worse than, it was during the days of slavery. Though today we are enjoying nominal freedom, we are literally slaves' (Aptheker 1951: 46–7). Specifically, the reasons for her considering herself as a slave are her long hours – up to 16 hours a day; the fact that she has to live in and be available at any time of the night for the employer's baby while she can only visit her own children every two weeks; she has no written contract and cannot rest when the baby sleeps; she has to look after four children and do all the tasks of the household and garden: 'You might as well say that I'm on duty all the time – from sunrise to sunrise, every day in the week. I am the slave, body and soul of this family. And what do I get for this work – this lifetime bondage? The pitiful sum of ten dollars a month!' (Aptheker 1951: 47). She had lost her first job because she refused the advances of her employer's husband, and when the case went to court the judge stated: 'This court will never take the word of a nigger against the word of a white man' – whatever her rights in law, in substance they were extremely limited.

Racism dubs black people natural slaves, immigration legislation makes of them 'legal slaves' in the Aristotelian sense. One might want to take the contemporary reach of the Aristotelian approach further: conquest in global economic terms makes contemporary legal slaves of the poor of the Third World, giving the middle class of the First World materialistic forms of power over them. Racism also continues to make of certain people 'natural slaves', however, regarding them as suited by nature to subjugation and labour. This is particularly true of domestic work. Domestic work is 'naturalised' as an extension of women's reproductive work – women do it naturally. Women from racialised groups, beng closer to nature, are 'naturally' good at domestic work, and domestic work in private households in the USA, Canada, Europe and the Middle East is heavily racialised. In the USA until the beginning of the Second World War domestic work in private households constituted the major form of employment for black women – the 1940 census shows that 60 per cent of all employed black women in the USA were domestic workers in private households. From the mid-nineteenth century until the First World War domestic work in private households outside the Southern States was performed predominantly by immigrants from Europe – though as a proportion of the total immigrant population, domestic service was less prominent than for black women (Eaton 1899: 433). Eaton's study includes an interesting comparison between black and immigrant (Irish, German, English, Swedish and Norwegian) domestic workers, noting that for women there was little difference between black and white pay, but among men, who tend to work as visible indicators of service (butlers for example) whites earned significantly more than blacks. Workers, both male and female, were more likely to be white immigrants in the fashionable quarters of Philadelphia, and were more likely to be employed by households with large retinues of servants. While some have drawn attention to the differences in this period in the women who performed domestic work in private households in the USA (Mexicans in the South West, African Americans in the South, Japanese in northern California and Hawaii) it is worth bearing in mind the similarities between their legal rights (or lack of them) and living and working conditions.[5]

In the USA today, while the proportion of native-born African-American women in domestic work has declined, there are again increasing numbers of immigrant women working in private households – in particular women from Mexico and from Central and South America. Numbers are extremely difficult to gauge. Romero cites the 1980 census putting the number of domestic workers in El Paso at 1,063, yet half the 28,300 daily trips on city buses are taken by domestic workers. The majority of these workers are undocumented. Similarly in Europe, domestic work in private households is increasingly being done by racialised groups – though it is not exclusively the work of such groups. In the UK in particular, it is still common for white working-class citizens to work as cleaners, and white middle-class citizens to work as nannies (Gregson and Lowe 1994). In Athens, Paris and Barcelona, older white female citizens also work as domestic workers, either because they can find no other work, or because they have worked in the sector all their lives. For migrants, however, domestic work and prostitution are the only work available on arrival. Those who continue to do domestic work when they have a settled immigration/citizenship status may choose live-out work, but they generally continue to work in private households, and it seems that they are accounting for an increasing share of the market. Why does domestic work figure so prominently in the employment of migrant women?

The most obvious reply would be cost, that migrant domestic workers are cheaper, and undocumented workers can be employed off the books. Certainly when there are figures available, it seems that citizens are likely to command higher salaries than migrants. It is a characteristic of paid domestic labour, however, that with the exception of professionalised work a large proportion of it is done off the books, whether the worker is a citizen or an undocumented migrant. Thus avoidance of tax and national insurance on its own does not explain the proliferation of migrants in this sector. Neither does their cheapness. Despite the relatively high wages of Polish workers in Berlin, they still account for a significant proportion of domestic workers. Filipino workers are the most popular and they are also the most expensive.

> Even in Athens we notice sometimes, Filipino, Filipino, Filipino, Filipino. But for Africans there is very little opportunity of getting job.... You do not see in Athens News advertising for Ethiopians or Africans. When they are advertising the work job, they always say, Filipinos or Europeans. They never advertise Africans.
> (Teshome, Ethiopian in Athens)

This suggests that wages are not the only consideration for the employer. One advantage of migrant labour is its flexibility. When the child of a live-in domestic worker is sick, if that worker is a citizen, she will leave her employing family to care for her child; not so the migrant worker for whom home and family may be thousands of miles away. A live-in migrant worker with limited access to life outside the employing home is less likely to form relationships that intrude on the employing family. As seen in Chapter 7, paid domestic workers are often constructed as 'part of the family', and migrants, removed from their own communities and relationships, are free to become a part of the family in a way in which a citizen is not. For the undocumented migrant worker there is not even the possibility of family reunification. One could also argue that, because personalised networks and word of mouth are so important for finding employment in domestic work, once a group has made its connections it is very difficult for outsiders to make headway in a system that relies on personal recommendations.

But if this explains why migrants become domestic workers, it does not explain why many continue to work in private households even when they are well established in the country with rights to family reunification and other advantages. Many of the Filipinas in Italy and Barcelona had settlement status and were highly educated, with professional experience as teachers or midwives, or in modern sectors such as telecommunications, yet continued as domestic workers. Similarly, evidence from placement agencies in Paris suggests that naturalised French citizens are disproportionately represented in domestic work. One of the problems faced is non-recognition of professional qualifications. This in turn is part of more general labour market racism. For migrant domestic workers are members of racialised groups. It is not only their status as (im)migrants that determines their opportunities (or lack of them) in the labour market, but also their 'race' and gender.

Racialised hierarchies and reproduction of racism

Bakan and Stasiulis (1995) have examined how the racialisation of domestic work means, on the one hand, the construing of a 'fictive, universal, nonwhite, female, noncitizen Other' who is in some way naturally suited to domestic work, but, on the other, the hierarchising of women by distinctions such as skin colour, ethnicity, religion and nationality, as being appropriate for different types of domestic work and as meriting different levels of wages. Rina Cohen (1987), too, refers to the 'racial division of labour' among employers of domestic workers in Canada, with the 'lighter' women being employed for childcare and cooking, and black women for housework. So while on the one hand the Other is constructed as a homogeneous creature, well suited for domestic labour, on the other a nineteenth-century hierarchy operates in which one 'race' is very clearly differentiated from another 'race'.

Table 8.1 Wages in Athens by country of origin (drachmas)

Pay per hour	Less than 450	450–500	500+
Filipina	0	4	4
Non-Filipina	11	2	4

Source: Questionnaires distributed to domestic workers in Athens

This invidious hierarchy is very much in evidence in Europe. To some extent it is a recognised hierarchy among both employers and workers, with Filipinas generally at the top and black Africans at the bottom, and it is most clearly manifested in pay. In Athens, for example, salaries ranged between 50,000 and 150,000 drachmas (£140–£422) a month, but Filipinas (and, it was reported, Poles) generally earned more than other nationalities (Table 8.1). This was true not just of Athens, but also of Barcelona and Paris (even though in Paris most Filipinas were undocumented): 'It is a little bit different situation between Filipinas and other nationalities, firstly because you are a large group, you are a majority, and you have been here for longer than other nationalities. Also you are very united' (Edita, Peruvian in Barcelona).

With the exception of Filipinos the position of national groups in the racist hierarchy varied from city to city. Broadly speaking, as the woman quoted above indicates, the lighter one's skin the better one's wages and the easier it is to find work:

> One African woman I met. Her fingers were very scratched and raw. She said her woman didn't let her have gloves. She was working for an old lady. When she dirtied herself she had to clean her and she had to pick the dirt with her hand. I said, 'But why don't you leave her after she did that to you?'. She said to me, 'You are lucky you are light skinned, it is easier for you to find employer.'
> (Alem, Ethiopian working in Athens)

While employers and agencies generally expressed their preferences in terms of 'nationality', this often seemed to be code for the precise shade of skin colour. Placement agencies, whether voluntary or commercial, play an important role in perpetuating such racist stereotypes. Their racism is overt and unashamed:

> The Ethiopians are very sweet. They are not like the African Africans, they are ugly.... Black means without light, and if the old woman does not see so well, if she has mental problems, then that person like that colour can cause psychological problems. For a mental person or an old person, someone who will not take their medicine, if they see black they see darkness and they are afraid. It is not because they are ugly.... but black become more black if you cannot see properly.
> (Caritas volunteer, Athens)

> Moroccans are difficult to place.... Their religion is very different, they observe Ramadan.... They are very different, though like Peruvians they are brought up to be servile.... Filipinas are easiest to place. They are cold [an advantage], efficient but not affectionate, they don't care about anything, hardworking, they speak English, are discrete, they have integrated to some extent. But they are disloyal.... They only care about money.
> (Agency R, Barcelona)

> You know the black people are used to being under the sun, and the people in France think they are very lazy, they are not going very quick, and you know, another breed. But they are very good with children, very maternal.
> (AGF volunteer Paris)

Employment gatekeepers, therefore, formal and informal, play an important part in the perpetuation of the racialisation of domestic work in Europe as elsewhere (Bakan and Stasiulis 1995).

But the hierarchy is not only based on skin colour: Albanians and Ukrainians in Greece were low on the hierarchy although white-skinned: 'It is not only a matter of the skin colour. We are white, we are not black, but we are discriminated in the same way, as foreigners' (Ana, Romanian working in Athens). In Paris, many employers expressed a preference for Haitians, generally darker-skinned than people from Morocco and Algeria, who were often expressly not wanted. The particular racist stereotype attached to particular nationalities in different European states also therefore seems to have an impact (thus, for example, in France Algerians in particular are often associated with terrorism). Religion and 'culture' can also play its part. Employers and agencies in Barcelona and Paris explained that it could be difficult to employ Muslims because of this different 'culture'. Anne Marie in Paris explained that her worker was a Muslim:

> She observes Ramadan. One day she came to work looking and feeling sick because her clock hadn't rung before the rising of the sun and she hadn't had anything to eat since the day before. She didn't work properly that day. Ramadan days are very difficult days.

Josee from Mauritius believed that her religion counted against her:

> The Greeks don't want Catholics to work for them. They will ask you, are you a Catholic, before you work for them. Catholics are not well regarded. If you are a black Catholic it is the worst.

Physical appearance, too, mattered. Clearly this intersects with racism, but it also included factors such as weight (generally workers felt employers didn't want them to be 'fat' because they might cost too much in food) and 'prettiness'. One agency in Barcelona explained that levels of pay depended 'por aspecto' – on the way you look.

> So one señora looking for a worker, they will ask you for your CV of course, but first they look at her. It depends on what colour she is, if she is pretty, or if she is ugly, that is all important. The agencies look at her, the product, to see if such a person is suitable for the employer.
> (Magnolia, Dominicana in Barcelona)

> Sometimes when a señora wants to employ someone she says, 'Do you know someone who could work in my home? But I want someone very presentable'.
> (Carmelita, Filipina in Barcelona)

> Because they said I am very small.... Maybe they are thinking that I cannot do the job because I am too small.
> (Rita, Filipina in Paris)

'Race' and nationality, however, seemed to be the crucial factors in determining the desirability of workers. The position of national groups in the racist hierarchy varied not only from city to city, but also from household to household – one might display an 'eccentric' liking for Zaireans, for example. Household myths about different nationalities assumed an

154

almost folkloric character. A 'bad' experience with a domestic worker would be used to extrapolate the 'bad' characteristics of her nationality.

> I have a problem with women from Ethiopia: they are lazy, have no sense of duty, though they are good-hearted.... I have a lot of experience. I have ten girls from Ethiopia. They like to be well-dressed, hair, nails, for that they are good.... Then the Albanians – that was terrible. They are liars, always telling lies. And telephone maniacs because they have never had. And they have no knowledge of electrical appliances. For seven months I had that girl.... Then I had from Bulgaria. They are more civilised, more sincere, more concerned about work. But they are very unhappy. They have so many problems, they cannot forget their families who suffer. I had two girls from Bulgaria, one was here for ten months.
> (Employer in Athens)

Employers thus commonly moved from nationality to nationality until they found one that suited them. In some ways this is an extension of the naturalisation of domestic work – to find a good worker one has simply to find the right genes. This is remarkably similar to Eaton's findings in the 1890s when she interviewed 55 employers asking for their opinion on their domestic workers: 'The Germans drink and the Irish order you out of the house, but the colored people are more respectful and anxious to please' (employer quoted in Eaton 1899: 487). Moreover, as the worker is doing the work in a style (allegedly) that the employer attributes to some perceived 'racial' identity, so 'racial characteristics' become self-fulfilling prophecies: my domestic worker is smiley because Haitians are smiley, and I know Haitians are smiley because my domestic worker is a smiley Haitian. The employment of migrant domestic workers thereby both enables the perpetuation at a household level of the myth of racial characteristics and expresses and reproduces the subordination of non-Europeans to European households, or of non-whites to white households – one of Eaton's employers claimed that white workers performed better but she employed three black workers 'because they look more like servants' (Eaton 1899: 484). Skills or attitudes which have very concrete reasons are racialised: Bakan and Stasiulis (1995) have given the example of the shift from Caribbean to Filipino domestic workers in Canada and the move from the stereotype of black mammy to cunning criminal which coincides with the organised resistance of domestic workers, at the time predominantly from the Caribbean. In a similar vein the commonly expressed notion that Filipinas are 'good with children' may have more to do with the fact that American colonisation of the Philippines means that education is in English and the majority of Filipino domestic workers speak excellent English and can consequently be prevailed upon to give free English lessons.

A very specific socially constructed and inferior identity is made use of in relating to the migrant domestic worker. In Europe domestic work is women's work. It is not just that women do it, but that it expresses and reproduces gender relations between women and men. In the case of paid domestic work it often reproduces class, gender and 'race' relations. So it is not only gender and class, but 'racial' identities that are reproduced through household labour. Lebanon's estimated 150,000 migrant domestic workers are known as 'Sri-Lankaises', wherever they come from. The only exceptions are African workers who are called simply *abed*, slaves. As different meanings are assigned to different jobs, so notions of what is deemed appropriate in terms of gender and 'race' are played out, and the identities of workers and employers are confirmed. As one woman put it: 'they give every shit work to you as the black in the house'. So the employment of a non-European Union domestic worker enables the expression and reproduction of the proper role of racialised groups, and their proper relations to European households, as servers, doers of dirty work that citizens are too important to do. Racism both reinforces and gives a new aspect to social divisions and the debasement of the worker; and when the worker is charged with looking after children these identities are quite literally reproduced. Cock (1989) has commented that: 'Many white South African children are socialised into the dominant ideological order and learn the attitudes and styles of racial domination from relationships with servants' (Cock 1989: 8). A similar process can be observed in Europe, where, as in South Africa, a domestic worker may well constitute the sole interpersonal relationship for the employing family between white and black. A Filipina in Athens described this process:

> I heard children playing, they are playing house. The other child said, 'I am a Daddy', the other child said, 'I am a Mummy', and then 'She is a Filipina'. So what does the child mean, even the child knows or it's already learning, that if you are a Filipina you are a servant inside the house.

The domestic worker has had to give up her personhood, her honour, which may be manifest in abuse but also in 'friendship', in becoming 'part of the family'. As one worker remarked: 'What they [employers] have to understand is that when you employ a domestic worker, your house changes. So even if the man usually walks round naked, he cannot do that any more' (Speaker at RESPECT conference, Paris, 7–9 May 1999). Yet employers do not acknowledge that their 'personal space' has changed, that it has become another's workplace. It is the worker who must change (into a family member, an invisible servicer) a re-make facilitated by this denial of personhood. Racism both facilitates and is bolstered by this effacement. A black person in a subordinate relationship to a white person may conduct themselves in ways, and in particular may be in spaces, normally reserved for whites. The worker is allowed into privileged places (employers' homes) which she never would be granted access to as an equal. Domestic service ensures that people are assigned their right place, which is granted priority over the physical space that they thereby occupy. A former slave commented on this phenomenon in the USA:

> but as soon as I did not present myself as a menial, and the relationship of master and servant was abolished by my not having the white children with me, I would be forthwith assigned to the 'nigger' seats... [A] Negro coachman or carriage driver huddled up beside some aristocratic Southern white woman, and nothing is said about it, nothing is done about it, nobody resents the familiar contact. But let that same colored man take off his brass buttons and his high hat, and put on the plain livery of an average American citizen, and drive one black down any thoroughfare in any town in the South with that same white woman, as her equal or companion or friend, and he'd be shot on the spot! (Aptheker 1951: 50–1)

On a larger scale, Romero remarks that in El Paso on the US Mexican border Monday was referred to as the border patrol's day off, because of the institutional ignoring of the large numbers of undocumented Mexican women crossing the border to return to their employers' homes having had the weekend off. Such practices allow large numbers of undocumented migrants to enter both the USA and the European Union.

'Slavery' works at several different levels to describe the situation of contemporary migrant domestic workers. First it may describe extremely abusive and exploitative living and working conditions endured by some but not all workers. It also encapsulates the personal dependence of the worker on the employer, the fact that many workers are not free to leave their employers experienced in a multiplicity of ways from actual imprisonment to having a dependent immigration status. The power of the employer over all aspects of the worker's life, and in particular the attempted commodification of her personhood as discussed in the previous chapter, are also elements of slavery. I have already mentioned 'race' as implied in media reports of the 'slave trade', and there is another implication which offers some way forward: the situation of the 'slave' is unacceptable. 'Slavery' in this sense is being used as a term of opprobrium. 'We' cannot tolerate slavery, it is not 'civilised'. Like 'genocide' it can never be condoned. One of the common themes of media pieces that use the 'slave' theme (and not only of domestic workers but commonly of prostitutes, for example) is exposing that this enslavement is taking place now, in Europe/USA in the twentieth century, at a time and in a place where it is unacceptable. It is the successful struggle against the Atlantic slave trade that is being called upon in the use of the term 'slavery' as designating an unacceptable form of labour.

Notes

1 Communities, Vol. 3, No. 3-4; *Washington Post* 5 January 1999.
2 See A. Robertson, 'Domestic Work – A Modern Form of Slavery?', paper presented to the International Seminar on Domestic Workers, organised by World Solidarity and An Hermans, Leuven, Belgium 14 April 1997.
3 B. Anderson, 1997(a).
4 *Nowhere to Turn to: a Case Study on Indonesian Migrant Workers in Hong Kong*. Hong Kong: Asian Migrant Centre (AMC) 1994.
5 Glenn 1992.

9

'Just Like One of the Family'
Status and Contract

Domestic workers' organisations and their supporters have called for the recognition of rights of domestic workers as *workers* in their campaigns. In her MA dissertation on migrant domestic workers, the then Kalayaan worker Margaret Healy wrote:

> For me one of the most startling aspects is the complete non-comprehension by the employer that these women are workers first and foremost needing to earn a living wage. The fact that they live in on the job should not detract from that reality. Many of the employers in this survey are business people and professionals themselves who wouldn't dream of treating their business staff in the same way.
>
> (Healy 1994: 32)

This is the position I have adopted myself – using 'domestic *workers*' rather than traditional terms such as 'servants' or 'maids'. While I have chosen the term deliberately, I accept, however, that it is not unproblematic. There are difficulties, both practical and philosophical, in applying the notion of the employment contract to domestic workers in private households. In its negotiations with the British Home Office, despite its emphasis on its members being workers, Kalayaan, with support from domestic workers, lobbied for migrant domestic workers to be admitted to the UK on the basis of their 'special relationship' with the employer. This points to a deep contradiction embedded in the application of employment relations to domestic work.

To begin to understand this contradiction one must first examine the origins of the notion of contract itself, and the implications of this for women, for workers and for women workers.

159

Gender and contract

Social contract theories originate in stories told to explain the formation of civil society and why citizens submit voluntarily to the state. The basic story tells of how inhabitants of the state of nature, each motivated purely by self-interest, agree to a social contract whereby civil society is created and the behaviour of each is regulated for the benefit of all.

> If man in the state of nature be so free as has been said; if he be absolute lord of his own person and possessions, equal to the greatest, and subject to nobody, why will he part with his freedom ... to which 'tis obvious to answer that, though in the state of nature he hath such a right, yet the enjoyment of it is very uncertain, and constantly exposed to the invasion of others.... This makes him willing to quit this condition which, however free, is full of fears and continual dangers. And 'tis not without reason that he seeks out, and is willing to join in society with others who are already united ... for the mutual preservation of their lives, liberties, and estates, which I call by the general name property.
> (Locke 1993: 324)

While there are many versions of the story – Hobbes, Kant, Rousseau – patriarchal subordination is central to all of them (Pateman 1988). For consistency and because I have referred previously to his concept of 'property in the person' I shall refer to Locke.

Between Locke's state of nature and civil society lies a 'mistake: monarchies' (Locke 1993: 314). Monarchies arose as an extension of paternal authority, this being the form of government to which all men were accustomed. But men do not accept such 'natural' subjugation:

> For there are no examples so frequent in history, both sacred and profane, as those of men withdrawing themselves, and their obedience, from the jurisdiction they were born under, and the family or community they were bred up in, and setting up new governments in other places.... All which are so many testimonies against paternal sovereignty, and plainly prove that it was not the natural right of the father, descending to his heirs, that made governments in the beginning.
> (Locke 1993: 320)

Patriarchy (or relations regulated by birth and status, as under monarchies) is thus incompatible with civil society, where relations are regulated by (voluntary) contract. Social contract theorists, then, are charting the movement away from the relations of status in which identities are given to individuals through their position within a community and in which social identity and individuality are the same:

Everybody is somebody's kin, somebody's slave, somebody's client, and these relations establish individuals' very being. Such sociality is internal to personal identity, and subjectivity is experienced as immediately social. Personal dependence is the groundwork of society and individual identity. (Sayer 1991: 57)

What is emerging is the juridical subject, the property owner, the individual who contracts.

But where do women figure in this? For Locke 'conjugal society' predates civil society and may be present in the state of nature:

But the husband and wife, though they have but one common concern, yet having different understandings, will unavoidably sometimes have different wills too; it therefore being necessary that the last determination, i.e. the rule, should be placed somewhere, it naturally falls to the man's share, as the abler and the stronger.
(Locke 1993: 302)

For Locke, then, women are constructed as 'natural subjects', unlike men, who will not accept such subjugation. The gendered nature of the social contract, being 'natural', therefore remained largely unexplored until Carole Pateman's seminal work *The Sexual Contract* (1988). Pateman examined the notion of social relations as regulated by contract, and critiqued social contract theorists' ignoring of the 'sexual contract'. She builds on and significantly develops the work of social contract theorists, providing a feminist reinterpretation of modern political theory. In her version of the story:

The sons overturn paternal rule not merely to gain their liberty but to secure women for themselves. Their success in this endeavour is chronicled in the story of the sexual contract. The original pact is a sexual as well as a social contract: it is sexual in the sense of patriarchal – that is, the contract establishes men's political right over women – and also sexual in the sense of establishing orderly access by men to women's bodies.
(Pateman 1988: 2)

She argues that the relations of domination and subordination between men and women are assumed by the social contract. According to her story, the original contract was a social–*sexual* contract, and the women were the *subjects* of the contract, not the parties to the contract. So while the original story describes the emergence of the public sphere of civil society, indeed it constructs civil society, it cannot account for the relations of the private sphere. Neither does it allow for the dependence of the public on the private. Its character as a story about domination (by men) and subordination (of women) is forgotten, and instead it is a story only about male freedom:

The social contract is a story of freedom; the sexual contract is a story of subjection. The original contract constitutes both freedom and domination. Men's freedom and women's subjection are created through the original contract – and the character of civil freedom cannot be understood without the missing half of the story that reveals how men's patriarchal right over women is established through contract.
(Pateman 1988: 2)

Patriarchal relations do not just dominate in the private. At the time of Locke women were not juridical subjects, wives belonged to their husbands under the common law doctrine of coverture. The 'individual' who enters into contracts, who is freed from relations of status, who owns the property in his person, who roams the public, is not gender neutral, he is a man. The 'worker' who enters into employment contracts is also a man:

> the construction of the 'worker' presupposes that he is a man who has a woman, a (house)wife, to take care of his daily needs. The private and public spheres of civil society are separate, reflecting the natural order of sexual difference, and inseparable, incapable of being understood in isolation from each other. The sturdy figure of the 'worker', the artisan, in clean overalls, with a bag of tools and lunch-box, is always accompanied by the ghostly figure of his wife.
> (Pateman 1988: 131)

But although Pateman argues that a woman cannot become a worker in the way that a man can because the construction of 'worker' presupposes that he is a man who has a woman to take care of his daily needs, to do his reproductive work, women *may* become workers in the same sense as men – but it is the ghostly, often racialised figure of the domestic worker/nanny/carer that accompanies them.

Domestic workers and the sexual-social contract

If both the public and private spheres depend on an original sexual division of labour in which women are subordinate to men, as Pateman stipulates, what happens when paid domestic labour is introduced into this equation? In social/sexual contract theory terms, given that the private sphere is ultimately governed by the sexual contract, it is women/wives who have responsibility for domestic labour. This explains why, when a household employs a domestic worker, she is managed by the woman of the household. But what governs relations between domestic workers and their (predominantly female) employers – the sexual contract, with its relations of status, or the social (i.e. employment) contract?

162

Wives and servants

It is occasionally noted that contract is not a device for 'servants' (see Baier 1986 cited in Pateman 1988: 62) but this is rarely problematised. Wives were commonly classed together with 'servants' in the seventeenth century: both came under the authority of the male householder, together with the household's children (Kussmaul 1981). Pateman takes the point of view of the wives and early feminists such as Mary Astell, Lady Chudleigh and Mary Wollstonecraft that a wife was 'the chief menial of the household' and contemporarily the 'sole servant of the household' (although the number of employers of domestic workers suggests that this is not really so). Both wives and servants are subordinate to the man. But though both subordinate to the man, they are not themselves *equal*. While wives considered they were treated as servants –

> 'Wife and servant are the same,
> But only differ in the name.'
> (Lady Chudleigh 1703 cited in Pateman 1988: 125)

– servants were not treated as wives. The wife/servant comparison was more apparent to the wives than to the servants. Domestic workers today are not struck by Pateman's comparison: 'You don't feel you have anything in common, not too much, because you work for them. I feel a little different to them because maybe if I have what she has, she's not going to stand on my back saying "do this" or "do that"' (Anderson 1996: 3). While Pateman cites American suffragists such as E.C. Stanton who compare the situation of women to slaves (Pateman 1988: 121; 124; 154), bell hooks (1981) criticises those same suffragists for expressing

> outrage that inferior 'niggers' should be granted the vote while 'superior' white women remained disenfranchised ... .White suffragists felt that white men were insulting white womanhood by refusing to grant them privileges that were to be given black men. They admonished white men not for their sexism but for their willingness to allow sexism to overshadow racial alliances. Stanton, along with other white women's rights supporters, did not want to see blacks enslaved, but neither did she wish to see the status of black people improved while the status of white women remained the same.
> (hooks 1981: 127)

Similarly, wives' equation of wives with servants does not necessarily have as a corollary wives' demands for the rights of servants.

What are the similarities and differences between wives and servants? According to Pateman, the wife does the same tasks as a household servant and works the long hours of a servant in exchange, not for a wage, but for the protection of her master:

what being a woman (wife) means is to provide certain services for and at the command of a man (husband). In short, the marriage contract and the wife's subordination as a (kind of) labourer cannot be understood in the absence of the sexual contract and the patriarchal construction of 'men', and 'women', and the 'private' and 'public' spheres.

(Pateman 1988: 128)

This elision, between being a wife and labouring in the home, is not justified, however: some wives only manage, most wives both manage and labour. The 'wife' may (crucially, of course, husband permitting) not bother to do the ironing, nor ever clean the windows, while domestic workers/servants only labour (although they may manage their time). Pateman holds that contracts like the marriage contract, which are about property in the person (rather than labour power), take the form of obedience for protection. So the wife puts her personhood at the disposal of her husband in return for his protection. But this is not simply a question for wives, for, as has been seen, the domestic worker 'contract', too, is about property in the person (see Chapters 7 and 8). Employers of live-in domestic workers will often attempt to strike the bargain of obedience for protection: 'for example, talking of people who live-in sometimes people offer a room for the worker to look after an old woman, and in exchange they won't pay anything' (Caritas volunteer, Barcelona). According to Davidoff (1983) at the turn of the century in the UK the payment of a domestic worker had to be stipulated in the contract, if not it was assumed that the worker was working for nothing. Palmer (1989) also found that full-time work was demanded in return for housing. When I worked live-in for a year in London I was not paid a wage for my six hours a day, five days a week plus babysitting, but this was 'in exchange' for my accommodation and bills. My 'socialist' employer explained that this was not exploitative because there was no money involved! In June 1998 it was revealed that the UK Low Pay Commission was seriously considering allowing the 'cost' of providing live-in accommodation as part of a worker's wage. (This could mean a handsome profit for employers living in expensive parts of London who could reasonably demand that workers pay the difference between their wages and the cost of renting their room!) Obedience for protection is a 'family' relation and underlies the worker becoming 'part of the family' (see Chapter 7).

Despite these similarities (in tasks performed; in subordination to the man of the house, in exchanging personhood) wives and domestic workers are differently constructed. Pateman states:

Housewives see freedom from control as their great advantage; they stress that they can decide what to do and how and when to do it, and many housewives have strong, internalized standards of what constitutes a good

job of work.... Discussions of housework often overlook the expectations and requirements of the husband. The demands of his work largely determine how the housewife organises her time.
(Pateman 1988: 130)

But this analysis fails to appreciate that housewives are right. 'Freedom from control' is management. Wives manage households. While women are oppressed and confined within the private sphere, they may also be affirmed and can express themselves and their affective relations within the private sphere. As Bubeck (1995) explains, some women can be empowered through caring, for example, and it does offer the opportunity of some non-alienated work. This is to be contrasted with the situation of migrant domestic workers who do not manage households, and are not empowered by caring. As men's identity is reinforced and confirmed by the public sphere, so women's can be by the private. 'Wives' can have an interest in not relinquishing control of the private sphere, particularly when they are not fully accepted by the public, or have a sense that the alienated labour of the public sphere is ungratifying. The decision to 'go out' to work after having a baby is not an easy one for many women, because of the pleasures and responsibilities of the private sphere. 'Wives' may therefore hold on tightly to the private sphere, through internalised standards, expertise and professionalisation, as tightly as men will to the public sphere. The identity of servants, in contrast, is constructed as degraded. Some migrant workers continue to be able to affirm themselves through maintaining a sense of the dignity of their work. Gisela from the Dominican Republic, for example, who worked in Barcelona, felt domestic work was: 'Good work, honourable, you can hold your head up high, because it is a worthwhile job.' Notably she described her employers as 'humanitarian': 'They treat me very well, as if I were a worker.' But, more usually, workers felt that they were treated as less than human:

> No reasonable hours, no employers and their children treat us with respect. No, none of them. No domestic workers we know are treated with respect by the employers. None of them. Nobody cares. If you work, work, and that's it. You don't get respect. No respect you: they pay you, so you work.
> (*Clapping*)
> (Regina, Ghanaian, Athens)

It is not simply that domestic workers are subordinate to wives, but that their role as 'domestic worker' to 'wife' is to act as a foil, to enhance status, to give honour through dishonour. As has been discussed previously, domestic workers are reproducing a status hierarchy which is profoundly antagonistic to their own interests. This is less clear in the case of the housewife/wife, whose status is bound up with her husband

and with the management of her own household. The housewife, unlike the migrant domestic worker, is not 'natally alienated'. She is bound up in a network of responsibilities and rights around the household (as a description of kin relations), while for a worker all responsibilities are discharged through cash. There may be 'economic and social advantages' to marriage, as Pateman acknowledges, but there is only an economic advantage to domestic employment, and sometimes not even that.

The relations between female employer and worker are not simply governed by the employment contract but by relations of status, and the confusion between the two benefits the employer. The possibility of slippage from affective to instrumental relations – that is, from sexual to social contract – increases the employer's control over her worker. The fact that she (the employer) is a woman facilitates this slippage. The domestic worker/employer relation is not a 'real' employment contract because it is between women about women's work in the home: 'I ask my señora, "There is no year in the contract. I can leave any time I want." And then my employer told me, "Adel, I think the contract is only paper. The most important thing is the one between us"' (Adel, Filipina in Barcelona). It is thus true that an employment contract cannot capture female relations, to the extent that domestic work is about status and status reproduction and hierarchies between women. And there is a third element to the sexual-social contract that Pateman touches on only briefly:

> The men who [are said to] make the original contract are white men, and their fraternal pact has three aspects; the social contract, the sexual contract and the slave contract that legitimizes the rule of white over black. (Pateman 1988: 221)

The notion of a 'slave contract' at first sight seems a contradiction in terms. Contract is about freedom, about individual subjecthood, so surely slavery, when a person becomes a thing, is its antithesis? But, although Pateman does not discuss this, I suspect that in her analysis 'slaves' are the subjects of the slave contract, as women are the subjects of the sexual contract – neither women nor 'slaves' are contractors. Like the sexual contract, the slave contract is assumed by the social contract – Locke himself was secretary to the 'proprietors of Carolina' and in this capacity drew up the *Fundamental Constitutions of Carolina* – an outline of his political ideas, in effect, in which he was given free rein to draw up any constitution on which the proprietors could agree and for which they would obtain royal consent. Article 110: 'Every freeman of Carolina shall have absolute power and authority over his negro slaves, of what opinion or religion soever.' (Locke 1993: 230). None of these aspects of the original contract are discrete – and negotiation is always possible. But Pateman does not explore this third element. Rather, her discussions of the 'slave contract' are concerned with the contract of 'civil slavery'. This does not refer to the original slave contract, but is used to shed light on the employment contract.

The employment contract

The work of organisations such as Kalayaan is in part an attempt to assert the relations of the employment contract over the relations of status that regulate domestic workers and their employers. For the relations of the employment contract to hold, the domestic worker must be constructed as selling her labour power rather than her personhood – but this is extremely difficult within the private domain as it is currently imagined. This manifests itself in all kinds of practical difficulties in applying employment contracts to the private sphere and in the ideological problems around constructing reproductive work as work at all. More concretely, tasks, hours and value – all very basic conditions of the employment contract, delineating limits to employers' power – are all very difficult to set with reference to domestic work. I have already discussed the difficulties around a task-based definition of domestic work. When domestic workers were shown the International Labour Organisation definition of domestic work they were unequivocal in saying that this was not an adequate definition of their work, that they did 'everything'.

There are also particular problems around the notion of 'hours of work' as applied to the household. As Nina, an employer in Athens, said: 'in a house there are no hours'. This is partly because so much of the skill around domestic work is concerned with time management, with doing the work associated with several different processes at once, so there is no simple clear relationship between hours and tasks. In France, where they have made some attempts to regulate domestic work in private households, working conditions are (allegedly) determined not by the French *code du travail* but by the Convention Collective Nationale de Travail du Personnel Employé de Maison. This Convention Collective enshrines the notion of *présence responsable*, defined as: *les heures de présence responsable sont les heures de garde à caractère familial auprès d'une personne physique sans travail effectif* (Article 6). An example is the situation – often referred to by workers as being 'on call' – when a child is asleep and not requiring any attention, but nevertheless requiring an adult's presence given the possibility of the child's waking up at any time. The Convention distinguishes between this time and the time of *travail effectif*, and sets payment

167

at two thirds of the minimum wage. *Présence responsable* is not a peculiarly French invention, but an attempt to deal with a very real problem in applying the employment contract to domestic work. In Spain this kind of time was described as *tiempo de presencia*, and the employer is entitled to require the worker's presence in the house (but not to 'work') for a certain number of hours a day unpaid. This fails to recognise that women working in the house very rarely have time off other than when they themselves are asleep. Time is a precious resource and there is always a job that could be done as a response to one's own or imposed standards. So *présence responsable* time is often used as an opportunity to finish household chores. The diaries kept by domestic workers provided many examples of this. Sally is an undocumented Filipina working in Paris:

> Monday 15 January 1996
> *9.00–11.10 a.m.*: I prepared the orange juice of the little boy, change his clothes and diaper, clean his room and put him on the bed to sleep. I started to clean the kitchen then the rooms, toilet, salon and the bathrooms.
> *11.10–12.00 a.m.*: while the baby is still sleeping I wash the windows and put all the clean clothes from the suitcases to their cabinet.

Now theoretically, of course, and assuming Sally fell under the Convention – which in reality, of course, she does not because she is undocumented – she could deem this *présence responsable* time, and put her feet up and read the paper while the little boy was sleeping, saving the cleaning until he was awake. But anybody with experience of tidying up with a young child knows this is a sisyphean task and she would thereby only be creating work for herself. Or she could omit to tell her employer about the boy's sleep and count it as *travail effectif*, for enforcement of contracts poses particular difficulties in the private sphere, as will be discussed below. But the employment contract is instructing her to do the former, which is simply not realistic. It is evident from many interviews with domestic workers that *présence responsable* is not time for oneself, nor is it rest time, it is even not rest time at night for those caring for small children or the mentally confused, because one can always be interrupted by something that must take priority. Indeed it is precisely the element of *présence responsable* that accounts for much of the bind of domestic work, one's freedom and time completely subsumed to another's. Unable to use the time as one would 'free time' because of the priority of the other person's needs, it is only to be expected that, unless it is the middle of the night, *présence responsable* is spent doing interruptible household tasks. *Présence responsable* exemplifies the difficulties in applying the employment contract to the private sphere. These difficulties have an important impact on the relations between domestic worker and female employer.

Professionalisation

Professionalisation may be seen as the way forward, clearing the muddied waters of maternalism by stating that the domestic worker is a professional, thereby improving her status *vis-à-vis* her employer and allowing for the application of an employment contract. This seems to benefit everybody, but leaves the sexual contract undisturbed: men continue to benefit from female domestic labour, it gives domestic workers status and limits the employers' powers of command, while allowing employers to expect the scientific standards of the public sphere applied rigorously to the private. This 'solution' is advocated by the French employers' federation, FEPEM, and they portray a coincidence of interests between women, between the domestic worker and the housewife: 'Préservez vos droits en respectant les siens', as a FEPEM leaflet says. In this view professionalism benefits both parties – the employer (assumed to be female) can be sure of a trained and competent worker, while the worker is respected, and may choose to enter the profession rather than seeing it as a last resort.

Now this, of course, begs several very important questions – crucially, professionals come very expensive! And who is the professional, the wife/housewife, or the domestic worker? If the domestic worker must be trained for her employment, how can domestic work continue to be a natural ability of women in general? In substituting a trained professional for herself, is a wife/housewife getting in someone who is better at 'her' job? It is not as straightforward as it would appear, then, to professionalise domestic work and maintain the current gender and class ideology.

The implications of professionalisation become clear in the Convention Collective, which divides domestic work into specialisms and hierarchies, though notably leaving the specifics of the job description to individual employers. From 1 October 1995 (previously a slightly different classificatory system had operated) the worker was distinguished from the *débutant* through different levels to level five. In 1998, the minimum salary for the *débutant* was F40.22 an hour, and for level five, F44.82 an hour. The classification represents a basic two-tier system, with levels *débutant* and one being unqualified workers *sous responsabilité de l'employeur* and levels two to five qualified employees with *employeur présent ou non*. Caring responsibilities are taken on only by level two upwards. At this stage workers are said to occupy *postes d'emploi a caractère familial* when, as well as working, they provide a *présence responsable*. The specific responsibilities of workers become clearer as one progresses up the scale – while a *débutante* has no specific jobs, level two can help children with homework, while level three includes sewing, ironing (qualified) and private

169

secretary. Difficulties in applying public sphere categories to the private sphere realities are immediately apparent – or, rather, the private sphere reveals the inherent shortcomings of the industrial mode of production characterised by the division of labour into precisely specifiable and timetable-driven tasks. While workers at the bottom may well be multi-skilled, that militates against their being considered specialised professionals. The Convention Collective also enshrines the contradiction that one's work becomes more specialised and defined as one's status and salary increases – chauffeurs and chefs, for example, are level five. The classification may be appropriate for reflecting distinctions between *cuisinier qualifié* (level three) and *chef cuisinier* (level five), but all unqualified workers are grouped at the bottom of the scale. The difficulty with a hierarchy based on specialisation is that workers who are concerned exclusively with looking after children are paid more than those who have to care for children and do the housework. It could be argued, then, that in encouraging the recognition of professionalism the Convention in fact validates a two-tier system which does not recognise the skills and experience of a large group of workers which includes the vast majority of foreign domestic workers.

The vast majority of domestic workers have no formal qualification in domestic work. Such qualifications, when they are available, only apply to certain aspects of domestic work, usually those with a caring function. In general, domestic work is constructed as unskilled – one cannot, to my knowledge, be qualified in dusting, though one can be experienced in it. Although migrant domestic workers may be technically *sous responsabilité de l'employeur*, the employer, more often than not, is not actually present while they are working. It is those who are at the bottom of the hierarchy who have to do everything, and who in reality often have the greatest responsibility, for very rarely are they supervised by their employer. Professionalised domestic workers are extremely expensive: not only are their wages higher than non-professionalised, but they are also likely to be declared, meaning the employer must pay tax and national insurance, and give them certain employment rights such as sick pay. Professional workers are less flexible: so, for example, a person who employs a professionalised carer will not get the cleaning thrown in, and may well 'have' to employ a cleaner in addition. An unprofessionalised carer, on the other hand, will combine care and the household chores, which are in reality a daily part of care. Professionalised domestic workers may be financially out of reach for many middle-class families, particularly those needing a full-time carer for children or the elderly. Yet this is precisely the sector that is growing. So, while citizens may take advantage of training and professionalisation to enable them to take up better paying and higher status jobs, migrants continue to fill the main area of need. The professionalising of domestic work can end up as its 'whitening' –

> we do all kinds of household chores ... unlike the European like the British that come here. If they hire a babysitter they just do the babysitting and not even wash their plate that they are eating. They don't even know how to wash their spoons.
> (Sandy, Filipina in Athens)

Workers' contracts

Despite the difficulties of applying the relations of the employment contract to domestic work, and the slippage between affective and instrumental relations, most workers did have individual contracts with their employers, even when they were undocumented. Given the difficulties that workers had in extracting official documentation from their employers if the latter did not want to register them, I would hypothesise that these contracts were at the instigation of the employer. But what is the point of having a contract that is in many cases invalid in law (such as when the worker is undocumented)? The majority of workers said that their contracts were not kept, and that what was important in determining living and working conditions was whether or not one had a 'good' employer, not the existence of a contract. Notably a 'good' employer was characterised as someone who left you alone, suggesting a certain freedom from both supervision and intrusive affective relations! For the employer an employment contract maintains the fiction of consent, while also providing a psychological, if not in the final instance a legal means of enforcing requirements beneficial to the employer, such as a minimal period of notice for example.

Some workers did not think much of contracts:

> *Alem:* I think sometime most of the people that sign contracts, the employer have you on paper. This is a big mistake.

> *Regina:* Once we sign contracts in Africa it's like you sign to be a slave.
> (Pan-African Association members, Athens)

Three aspects of the contractual relation account for this negative assessment.

Coercion

Pateman's description (citing Buchanan) of the civil slave contract has uncomfortable resonances with the situation of migrant domestic workers in Europe:

The strong – in their own interests – will conquer, forcibly disarm and seize the goods of the weak, and then make a contract in which the conquered agree henceforth to work in return for their subsistence or protection. The strong can present the contract as being to the advantage of both: the strong no longer have to labour and the weak now can be assured that their basic needs will be provided for.
(Pateman 1988: 61)

People are forced to migrate for reasons of poverty and violence that arguably often stem from the interests of the global strong, including the states of the European Union. Some of the benefits of such plunder are reaped, albeit often unintentionally, by the middle class of those states, who are also counted among the employers of migrant domestic labour. These employers may offer employment in the household as a kindness, labour for protection, being part of the family. Statements such as Nina's encapsulate such a contract: 'when there was a war in Ethiopia I pitied them'. There are different degrees of coercion, some of which one might not want to count as coercion at all. So a woman who is debt bonded to her employer, living in with an immigration status dependent on her employer, is in a very different position to a woman working live-out with settlement rights in the host state. A worker who is emotionally manipulated into remaining with her employer ('How can you leave me, have you no conscience?') is in a very different position to the worker who is threatened with death should she leave.

On the face of it, if someone has been coerced into a contract, it is not really a contract – though clearly many people, not just domestic workers, could be said to be forced into 'employment contracts' through poverty. But the flip side of coercion is the freedom to retract from a contract. It is the freedom to retract that is legally denied to so many migrant domestic workers through immigration legislation and regulation.

Specification

The employment contract specifies time and tasks to be done. It is this that limits the employer's power to command. The looser the contract, the easier it is for the powerful party to exploit the worker. The difficulties around specification of domestic work are significant; hence the contract is in practice always being negotiated to the detriment of the worker:

OK Greeks take an advantage sometimes. You feel that they are giving you a little respect or sometimes you feel happy to help them. They tell you to feel at home. She ask you once to help ironing. I happy to make one change. The next day they will add trousers. The next day add another one. Another time, a full bowl. They taking advantage, if you give them a little chance they will use you as a donkey.
(Vivian, Nigerian in Athens)

Enforcement

Given the weakness of the position of workers, while 'good' employers may keep to the contract, 'bad' employers may ignore it with no effect on themselves. In the UK some domestic workers, supported by Kalayaan and other groups, have taken employers to court over physical abuse and non-payment of wages. Some, but not all, of these cases have been successful. The first step has always been to win the worker's right to stay, even though they have left their employer, while their case against their employer is being heard. While this has been won in some cases – with legal support and campaign mobilisation – victory is extremely unusual. The fact that, even when the case against the employer has been heard and won, the worker can be and is deported because she has left her employer, means that women are extremely reluctant now to demand through the courts that most basic of employment rights, to be paid the agreed wage. If this is the position of well-organised women who have political support, then clearly that of the majority of domestic workers is likely to be far weaker.

Yet what is being recognised by the attempted imposition of these public sphere concepts is that the boundaries between the private and the public are not real; they shift; they are negotiable. The boundaries are culturally specific (Yuval-Davis 1991) but even within a dominant culture, where boundaries are drawn by the state, they depend on gender, class, 'race', sexuality, age and other variables. For example, consider the ban on gays serving in the army, or the scrutiny directed at the private life of the poor in determining access to benefits (Lister 1990). The most intimate details of a person's life may be publicly explored in an immigration appeals tribunal – I have heard Home Office lawyers inquiring in such circumstances, for example, at what age a woman 'lost her virginity', who to and under what circumstances (of course the woman asking the same questions to the Home Office lawyer is a total impossibility). Domestic workers are caught within these shifting boundaries. This is a particular problem for live-in workers because they have no escape; the boundaries are constantly indeterminate. While the precise relations governing live-out domestic workers and their employers are still unclear, at least there is an enforceable distinction between work *time* and private *time*.

Domestic workers in private households exemplify the problematic nature of employment contracts in general, and the importance of gendering contract. They also indicate that contracts are racialised. So, while Pateman demonstrates the workings of the sexual contract, she does not sufficiently allow for its complexities, negotiations and trade-offs,

173

which are given an added dimension once one allows for the 'slave contract'. Contracts are constantly up for renegotiation; new bargains may be made, new alliances formed; the relations between them are complicated. It is not simply that the sexual contract has an 'opt out clause' on the labour of domestic work (although not on its management), but that it enables some women, as women, to command other/ Other women. Pateman touches on this:

> His [the employer's] task is much easier if the wage includes protection that binds the subordinate more closely to the contract. Extra-monetary benefits, or, in the case of the marriage contract, 'generous' housekeeping money or 'help' around the house are obvious examples.
> (Pateman 1988: 148)

This suggests that women, or at least some women, are subjected to obligations that extend beyond the original contract. To facilitate the reproduction of the sexual-social contract at a time of 'equality' between certain groups of women and men, the slave contract is renegotiated.

10

'Your Passport Is Your Life'

Domestic Workers and the State

The fact that domestic work in private households is often being under-taken by third country nationals is not only evidence of the racialisation of reproductive work, but presents a serious challenge to notions of citizenship. Much of the reproductive labour of Europe is now being done by non-citizens: 'racialisation', therefore, is not simply an indicator of employer preference, but places this segment of workers in a certain relation to the state. Debates on citizenship have focused on differential access to the rights of citizenship (of the poor, disabled, and women in particular); but have rather taken for granted the right to citizenship in the formalised sense of what passport a person holds and an individual's right to be present and work in a particular nation state. This meaning of citizenship may be more narrowly defined as the formal ascription of membership through nationality laws. This formalised sense of citizenship demonstrates that citizenship is inextricably linked to particular nation states which have different grounds for entitlement to membership. In particular, some nation states grant citizenship by descent, *ius sanguinis* (the 'law of blood'), others by place of birth, *ius soli* (the 'law of land'). It also demonstrates that citizenship is exclusive. In this chapter I want to refer to the position of domestic workers in relation to this formal sense of citizenship. This is only half the story, in that it focuses on migrant domestic workers as providers of the necessary labour of care, but it helps to throw light on the broader debates around citizenship and to show how the relationship of domestic workers to the state encourages and reinforces the racialisation of domestic work.

Domestic workers and immigration status

It is important to distinguish immigration status from nationality. While nationality defines the country of which people are citizens, and how individuals can become citizens, immigration is the system of laws, regulations and practices by which a state sets out who can live within its territory and under what conditions. A person's immigration status refers to how they are positioned within that system, and in particular whether they are 'regular', with a legal right to be present (though not necessarily to work) in the country; or 'undocumented', in which case their presence in the country constitutes a criminal act. Although distinct, immigration and nationality are related since in some states migrant workers can take out citizenship after a period of residence and become 'naturalised'.

Speaking very broadly, people who end up as domestic workers in Europe may enter legally as tourists or students (who then go on to work, thereby becoming liable to deportation) or as workers in Spain and Italy, where it is possible to get a permit as a domestic worker. Workers who enter on a permit may overstay the fixed period of time allotted them, in which case they become undocumented. People may also enter illegally by evading immigration controls. It is also possible for some people to enter as the spouse of a migrant (usually a 'wife'). In this case they are usually prohibited from working and from having recourse to public funds. Those who have entered legally may in some states have the right, after a certain period, to naturalisation and formal citizenship. This right does not apply to all states, however, and the law may be so formulated as to make the right impossible to exercise.

As is clear from Chapters 5 and 6 the immigration status of migrant domestic workers varies from state to state. There are two aspects of domestic workers' immigration status that are common, however. First, that those who have legal status are often dependent for that status on their employer; and second, that a large proportion of domestic workers are undocumented.

Dependence

Where it is possible to get a permit for domestic work – for example, in the USA, Spain and Italy – workers are often legally bound to their employers. It is the employers who must apply for the permit, proving that they have the income to pay for and can accommodate their workers. It is also the employer who renews the permit – should there be a problem in the fraught domestic worker–employer relationship, the employer can simply refuse to renew the permit, and the worker must leave the country. A change of employer or of type of employment is not permissible. This dependence on employers to renew work permits has been true historically – in Greece, for example, under the nursing aide system of the 1970s and 1980s, and in the UK when work permits were available to resident domestic workers in the 1970s. Dependence is not restricted to domestic workers. Currently in the UK work permits are available, mainly for employees in high-level posts, and these too are granted to employers not to workers. If a person changes jobs, even within the same company, the employer must apply for a new work permit. This work permit system is allegedly a means of tying workers to the national economy, but it also ties workers to their employers. Annual renewal effectively gives the employer the sanction of the annual possibility of deportation should they be dissatisfied with their employee. Although work permits ostensibly impose the same restrictions on all employees, whether board members or domestic workers, they have different implications for executives in multinational companies than for those who have indebted themselves in order to migrate. Being formally dependent on their employers has particular implications for domestic workers. It is in the nature of the type of employment that they are cast in a status relation to their employer. Live-in domestic workers are dependent on their employers for accommodation and food. I have argued elsewhere that domestic work is not only a job but a role. The domestic worker, unlike the executive, cannot return home after a difficult day with her employer, but must continually negotiate her relationship with her. This is legally sanctioned through her permit: she cannot change jobs; she, quite literally, *is* a domestic worker; those are the grounds on which her presence is tolerated. But she is also a domestic worker attached to a particular named person, a person whose status she is expressing and reproducing in part by herself being of 'lower status'. A migrant domestic worker's legal dependence on her employer for her presence in a particular European state gives the employer direct control over every aspect of the migrant's life. The worker's physical presence in Europe is a personal favour which may be withdrawn at the employer's whim by non-renewal of the work permit. Unlike deportation by the state, the worker has no possibility of appeal against this deportation by default, but must return to her country of origin. The presence of domestic workers is tolerated by the state for as long as it is wanted by the employers. The immigration status of migrant domestic workers therefore reinforces the status relations that oppress and exploit them within their employment, legally sanctioning such relations and weakening the workers' position still further.

The difficulties this can cause have been well documented in the UK, where workers' dependence on their employers was institutionalised in the Concession. This leads to situations such as that of Mahesh Kumari Rai, who left her home in a Nepalese mountain village at the age of thirteen to avoid an arranged marriage. After work as a carpet weaver in Kathmandu she made her way to Delhi where she found domestic work. She accompanied the family to London, promised an easy life with good pay and a chance of education. The reality was very different: long hours, imprisonment, no pay at all, no education and constant physical and psychological abuse. Two years later she escaped, and with the help of a law centre she took her former employer to court for compensation and her unpaid wages. The matter was settled out of court. Mahesh received £1,349, the equivalent of £13 a week. For the two years Mahesh was with them her former employers had neglected to keep her visa in order; she was therefore liable for deportation. In April 1991 she was picked up by the police and detained, and in August 1992 Mahesh was finally deported to Nepal, where she had neither family nor friends and had not been for more than fifteen years. Mahesh was supported by a large campaign, including 25 MPs, several peers and other public figures, Cardinal Hume and organisations such as Kalayaan and Anti-Slavery International, yet this did not protect her from deportation. It is scarcely surprising, then, that most of those in her position should avoid the risk of drawing the attention of the authorities by exercising their civil rights.

'Illegality'

There are significant numbers of undocumented domestic workers in all the European Union cities I visited, both in countries where work permits are available and in those where they are not. Immigration restrictions do not stop movement, and once migrants have entered a country only a minority are deported. The difficulty with stringent and restrictive immigration laws is that since they cannot stop migration, they mean that migration is forced to come through irregular channels and that state control over patterns and directions of migrant labour is relinquished rather than increased (Collinson 1994: 14). This is clearly apparent when one contrasts Spain, where it is possible for domestic workers to enter legally, with Greece and France, where this is not so. In Spain the nationalities working in domestic work are clearly demarcated – even those working illegally – since usually they have come through networks established by migrants before them. This is not to say that there are not women of other nationalities working in the sector, but the state has had a significant impact on the nationality of groups deemed suitable to be domestic workers. This is to be contrasted with Greece and France, where the state has ignored the existence of migrant domestic workers and exercised no control over who will fill the demand for domestic labour, and consequently the nationalities doing this work are far more varied.

Unlike workers in this sector who are undeclared (who may or may not be citizens) being undocumented never serves the workers' interest. Undocumented workers are extremely vulnerable. If they are sick they cannot get health care; they must continue to work or they risk losing not just their wage but their accommodation too – even if their sickness is a direct result of their work. They are subject to constant fear and insecurity which can make it difficult to sustain personal relationships, even if the opportunity to make friends is there. If their rights are abused they have no recourse to authority, since they are likely to end up in prison. As women they face particular problems with pregnancy, often losing their job in consequence, and with no rights to state health care during their pregnancy and birth. When born their children often have no rights to health or education. Being undocumented does not mean that workers are independent of their employers; indeed it gives the employers a direct hold over the workers: if they are dissatisfied with them they may simply report and deport them, or may even do so to avoid paying their wages.

> I know some friends who work about two months in this country. Later on they say to them, go away from our job, not giving any money. Because they know we are illegal here, we are not going to police. Because immigration will deport us. I cannot go nowhere. When somebody is holding your passport, where do you go? Your passport is your life. I know places will not give you any money because they know we will not go to the police because police will deport us.
> (Daniel, Eritrean in Athens)

Some undocumented workers who have been living in Europe for a while have the confidence to use their position to threaten their employers:

> my first employer threatened me with the police. 'I will call the police and tell them you don't have a working permit', and I said, 'And I will tell them you didn't arrange my papers and you will have to spend money.' Then the employer said, 'I am only joking', and I said, 'I am only joking also, but if you tell, then I will tell also.'
> (Aida, Filipina in Athens)

But this is not easy, for in reality the worker has much more to lose than the employer. Although employing undocumented workers is a criminal offence in many European countries, including France and Greece, I came across no examples of employers incurring any problems as a result, though there were many instances of domestic workers being deported and imprisoned.

Live-in domestic work seems to offer some advantages to undocumented women. It solves problems of employment and accommodation at one go, and enables them to maximise their savings to repay loans incurred in their travels to Europe. Crucially, although living and working in the home places them directly and constantly under the authority of their employer, it also protects them against the state – so while the state is not available to protect them from abuse, neither will it remove them from the country. Being undocumented, however, means that domestic workers, already engaged in low status work, are cast as needy and victimised, requiring benevolence and charity from those kind enough to offer it. This latter point has been demonstrated in the responses to publicity around the issue of migrant domestic workers put about by Kalayaan. Margaret Healy, former worker with the organisation, has observed that one response to publicity about the plight of domestic workers was to contact the organisation offering accommodation in return for work (employment as a favour) rather than supporting demands for the right to change employers.

Naturalisation

In some European states third country nationals who have fulfilled certain criteria (usually language and a minimum number of years as a legal immigrant) may apply for citizenship of the state where they have been resident. Naturalisation is extremely difficult for migrants in general and depends on many factors – the state within which they are working, the state they come from, and the historical links between these two states. One of the easiest routes (at least in legal terms) to citizenship is through marriage – the fact that so many domestic workers in Barcelona were reported to be interested in going out with Germans in search of brides suggests that citizenship is actively desired by many. For domestic workers, two factors are usually crucial: whether or not the state recognises domestic work as legitimate employment; and their relation-ship with their employers.

My research was on migrant domestic workers, implicitly targeting those who do not have citizenship, but I think a measure of the problems of access can be gauged by difficulties experienced in regularisation procedures:

> I tried to deliver my papers to the Ministry of Work, but they would always say, this piece of information's missing or that bit of information.... Then one night she (*employer*) just told me to get out of the house, that she was tired of me. And I said, 'Why Señora, I haven't said or done anything, why are you doing this to me?' 'I'm tired of you and your papers.' And we're going, of course, she doesn't want anything more to do with us.
> (Men, Filipina in Barcelona)

Interaction of immigration status and employment: the German case

For migrant domestic workers immigration status is important in determining employment. This is tautological for those holding work permits but, as mentioned above, undocumented women may actively seek live-in domestic work. Notably when domestic workers have an independent right to stay they often try to move out of live-in to live-out work. This bears out the workers' point of view, that it is not their 'race' (as the employers would have it), but their immigration status that pushes them into domestic work.

Germany now has four means of entry for labour migrants: project-linked employment (*werkvertragsarbeitnehmer*) mainly in the construction industry; guestworker contracts (*gastarbeitnehmerbeschaftigung*) designed to encourage the exchange of young skilled labour between Germany and former Eastern Europe countries (80 per cent of the workers are male); seasonal workers (*saisonarbeit*) for agriculture, forestry, construction and vineyards (again, 80 per cent are male); and commuters (*grenzganger-beschaftigung*), work permit holders who live up to fifty kilometres from the German border. Those who work under this last system are mainly male Czech workers in Bavaria (Rudolph 1996). It is striking that these legal means of working in Germany are all for areas of work dominated by men, and that the majority of migrants taking them up are male. The single exception to this is the employment of nursing staff for the sick and elderly. In 1994, however, this accounted for only 412 people, 390 from Croatia and 22 from Slovenia. So, as with the earlier *gastarbeiter* system, Germany's attempts to regulate foreign labour are principally directed at male migration. This does not mean, of course, that women do not migrate, but that women migrants are likely to be undocumented and to work in unregulated sectors such as domestic work.

The most visible paid domestic workers are the Polish, who work as cleaners. Domestic work in private households is said by migrants' organisations to be the chief employment of Polish women in Berlin. Although no visa is needed for Polish citizens for a stay of under three months, working is forbidden. So many workers, although residing legally, are working illegally. Employers in private households do not require that their worker has a working visa, however, particularly since Polish women are likely to live out and work for several employers a few hours a week. The short distance between Berlin and western Poland means that they are often pendular migrants, working in Berlin for short periods, sometimes on a weekly basis, with weekends spent back in Poland.

So workers regularly renew their three-month stay in Germany and minimise their social costs: since they can still have family and community support, they are not faced with the difficulty of learning a new language, and can return if in difficulties. Although working illegally, Polish domestic workers do have the right to be present in Germany, and this, coupled with the advantages of geography, accounts for Polish women's relatively privileged situation (although they are still confined to domestic work). They seem to escape many of the abuses and exploitation that are the lot of other migrant domestic workers. Although they cannot pursue cases of abuse through the courts because they are working illegally, they are less dependent on individual employers since they do not live in and can leave particular employers should there be any difficulties. Notably they are the best paid among the migrant domestic workers in Berlin.

The impact of immigration legislation goes beyond Germany. According to the Polnischer Socialrat in Poland many Polish families employ Ukrainians as domestic workers to cover for them while they are away working (as domestic workers) in Berlin. Unlike Polish citizens, Ukrainians need a visa to enter Germany. They do not, however, need a visa to enter Poland. The 'Northern route' for migrants from Ukraine and Belorus through Poland to Germany is now receiving full attention from immigration officials (Forschungsgesellschaft Flucht und Migration 1998: 63). Those Ukrainians who are caught are deported to Poland as a buffer state (that is, a state which has an agreement with the European Union to readmit foreigners rejected by the European Union member state). Work in Poland is less remunerative, but is a fall-back for those who are unable to enter Germany. The wage differential between Germany and Ukraine is 100:1; between Germany and Poland it is 10:1 (Forschungs-gesellschaft Flucht und Migration 1998: 62).

> The new border regime and the amended legislation on aliens not only cement the economic hierarchy between states but, as 'black' labour markets expand in all countries, also give rise to a whole continuum of exploitation ... which leads to the 'illegalisation' of people from more distant countries.
> (Forschungsgesellschaft Flucht and Migration 1998: 62)

In Berlin, Ukrainians and other women from Eastern Europe and the former Soviet Union are thought to be mainly live-in workers. The Polnischer Socialrat at the time of interviewing was attempting to extend its work to this group, very much a hidden population in Berlin:

> The problem is when they stay with the families, they are very badly paid and very badly treated.... A lot of people do live-in but it is difficult to

182

contact them. As far as I know this is a closed story, they have no contact with other people, no information, they don't know where to get help for their problems.

Although settled and maybe even born in Germany, most of those who came to the country under the *gastarbeiter* system are not eligible for German citizenship, which is based on the principle of *ius sanguinis*. A baby born in Germany of 'Turkish' parents (who themselves were born in Germany) is not represented in official statistics as a birth, but as a migrant of one day's stay. Under current legislation, were the baby in fifteen years time, say, to commit what the German government deemed an offence, the child and parents would be liable to deportation. Indeed, the birth of the baby itself might constitute a reason for deportation, since migrants have to prove that they occupy a minimum number of square metres per residence. However many years those of 'Turkish' parentage work, even if they were born in Germany, they do not have the right to German citizenship. Yet *Aussiedler*, those of 'German' descent, may become German citizens on the grounds of descent, even if their family left Germany hundreds of years ago. *Aussiedler* can prove their 'Germanness' and hence right to citizenship by presenting papers in which they are defined as Germans, some of which derive directly from the Nazi period. The *Volkslistes* which were drawn up after the occupation of Poland register the population according to their 'German blood' – 'the wheel has come full circle, only now it is the Social Democrats who reproduce the purely biological construction of German citizenship that was first enacted by the *Nurnberger Reichsgesetze* in 1934' (Rathzel 1991: 42). Although they, too, are migrants, specific attempts are made to integrate them into Germany public life, with German classes and priority access to housing. *Aussiedler* from Poland, Russia and other countries do not work in private households, but they do operate in employment networks in informal but commercialised arrangements. An *Aussiedler* from Poland or from Russia will travel back to Poland or Russia and bring non-*Aussiedler* Polish/Russians to work for families in Berlin. Of course, while they can arrange employers they cannot arrange work permits, so this work is almost always illegal. Although ostensibly they do it as a favour, these fixers earn well from this work – and cannot offer any support or security to the woman once she has a job. According to one informant:

> *Aussiedler* go to Poland regularly and bring Polish people to Berlin to find work because they want to help them. For example, a woman from Belorussia comes with a visa to Germany because she has friends who are *Aussiedler* here. She stays here and organises work as a domestic worker. She must earn money for herself, her husband and her sick child. She was

paid very badly, and sexually abused a lot over three months. It was not just by her employers – the man and the woman – but they used to bring in people they knew and make her have sex with them. This was a German family. I knew this woman. She ran away, but I don't know what happened with her in the end, because she didn't contact us any more.

Aussiedler, then, can use their contacts in the communities where they grew up, their knowledge of their language and culture, and their personal relationships to access potential domestic workers. Their German citizenship means they can move freely across borders, enabling them to maintain and develop their networks with potential migrants while being based in Germany. They do not have to work as domestic workers themselves, but use their dual access to contacts to act as mediators. *Aussiedler*, as citizens, have privileged access to and knowledge of the market and can travel in and out freely. They can use this to profit from non-citizens. They have the best of both worlds – access to employment networks, and freedom of movement.

Women and the citizenship debate

Discussions around the rights and obligations of the citizen often ignore the legal sense of citizenship. In political theory citizenship is often talked about as if it was fundamentally concerned with issues of belonging and equality, a universal concept through which societies recognise that they have a duty to meet basic human needs. Citizenship is treated as an inclusive concept: everyone has citizens' rights even if they are more difficult for some to exercise than others. The current debates on citizenship take as their classic text T. H. Marshall's analysis of citizenship and social class. He developed a theory of citizenship which attempted to accommodate class differences within a liberal democracy, allowing that people may be equal citizens despite the inequalities generated by capitalism. He argued that while feudalism offered rights and duties subject to status, under capitalism everybody is equal and free within the market – even if this equality and freedom is simply expressed in the ownership of one's own labour. Marshall defined citizenship as having:

> three parts, or elements, civil, political and social. The civil element is composed of the rights necessary for individual freedom – liberty of the person, freedom of speech and thought and faith, the right to own property and to conclude valid contracts, and the right to justice.... By the political element I mean the right to participate in the exercise of political power, as a member of a body invested with political authority or as an elector of the members of such a body.... By the social element I mean the whole range

from the right to a modicum of economic welfare and security to the right to share to the full in the social heritage and to live the life of a civilised being according to the standards prevailing in the society.
(Marshall 1950: 10–11)

Marshall puts the development of these rights within a historical context: civil rights were developed in the eighteenth century, political rights in the nineteenth century, and social rights in the twentieth century. Although rights were thus built up steadily, he does not deny that there can be conflicts between these rights, in particular between social and civil rights. So, in the UK at the end of the eighteenth century, there was a conflict between pre-capitalist social rights deriving from membership in local communities and finding expression in, for example the Elizabethan Poor Law, and burgeoning civil rights – to work, make contracts, own property. He argues, however, that through exercising civil rights workers were able to re-establish entitlement to certain social rights, and that these social rights were incorporated into the status of citizenship.

Marshall's analysis has had a profound effect on the framing of debates on citizenship – and continues to have resonances today.[1] Patricia Hewitt writes of the conflict he perceived between social and civil rights:

> Two hundred years later, we find ourselves engaged in a latter-day version of the same battle. On the one side, the neoliberals – the champions, in Marshall's terms, of civil rights – who argue that Europe can only survive in the modern global economy by slashing its social costs, deregulating its labour markets and dismantling its welfare institutions. On the other, social and Christian democrats alike who believe that an extension of social rights must go hand-in-hand with the expansion of the market, if economic efficiency as well as social justice is to be served.
> (Hewitt 1996:250–1)

While the division of the rights of citizenship are generally found useful in analyses of citizenship, however, Marshall's generalisation of the three-stage attainment of citizenship has had many critics. In particular, it is clear that this is not an adequate description of women's achievement of citizenship. So, as Walby points out (1997: 168) women in Britain before 1928 did not have many of the rights associated with either political or civil citizenship, and she argues that for most First World women political citizenship (specifically the right to participate in elections) is achieved before civil citizenship (such as the right to bodily integrity, the right to all forms of employment, or the right to terminate a marriage). Women citizens still lack some aspects of civil rights, such as the right to justice from male violence (Walby 1997: 175), and women's participation in formal political process is restricted because of the obligation of the private sphere. For women of the Third World, political citizenship was often achieved at the same time as men, at national independence:

> in many countries citizenship did not arrive at one moment for all people; rather, different groups gained different aspects of this in different periods. Countries vary as to whether White men, White women, men and women of minority ethnic groups, gained citizenship at the same time or not.
> (Walby 1997: 171)

That Marshall's model does not work for women is an indication that he has failed to understand that women's relationship to the state is fundamentally different to men's, or rather, that he has not problematised this different relationship. Women's access to the rights of citizenship is different from men's, and mediated by men. The social rights of citizenship (the right to unemployment benefit, pensions and so on) are tied to the individual's position in the labour market and generally to male patterns of employment. Women's responsibilities in the private sphere make it difficult for them to participate equally with men in the public sphere, including in the labour market. Pateman argues that as the social contract is gendered, so is citizenship, for citizenship is what is attained by men under the social contract. 'The social contract brings the public world of civil law, civil freedom and equality, contract and the individual into being' (Pateman 1988: 11). Citizenship is participation in the public arena that presupposes and depends on the private. In order to have access to the public – the world of official employment and political meetings – one must have one's reproductive needs catered for. This demonstrates that in liberal democracies people have differential access to citizenship, and this is not simply a question of gender. Along with a broad stream of other groups (disabled, elderly, children, and, more recently, 'the poor') some feminists have sought emancipation through struggles conceptualised in terms of participatory citizenship.[2] As Lord Hylton said (quoted above with reference to overseas domestic workers in the UK), rights are useless unless one can exercise them. So citizenship has moved from Marshall's essentially passive conception towards a participatory model – to gain access to the rights of citizenship and to exercise those rights, one must be able to participate directly in the social, civil and political spheres.

Women have a very particular relation to the political order, however. As Pateman puts it: 'Women's political standing rests on a major paradox; they have been excluded and included on the basis of the very same capacities and attributes' (Pateman 1992: 19).

While women are excluded from the public sphere because of their role as reproductive workers, it is precisely this role that allows for their formal incorporation into the political order; so women are not completely excluded from citizenship, but rather have an ambiguous relationship to it through their participation in the private sphere. Thus the Beveridge Report of 1942, which formed the basis of the British welfare state and the rights of social citizenship, recognised that 'the great majority of married women must be regarded as occupied on work which is vital though unpaid, without which their husbands could not do their paid work, and without which the nation could not continue' (Beveridge 1942 para 107). Women's distinctive contribution was therefore recognised and formalised as subordinate to men's, and married women were to have access to the social rights of citizenship, only mediated by their husbands. Women citizens, therefore, have a particular role in the political order; their rights and duties are different from those of men. This role is encapsulated in the importance attached to the woman citizen's responsibility for reproduction in its literal sense. In the late nineteenth and early twentieth century in France, for example, feminists argued that motherhood was a duty that should be supported by the state, and in return for which mothers should be given the rights of citizens. Notably this particular duty of citizenship is associated with 'quality' of 'racial' reproduction. It is the responsibility of female citizens to reproduce the 'race'. 'In the next thirty years housewives as mothers have vital work to do in ensuring the adequate continuance of the British race and the British ideal in the world' (Beveridge 1942: para 117). For citizenship is not only gendered, it is also racialised. Who 'belongs' and who is excluded from a particular nation state is a matter of 'race' and ethnicity.

Nationality and racialisation

Citizenship has been a particular issue in the UK because – in contrast to the situation in Germany, for example, where immigrant workers were non-nationals – 'immigrants' were on the whole British subjects exercising their citizenship rights to live and work in the UK (which had no citizenship legislation until 1948). The British government, therefore, had to redefine citizenship rights rather than immigration legislation in the first instance, in order to render some British citizens subject to immigration control. Consequently there are currently six categories of British nationality, of which only one has an absolute right to enter the UK. The British citizens subject to immigration control are almost always racialised groups. Concern about the social and political impact of 'coloured' immigration led to the Commonwealth Immigrants Act of 1962 which gave preferential treatment in the form of 'right of abode' to Commonwealth citizens with a UK-born grandparent (previous to that all Commonwealth citizens were free to enter the UK). Although not cast in terms of 'race', what this meant in practice was that in general Australians, New Zealanders and Canadians continued to have residence rights in the UK, while black British subjects were excluded. This replacement of *ius soli* with *ius sanguinis* culminated in the 1981 Nationality Act, which took away the automatic right of children born in the UK to UK nationality. The notion of citizenship by descent is similarly illustrated in the case of Germany.

The point is that, while it is agreed that the citizenship concept is predicated on a notion of community, the notion of community is not problematised, as Yuval-Davis puts it,

> as an ideological and material construction, whose boundaries, structures and norms are a result of constant struggles and negotiations, or more general social developments. Any dynamic notion of citizenship must start from the processes which construct the collectivity and not just assume it. (Yuval-Davis 1991: 59)

Nation states are not natural communities. Their historical development in some cases involved processes of assimilation of non-dominant groups, as for example in France, where the citizenship project was allied to assimilation – all citizens were French and equal, difference was reactionary. In other cases it involved processes of rejection – the development of the nation state in Spain was tied to the expulsion of the Moors and the Jews. Indeed, within Europe the historical development of particular nation states continues to have implications for the granting of citizenship today (Anderson 1997b: 126–9). It is not possible to divorce how nation states developed from how they are currently constituted, and the histories of nations have a direct impact on their immigration laws. In the UK, for example, its history of free movement of capital and labour within the Empire and its post-war interest in maintaining good relations with the Commonwealth led to the 1948 Nationality Act, which affirmed that all colonial and Commonwealth citizens were British subjects and could hold British passports. Once in the UK, Commonwealth immigrants had full citizenship rights, including the right to vote. In France, the 1947 *Statut Organique de l'Algerie* conferred French citizenship on all Algerians and confirmed the principle of free movement between Algeria and France itself. The imperial histories of Spain and Italy are also reflected in the presence of migrants from former colonies.

Membership within the constructed community of the nation state is constantly being negotiated. Yet it is surprising how the natural community of the nation state is assumed. So Walzer in his famous *Spheres of*

Justice can state that 'the link between people and land is a crucial feature of national identity' (Walzer 1983: 44) as if it were a self-evident truth, rather than a highly controversial not to say dubious assertion. He also states that, if immigration were left to the market, the communities within the state would become hostile and exclusionary and that this is true 'historically', whereas there is strong evidence that restrictive immigration controls are the precursor of xenophobia (Harris 1995). This is a complex argument not appropriate for here, but it does illustrate that much of what Walzer considers to be self-evident is in fact highly contentious, and depends on a static and uncritical notion of community, in which nation states are discrete and autonomous – so one's moral obligation to take in refugees, for example, is entirely dependent on one's humanity, and not on any political and economic links with the dictator of the state that produces refugees.

It is within this racialised framework that one must understand the role of women citizens in the political order. The political duty of mother-hood is racialised. Gisela Bock (1992), for example, has shown that National Socialist Germany combined the pro-natalist measures for those women who were suitable for 'race regeneration' with anti-natalist policies, including enforced sterilisation, for those deemed eugenically inferior.

> The state has been interested in the 'quality' and not merely the quantity of the population. If women have had the duty to give birth for the state, not all women have been seen as fit to be mothers. Middle-class white women, above all, as 'superior' genetic stock, have been seen as under-mining the nation by limiting the extent of their service, or avoiding service altogether by 'unnatural' means. Other women have been subject to measures to prevent them from fulfilling their duty; women from indige-nous, migrant or black minority populations in western countries have been sterilised without their consent, and arguments surface regularly about the deleterious effects of differential birth rates of women classified according to IQ or class.
> (Pateman 1992: 25)

In Italy the Labour Minister Carl Donat Cattin called on Italians to have more babies 'to keep away armadas of immigrants from the southern shores of the Mediterranean' (Anderson 1993: 77).

Migrant domestic workers and the citizenship debate

The relevance of migrant domestic workers to this debate is clear. For, particularly in their role as welfare providers, as carers for the elderly and young children, they are directly facilitating some members of the marginalised collectivity of women to exercise their citizenship rights. Thanks to the hidden labour of migrant domestic workers, some middle-class women gain access to the public sphere. They are able to participate *like men* in the labour market – not forfeiting such advantages as pension rights and national insurance (that is, social rights) because of 'withdrawal' to the private. Migrant domestic workers, therefore, enable some middle-class women citizens to participate in the labour force as men's equals, because they are liberated from the home. The fact that they are migrants is important: in order to participate *like men* women must have workers who will provide the same flexibility as wives, in particular working long hours and combining caring and domestic chores. For it is the woman's responsibility, otherwise, to cover when a child is sick, to do the housework, and to meet all domestic eventualities. Migrants are far more flexible than citizens. Through their labour women citizens have male access to the public sphere, but they continue to fulfil female citizens' role of motherhood. Migrant domestic workers enable women citizens to fulfil the political duty of motherhood at the same time as participating in the labour market. Notably, motherhood as a political duty, the birthing and upbringing of citizens, does not necessarily include motherhood as work. While a woman with good European genes must pass these on to the next generation, and should be involved in the moral and social upbringing of the child, this has been de-coupled from the labour of care. In the light of this, Signor Cattin's remarks seem rather ironic – it is precisely the immigrant armadas that are facilitating the reproduction of the Italian 'race'. In February 1997 Italy's General Accountant declared that over the next fifty years Italy would need at least 50,000 immigrants per year to balance the social security budget and support the economy in the face of a stagnant birth rate and an increasingly ageing population (*Migration News Sheet* March 1997: 5). As has already been noted, migrant women facilitate this reproduction of citizens but are directly prevented from becoming mothers themselves. This is not just because of the nature of their work, it is also because of their immigration status and access to citizenship. Undocumented workers have no possibility of achieving family reunification under European immigration regimes, and even when they are documented it is extremely difficult for their children to enter. Women migrants' access to possibilities of their own reproduction are directly influenced by the state. So, while female citizens' reproductive role is driven by political duty, and there is at least lip service paid to the importance of women's reproductive role when performed by citizens this reproductive responsibility simply disappears when it refers to non-citizens.

This brings a new dimension to the notion of the reproduction of

status. Migrant domestic workers are enabling female citizens to participate in the public sphere, thereby taking full advantage of the rights
attached to their citizenship status, but they themselves are often formally
denied citizenship rights. Immigrants are popularly presented as a threat
to a way of life – and this may be repeated uncritically by political
theorists:

> The distinctiveness of cultures and groups depends upon closure and,
> without it, cannot be conceived as a stable feature of human life. If this
> distinctiveness is a value ... then closure must be permitted somewhere. At
> some level of political organisation, something like the sovereign state must
> take shape and claim the authority to make its own admissions policy, to
> control and sometimes restrain the flow of immigrants.
> (Walzer 1983: 39)

But migrant domestic workers are engaged in the support and reproduction of the European way of life, not least its families. Migrants are
presented as a drain on the welfare state, again supported uncritically by
some political theorists:

> wealth and resources ... too, can be superfluous.... Are those inhabitants
> morally bound to admit immigrants from poorer countries for as long as
> superfluous resources exist?.... Once again there must be some limit, short
> (and probably considerably short) of simple equality, else communal wealth
> would be subject to indefinite drainage.
> (Walzer 1983: 47–8)

The case of migrant domestic workers demonstrates that this is by no
means one-way traffic. Not only do migrant domestic workers, documented and undocumented, contribute to the state, they are also providing the welfare that is the social right of citizens, but to which many of
these workers, however necessitous, have no right. By providing welfare,
one of the crucial social rights of the citizen, they are helping to give
meaning to the notion of citizenship status, while themselves being denied
any of its rights.

Contemporary debates around citizenship in the UK are increasingly
framed in terms of duties and obligations rather than universal rights
(Lister 1990), and in particular the citizen's obligation to work at whatever is available. That this political obligation overrides the political duty
of motherhood is clear in the current Labour government's attitude to
single mothers, who must be given the 'opportunity' to take up paid
employment. But what the position of migrants in Europe demonstrates is
that, while citizens' rights are increasingly cast by the state in terms of
fulfilling obligations to be available for work, work itself is not enough to
gain access to citizenship. It does not matter how many years a 'Turk' has

worked in Germany or Greece, this is not a sufficient criterion for member-ship. While citizens have an obligation to work, and may be denied social rights if they are regarded as not fulfilling this obligation, non-citizens who work are not thereby proving their suitability for citizenship, but are 'stealing' jobs. Neither is motherhood a sufficient criterion for member-ship: in the UK, for example, being the mother of a citizen is not a guaran-tee against deportation, let alone a reason for granting citizenship. In France, the mother of a citizen does in consequence have some rights, including, in general, not to be separated from her child by deportation, but she does not have a right to citizenship.

This emphasises a broader question in the debate around citizenship: there is a danger, in focusing all attention on the legitimate point of the importance of participation and access to rights, of being taken in by the rhetoric of citizenship. Because it seems that citizens have certain basic, fundamental and inalienable rights and duties, citizenship is represented in some discussions as an inclusive principle, which appears to cut through material inequalities and to offer some way forward. This is particularly true with reference to discussions around care; thus Bubeck, for example, suggests that caring should be a citizens' obligation:

> one might conceive of care as part of a citizen's obligation to contribute her share to one of the most, if not the most important function any self-governing society has, namely to ensure the well-being of its members. Citizenship would be redefined to comprise care as much as, or even more importantly than, defence, as every citizen's obligation.
> (Bubeck 1995: 260)

Yet this is precisely the labour that is increasingly being carried out by non-citizens. While it is important to look at new ways of social organis-ing and of arranging access to rights and participation, there are dangers in casting this within the framework of citizenship. In emphasising that citizenship is allegedly universal, while in practice many groups cannot avail themselves of the rights of citizenship, one risks forgetting that as long as citizenship is tied to the notion of belonging to a particular nation state, and as long as some states are richer and more powerful than others, citizenship will be formally exclusive. As Walzer puts it:

> Since human beings are highly mobile, large numbers of men and women regularly attempt to change their residence and their membership, moving from unfavored to favored environments. Affluent and free countries are, like elite universities, besieged by applicants. They have to decide on their own size and character.
> (Walzer 1983: 32)

Employers and citizenship

In this respect the UK exemplifies an interesting aspect of the intersection of citizenship, racism and domestic work. In my discussion of the situation of migrant domestic workers in other EU countries, it has been assumed that the employers are predominantly citizens – as indeed they are. Much of the power deployed in the relationship derives from their citizenship and the domestic workers' dependence as an immigrant – the employers' power to report and deport, not to renew work permits, to call the police if there's a dispute. The fact that employers are citizens and the workers are not citizens formalises their unequal power relations – even outside of the employment relationship, workers and their employers are not equal before the law. This facilitates the persistence of the master/mistress–servant roles. In the UK, too, the majority of employers of migrant domestic workers known to me are UK citizens, since the pattern is for workers to leave the employers with whom they entered the UK, and to 'go underground', working for other employers, predominantly UK citizens, illegally. In this case the original employers are often not citizens but wealthy visitors or businessmen, bringing with them their domestic workers. In fact this is also true, though less common, in other EU states (mention was made of it in Spain, Germany and Greece). Both employer and worker are non-citizens, but they are not equal before the law, since the worker is still dependent for her immigration status on the non-citizen employer. If the worker brings a case against her employers for abuse, they too may be deported, but this sanction does not help the worker. So, for example, when the Nigerian woman Helen Samuels was maltreated and exploited by her Nigerian employers she was successful in her case and won damages. She herself was deported, however, while her employers were imprisoned for two years, to be deported having served their sentence. But deportation is used extremely selectively against employers. Wealth and political influence, as well as citizenship, must be taken into account. When defending the Concession in 1990, Lord Reay, speaking for the government, said:

> Looking at our national interest, if wealthy investors, skilled workers and others with the potential to benefit our economy were unable to be accompanied by their domestic staff they might not come here at all but take their money and skills to other countries only too keen to welcome them.
> (Hansard Col. 1052, 28 November 1990, House of Lords Debate on Overseas Domestic Workers)

This continues to be an issue. In the 1998 negotiations between Kalayaan and the Home Office the government put forward Foreign Office concerns that wealthy people entering the UK should not have to leave their domestic workers behind because that would discourage them and their money from coming to the UK. So it is not just citizenship but wealth that gives the employer control over the worker.

The fact that these employers are not citizens has ensured a surprising breadth of support for the campaign for domestic workers to be given an independent immigration status, partly because the employers whom they accompany often belong to racialised groups from the Middle East. Employers were commonly portrayed both in the media and by parliamentarians as 'importing' slavery. Maltreatment and abuse of workers was presented as a consequence of allowing people with no understanding of what constituted civilised behaviour to bring in their domestic servants. There was a need to teach people that what was acceptable in 'their' countries was not suitable behaviour in the UK. This intersected with racist stereotypes of misogynistic, cruel Middle Eastern men, and victimised (pretty) Filipinas – the two groups most commonly portrayed. There has been no public interest in the fact that, having been forced into illegality by non-citizens, domestic workers are then exploited by British employers. Margaret Healy interviewed ten women before and after their change of employer. She found that two months after the first interview, six had left their British employers. Problems included:

> the negotiated salary was not adhered to. Likewise with the hours of work. For example when asked to change a day off or to do overtime, if the worker said she had an appointment with the doctor, the employer would say, 'well I can always call the Home Office'.... The treatment of the employers ranged from shouting at them, insults to their person, passing derogatory comments, constant complaints. One woman said she was treated 'as if I'm nothing'. One of the six had to sleep on the living-room floor and wasn't given any place to put her personal belongings. She had to keep everything in her bag. One of the women experienced overt racism by the employer making personal derogatory remarks about her, not allowing her to sit on the settee in the sitting room.... Another of the women complained that her male employer was constantly sexually harassing her by making suggestive comments and even offering her money for sexual favours.
> (Healy 1994: 29)

Following reports in the *Washington Post* about abuse of domestic workers by foreign nationals working in international organisations, one reader wrote:

> I have seen US officials in Central America and the Caribbean (some of whom, ironically, were abroad to advance US-style labor standards) quickly adopt the norms of the host-country elites and require their household staff to work 13 to 16 hour days with two days off every 15 days.
> (Letter from Keith Mines to *Washington Post*, 18 January 1999)

Conclusions

When rights are cast in terms of access to citizenship rights, the implication is that if a person is not a citizen, it is legitimate to deny her certain rights, even if those rights would be considered basic human rights by citizens. So while citizenship rights guarantee that citizens' basic human needs are met, these rights do not derive from humanity but from membership of the community. As well as a guarantee of rights, then, citizenship therefore becomes a device by which demands on the state are controlled and this denial is perceived as legitimate. Historically class inequalities may have been ameliorated through citizenship, but at the expense of other non-citizens. The access to social rights that mainly concerns Marshall was facilitated by the development of the welfare state after the Second World War. This development was largely financed, however, by the exploitation of Britain's colony in Malaya (T. Kaplan 1990). The labour for the tin and rubber that earned the British state so many dollars was predominantly migrant and first-generation Chinese and Indian. The majority of the members of these groups were deprived of their entitlement to citizenship by the Constitution of 1948.

While citizenship is tied to the notion of the nation state, these states are bound to each other in particular economic and political relationships which have direct implications for citizens' rights or lack of them. How to apply the universal principle implied in concepts of citizenship, when different people have such different access to resources in different societies, is a question that has been posed (Jones 1990). What remains unexplored is how the rights of citizenship in one state can be gained precisely because these are denied in another. The case of migrant domestic workers might be said to describe this process within a single state, and how this process is eased by what is perceived as the legitimate denial of rights based on ascription of nationality. A potential conflict between the rights of two groups of citizens (men and middle-class women) to participate in the public sphere is resolved without requiring restructuring of the public and private, by using the labour of non-citizens.

Notes

1. See for example Bulmer and Rees (eds) 1996.
2. Doyal and Gough 1991; Morris 1992.

11

Conclusions

The living and working conditions of migrant domestic workers are in large part determined by the intersection of workers' relations with their employers and the relations they have to the state. Citizenship and immigration status are crucial factors in this. The power of the state is often used to enforce a workers' dependence on her employer and to institutionalise master/mistress–servant relations, so the worker may be subject to her employer 24 hours a day. Citizenship and immigration are areas where there are at least possibilities of organising for change; they offer specific improvements and unifying organising principles. As someone engaged in a minor way in supporting such struggles, I know that they are not easy, but the winning of them and the struggle itself offers material gains. I would also put forward for the consideration of workers and activists that live-in domestic work, for all the benefits it apparently offers the worker, binds her into a relation of status and dependence mediated by racism. How to organise for rights, justice and equality within that relation – if it is possible at all – needs some serious thought.

Immigration status is not the only reason that migrant women are in domestic work, and it is not the only factor in their abuse and exploitation. The treatment of migrant domestic workers and the 'demand' for them in the first place is symptomatic of fundamental contradictions and tensions with capitalism which is both racist and patriarchal. The public/private divide, desperate poverty and ostentatious wealth, under-pinned by a history of ferocious imperialism and plunder: herein lie the roots of the problems confronted by women who work as migrant domestic workers. I began this thesis by noting that domestic work in private households is, together with prostitution, the most significant employer of newly arrived female migrants. The expansion and racialisation of prostitution, paid domestic work, and the 'mail order bride' phenomenon are a function of the expansion of global capitalism. This is disheartening and encouraging: disheartening because the forces to be confronted are so powerful, and encouraging because it offers possibilities for alliances with other groups, fighting the same enemy on different ground.

The theoretical challenges posed by migrant domestic workers demand that we re-centre reproductive work, and examine critically how and what we are reproducing, not just to make the personal political, but to make the political personal. There is a need for empirically based theory to help promote such alliances, to understand what binds some women together and drives others apart. Such theory must be located in the real, lived experiences of workers. I hope I have demonstrated that workers and employers have a sense, a social consciousness, of the contradictions they are attempting to manage. Unlike the workers, I have had the opportunity to listen to people from many migrant communities talking about domestic work in different European cities; I have had the opportunity to read about domestic work and paid domestic work throughout the world; I have had time to think and colleagues to talk to. It is these opportunities that help me to hope I have something to offer, food for organisational thought. It is largely an unpacking of what workers and their employers have told me, for it is grounded in their experience. As Josee said: 'We, the Third World, don't diminish them, rather it is they who diminish us.'

Bibliography

Abadan-Unat N. (1984) 'International Labour Migration and Women's Roles: a Turkish View', in *Women on the Move: Contemporary Changes in Family and Society*, Paris: UNESCO.

Andall, Jacqueline (1992) 'Women Migrant Workers in Italy', *Women's Studies International Forum* 15(1): 4–48.

Andall, Jacqueline (1996) 'Catholic and State Construction of Domestic Workers: the Case of Cape Verdean women in Rome in the 1970s' paper for ERCOMER Conference on New Migration in Europe: Social Constructions and Social Realities, Utrecht University, 18–20 April 1996.

Anderson, B. (1993) *Britain's Secret Slaves: an Investigation into the Plight of Overseas Domestic Workers*, London: Anti-Slavery International and Kalayaan.

—— (1996) 'Domestic Workers' Challenges to Feminism' unpublished group interview with domestic workers for Kalayaan/Solidar distribution.

—— (1997a) *Labour Exchange: Patterns of Migration in Asia*, London: CIIR.

—— (1997b) 'Western Europe' in Minority Rights Group (ed.) *The World Directory of Minorities*, London: MRG.

Anthias, F. and Yuval Davis, N. (1992) *Racialised Boundaries*, London: Routledge.

Aptheker, H. (1951) *A Documentary History of the Negro People in the US*, New York: The Citadel Press.

Arat-Koc, Sedef (1989) 'In the Privacy of our Own Home: Foreign Domestic Workers as the Solution to the Crisis in the Domestic Sphere in Canada', *Studies in Political Economy* 28: 33–58.

Arena, G. (1983) 'Lavoro feminile ed Immigrazione dai Paesi Afro-Asiatici a Roma', *Studi Emigrazione* 70, June.

Aristotle (1941) *The Basic Works of Aristotle*, ed. Richard McKeon, New York: Random House.

Asian Migrant Centre (1994) *Nowhere to Turn to: a Case Study on Indonesian Migrant Workers in Hong Kong*, Hong Kong: Asian Migrants Centre.

Athens University of Economics and Business (1996) *Labour Market Studies: Greece*, Luxembourg: Office for Official Publications of the European Commission.

Baier, A. (1986) 'Trust and Anti-Trust', *Ethics* 96.

Bakan, A. and Stasiulis, D. (1995) 'Making the Match: Domestic placement agencies and the racialization of women's household work', *Signs* Winter 1995: 303–35.

Bakan, A and Stasiulis, D (1994) 'Foreign Domestic Worker Policy in Canada and Social Boundaries of Modern Citizenship', *Science and Society* 58(1):7–33.

198

Bibliography

Bales, Kevin (1999) *Disposable People: New Slavery in the Global Economy*, London: Routledge.

Benston, Margaret (1971) 'The Political Economy of Women's Liberation', in Michele Hoffnung Garskof (ed.) *Roles Women Play, Readings Toward Women's Liberation*, Belmont CA: Brooks/Cole Publishing Company.

Berk, S. Fenstermaker (1980) *Women and Household Labor*, Beverly Hills: Sage.

Bernard Brunhoes Consultants (1997) Labour Market Studies: France, Luxembourg: Office for the Official Publications of the European Commission.

Beveridge, W. (1942) *Social Insurance and Allied Services*. Report by Sir William Beveridge, London: HMSO.

Black, Robert (1992) 'Livelihood and Vulnerability of Foreign Refugees in Greece: a Preliminary Report of Research on Iranian and Iraqi Refugees in Greater Athens', unpublished, lodged with the Refugee Studies Programme, Queen Elizabeth House, University of Oxford.

Bock, Gisela (1992) 'Equality and Difference in National Socialist Racism', in G. Bock and S. James (eds) *Beyond Equality and Difference*.

Bock, Gisela and James, Susan (1992) *Beyond Equality and Difference. Citizenship, Feminist Politics and Female Subjectivity*, London: Routledge.

Bolden, D. (1976) 'Forty Two Years a Maid' in Nancy Seifer (ed.) *Nobody Speaks for Me! Self-Portraits of American Working Class Women*, New York: Simon and Schuster.

Brenner, Johanna and Laslett, Barbara (1986) 'Social Reproduction and the Family', in Ulf Himmelstrand (ed.) *Sociology from Crisis to Science? Vol. 2, The Social Reproduction of Organisation and Culture*, London: Sage.

— (1989) 'Gender and Social Reproduction: Historical Perspectives', *Annual Review of Sociology* 15: 381–404.

Brettell, C. and Simon, R. (eds) *International Migration. The Female Experience*, New Jersey: Rowman and Allenheld.

Brooks, Sara (1986) *You May Plow Here: The Narrative of Sara Brooks*, Thordis Simonsen (ed.), New York: Norton.

Brown, Pam (1984) *Mutterings of a Char*, Watford: Exley Publications.

Bubeck, Diemut (1995) *Care, Gender and Justice*, Oxford: Clarendon Press.

Buchanan, J. M. (1975) *The Limits of Liberty: Between Anarchy and Leviathan*, Chicago: University of Chicago Press.

Buechler, Hans and Buechler, Judith-Maria (1985) *Carmen: The Autobiography of a Spanish Galician Peasant Woman*, Cambridge: Cambridge University Press.

Bulmer, Martin, and Rees, Anthony (eds) (1996) *Citizenship Today. The Contemporary Relevance of T. H. Marshall*, London: UCL Press.

Campani, G. (1992) 'International Perspectives on Migrant Women's Employment. The Example of Self-Employment and of Domestic Work' for International Seminar on Migrant Women in the 1990s, Barcelona, Spain, 26–29 January 1992.

— (1993) 'Labour Markets and Family Networks: Filipino Women in Italy', in H. Rudolph and Morokvasic, M. (eds) *Bridging States and Markets*, Berlin: Sigma.

— (1995a) 'Immigrant Women as Social Actors' for UNESCO Conference on New Trends in Migration, University of Warwick, November.

— (1995b) 'Women Migrants: from Marginal Subjects to Social Actors', in Robin Cohen (ed.) *Cambridge Survey of World Migrations*, Cambridge: Cambridge University Press.

— (1997) 'Immigrant Women in Southern Europe: Social Exclusion and Gender' for conference on Non-military Aspects of Security in Southern Europe: Migration, Employment and Labour Market, Institute of International Economic Relations and Regional Network on Southern European Societies, Santorini, Greece, 19–21 September 1997.

Caspari, Andreas and Giles W. (1986) 'Immigration and the Employment of Portuguese

199

Migrant Women in UK and France: a Comparative Analysis', in C. Brettell and R. Simon (eds) *International Migration: the Female Experience.*

Castro, Mary Garcia (1984) 'What is Bought and Sold in Domestic Service? The Case of Bogotá: a Critical Review'. Elsa Chaney and Mary Castro (eds) *Muchachas no More: Household Workers in Latin America and the Caribbean.*

Chabaud, D. and Fougeyrollas, D. (1984) 'A propos de l'autonomie relative de la production et de la reproduction' in *Le Sexe du Travail*, Grenoble: Presses Universitaires de Grenoble.

Chaney, Elsa and Castro, Mary (eds) (1984) *Muchachas no More: Household Workers in Latin America and the Caribbean*, Philadelphia: Temple University Press.

Clark-Lewis, Elizabeth (1985) 'This Work Had an End: the Transition from Live-in to Day Work' Working Paper No. 2, *Southern Women: the Intersection of Race, Class and Gender Series* Center for Research on Women, Memphis: Memphis State University.

Cock, J. (1989) *Maids and Madams: Domestic Workers under Apartheid*, London: The Women's Press.

Cohen, Rina (1987) 'The Work Conditions of Immigrant Women Live-In Domestics: Racism, Sexual Abuse and Invisibility', *Resources for Feminist Research* 16(1): 36–38.

Colectivo Ioe (1987) *Las empleadas de Hogar en España*, unpublished monograph, Colectivo Ioe Madrid, Spain.

—— (1990) *El Servicio Domestico en España entre el trabajo invisible y la economiá sumergida. Informe de investigación*, Madrid: JOC-E.

—— (1991) *Foreign Women in Domestic Service in Madrid Spain*, Geneva: ILO.

Colen, Shellee (1984) 'Just a Little Respect: West Indian Domestic Workers in New York City', in E. Chaney and M. Castro (eds) *Muchachas no More.*

Colen, S. and Sanjek, R. (eds) (1990a) *At Work in Homes: Household Workers in World Perspective*, Washington DC: American Ethnological Society Monograph Series.

Colen, S. and Sanjek, R. (1990b) 'At Work in Homes 1: Orientation', in Colen and Sanjek (eds) *At Work in Homes.*

Collinson, Sarah (1994) *Europe and International Migration*, London: Royal Institute for International Affairs.

Cornelius, Wayne (1982) 'Interviewing Undocumented Immigrants: Methodological Reflections Based on Fieldwork in Mexico and the US', *International Migration Review* 16(2):378–411.

Coulson M., Magas, B. and Wainwright, H. (1975) '"The Housewife and her Labour Under Capitalism" – a Critique', *New Left Review* 89: 59–71.

Croff, Brigitte (1994) *Seules: Genèse des emplois familiaux*, Paris: Métailié.

Daenzer, P. (1991) 'Ideology and the Formation of Migration Policy: The case of Immigrant Domestic Workers 1940–1990', unpublished PhD thesis, University of Toronto.

Dalla Costa, M. and James, S. (1972) *The Power of Women and the Subversion of the Community*, Bristol: Falling Wall Press.

Dalley, G. (1988) *Ideologies of Caring*, London: Macmillan.

DARES (Direction de l'Animation de la Recherche, des Études et des Statistiques) (1995) 'L'Évolution des Emplois Familiaux de 1992 a 1994', in *Premieres Syntheses* No. 109, 17 August.

Davidoff, L. (1974) 'Mastered for Life: Servant and Wife in Victorian and Edwardian England', *Journal of Social History* 7: 406–28.

Davidoff L. (1976) 'The Rationalization of Housework', in D. Barker and S. Allen (eds) *Exploitation in Work and Marriage London*: Longmans.

—— (1983) 'Class and Gender in Victoria England', in J. Newton, M. Ryan and J. Walkowitz (eds) *Sex and Class in Women's History*, London: Routledge and Kegan Paul.

Bibliography

Davis, Angela (1984) *Women, Race and Class*, London: The Women's Press.

Dawes, Frank V. (1989) *Not in Front of the Servants*, Guernsey: The Guernsey Press Co. Ltd.

Dawkins, H. (1987) 'The Diaries and Photographs of Hannah Cullwick', *Art History* 10(2): 14–187

Delcourt, J. (1975) *The Housing of Migrant Workers: a Case of Social Improvidence?* Brussels: Commission of the European Communities.

Delphy, C. and Leonard, D. (1992) *Familiar Exploitation: a new analysis of marriage in contemporary western societies*, Cambridge: Polity Press.

Dill, Bonnie (1980) 'The Means to Put my Children Through: Child-rearing Goals and Strategies among Black Female Domestic Servants', in Rose La Frances Rodgers (ed.) *The Black Woman*, London: Sage.

Dill, Bonnie (1988) 'Making your Job Good Yourself: Domestic Service and the Construction of Personal Dignity', in A. Bookman and S. Morgen (eds)*Women and the Politics of Empowerment*, Philadelphia: Temple University Press.

Divino, Cecile (1998) 'A Report on the Experiences of Overseas Domestic Workers with Work, Accommodation and Access to Health Services after Leaving their Primary Employer', unpublished mss, Kalayaan.

Doyal, R. and Gough, I. (1991) *A Theory of Human Need*, London: MacMillan.

Duarte, Isis (1984) 'Household Workers in the Dominican Republic: a Question for the Feminist Movement', in E. Chaney and M. Castro (eds) *Muchachas no More*.

Dudden (1983) *Serving Women: Household service in Nineteenth Century America*, Middeleton, CT: Wesleyan University Press.

Dumon, W. (1981) 'The Situation of Migrant Women Workers', *International Migration* 19(1/2): 190–209.

Eaton, Isabel (1899) 'Special Report on Negro Domestic Service in the Seventh Ward Philadelphia', in W.E.B. DuBois, *The Philadelphia Negro*, Philadelphia: University of Pennsylvania.

Ehrenreich, B. and English, D. (1979) *For Her Own Good: 150 Years of the Experts' Advice to Women*, London: Pluto Press.

Engels, Frederick (1884) *The Origin of the Family, Private Property and the State*, 1978 edition, Peking: Foreign Languages Press.

Escrivà, A. (1996) 'Control, Composition and Character of New Migrations to Southwest Europe: the Case of Peruvian Women in Barcelona', paper given at ERCOMER International Conference, Utrecht, 18–20 April.

European Commission Network on Childcare and other Measures to Reconcile Employment and Family Responsibilities (1996) *A Review of Services for Young Children in the EU 1990–1995*, Luxembourg: Office for Official Publications of the European Commission.

European Forum of Left Feminists (1993) *Confronting the Fortress: Black and Migrant Women in the European Community*, Brussels: European Women's Lobby.

European Race Audit, London: Institute of Race Relations.

Eurostat (1996) *Social Portrait of Europe*, Luxembourg: Office for Official Publications of the European Commission.

Fakiolas, Rosseetos (1997) 'The Impact of Migration on the Greek Labour Market', paper given at Conference on Non-military Aspects of Security in Southern Europe, Santorini, Greece, Institute of International Economic Relations, 19–21 September.

Fairchilds, Cissie (1984) 'Domestic Enemies: Servants and their Masters in Old Regime France', unpublished MPhil thesis, Johns Hopkins University.

Fee, Terry (1976) 'Domestic Labor: an Analysis of Housework and its Relation to the Production Process', *Review of Radical Political Economy* 8(1):1–17.

Finch, J. and Groves, D. (eds) (1983) *A Labour of Love: Women, Work and Caring*, London: Routledge and Kegan Paul.

Fondazione Giacomo Brodolini (1996) *Labour Market Studies: Italy, Luxembourg:* Office for Official Publications of the European Commission.

Forschungsgesellschaft Flucht and Migration (1998) 'Germany, Poland and Ukraine: asylum-seekers and the "domino" effect', *Race and Class* 39 (4) April–June: 62–76.

Fox-Genovese, Elizabeth (1988) *Within the Plantation Household*, Chapel Hill: the University of North Carolina Press.

French Ministry of Social Affairs (1984) 'The Employment Market and Immigrants in an Irregular Situation: Lessons from the Recent Legalization in France', *International Migration Review* 18(3): 558–78.

Gaitskell, D., Kimbie, J., Maconachie, M. and Unterhalter, E. (1984) 'Class, Race and Gender; Domestic Workers in South Africa', *Review of African Political Economy* 27 28: 86–108

Gálvez, Thelma and Todaro, Rosalba (1984) 'Housework for Pay in Chile: Not Just Another Job' in E. Chaney and M. Castro (eds) *Muchachas no More.*

Gardiner, J. (1975) 'Women's Domestic Labour', *New Left Review* 89 (January–February).

—— (1976) 'Domestic Labour in Capitalist Society', in D. Barker and S. Allen (eds) *Dependence and Exploitation in Work and Marriage*, London: Longman.

Gardiner, J., Himmelwiet, S. and Mackintosh, M. (1975) 'Women's Domestic Labour', *Bulletin of the Conference of Socialist Economists* 4(2).

Gerstein, I. (1973) 'Domestic Work and Capitalism', *Radical America* 7(4–5).

Gilbert, Olive (1991) *Narrative of Sojourner Truth, a Bondswoman of Olden Time: With a History of Her Labors and Correspondence Drawn from Her 'Book of Life'.* New York: Oxford University Press.

Glazer, Nona (1980) 'Everyone Needs Three Hands: Doing Paid and Unpaid Work', in S.F. Berk (ed.) *Women and Household Labour.*

Glazer-Malbin, N. (1976) 'Housework', *Signs* 1(4):905–21.

Glenn, Evelyn Nakano (1986) *Issei, Nisei, War Bride*, Philadelphia: Temple University Press.

—— (1992) 'From Servitude to Service Work: Historical Continuities in the Racial Division of Paid Reproductive Labor', *Signs* 18(1):1–43.

Goffman, E. (1968) *Asylums*, London: Penguin.

Golden, Janet (1987) 'Trouble in the Nursery: Physicians, families and wet nurses at the End of the Nineteenth Century', in C. Groneman and M. Norton (eds) *To Toil the Livelong Day: America's Women at Work*, Ithaca: Cornell University Press.

Graham, H. (1983) 'Caring: a Labour of Love', in J. Finch and D. Groves (eds) *A Labour of Love: Women, Work and Caring*, London: Routledge and Kegan Paul.

—— (1991) 'The Concept of Caring in Feminist Research: the Case of Domestic Service', *Sociology* 25(1).

Gregson, Nicky and Lowe Michelle (1994) *Servicing the Middle Classes*, London: Routledge.

Groenendijk, K. and Hampsink, R. (1995) *Temporary Employment of Migrants in Europe*, Nijmegen: Reeks Recht and Samenleving.

Grosvenor, Verta Mae (1972) *Thursdays and Every Other Sunday Off: A Domestic Rap* by Verta Mae, New York: Doubleday.

Gulati, Leela (1993) *Women Migrant Workers in Asia: a Review*, New Delhi: ILO-ARTEP.

Hansen, Karen Tranberg (1990) 'Part of the Household Inventory: Men Servants in Zambia', in S. Colen and R. Sanjek (eds) *At Work in Homes.*

Harris, Nigel (1995) *The New Untouchables: Immigration and the New World Worker*, London: I.B. Tauris.

Harrison, J. (1973) 'The Political Economy of Housework', *Bulletin of the CSE*, Winter: 35-51.

Harrison, Rosina (1975) *Rose: My Life in Service*, New York: Viking

Bibliography

Hartmann, H. (1981) 'The Family as the Locus of Gender, Class and Political Struggle: the Example of Housework', *Signs* 6: 366–94.

Healy, M. (1994) 'Exploring the Slavery of Domestic Work in Private Households', unpublished MA thesis, University of Westminster.

Hertz, Rosanna (1986) *More Equal Than Others: Women and Men in Dual-Career Marriages*, California: University of California Press.

Hewitt, Patricia (1996) 'Social Justice in a Global Economy', in M. Bulmer and A. Rees Citizenship Today, London: UCL Press.

Heyzer, N. and Wee, V. (1993) 'Who Benefits, Who Profits? Domestic workers in Transient Overseas Employment', *Issues in Gender and Development*, 5 April, Kuala Lumpur: Asian and Pacific Development Centre.

Himmelweit, S. and Mohun, S. (1977) 'Domestic Labour and Capital', *Cambridge Journal of Economics* 1(1).

Hochschild, A. (1983) *The Managed Heart: the Commercialisation of Human Feeling*, Berkley: University of California Press.

Hochschild, A. and Machung, A. (1990) *The Second Shift: Working Parents and the Revolution at Home*, London: Tiatkus.

Hondagneu-Sotelo, P. (1994) 'Regulating the Unregulated? Domestic Workers' Social Networks', *Social Problems* 41(1) February: 50–64.

hooks, bell (1981) *Ain't I a Woman: Black Women and Feminism*, London: Pluto Press.

Hudson, Derek (1972) *Munby: Man of Two Worlds. The Life and Diaries of Arthur Munby, 1828–1910*, London: Abacus.

Human Rights Watch (1992) 'Punishing the Victim: Rape and Mistreatment of Asian Maids in Kuwait', New York: Middle East Watch Women's Rights Project.

IFO Institute for Economic Research (1997) *Labour Market Studies: Germany*, Luxembourg: Office for the Official Publications of the European Commission.

ILO Interdepartmental Project on Migrant Workers Equality and Human Rights. Coordination Branch (1995) *Problems of Discrimination against Women Migrant Workers and Possible Solutions*, Geneva: ILO.

Iris de Rimini (1995) *Immigrati: pericolo o risorsa?*, Rimini: CGIL.

Jacobs, Harriet (1988) *Incidents in the Life of a Slavegirl*.

Joly, D., Nettleton, C. and Poulton, H. (1992) *Refugees: Asylum in Europe?*, London: Minority Rights Group.

Jones, P. (1990) 'Universal Principles and Particular Claims: from Welfare Rights to Welfare States', in A. Ware and R. E. Goodin (eds) *Needs and Welfare*, London: Sage.

Kalayaan (1996) *Briefing Notes on the plight of Overseas Domestic Workers*, unpublished.

Kaplan, Elaine (1987) '"I Don't Do No Windows": Competition between the Domestic Worker and the Housewife' in V. Miner and H. Longino (eds) *Competition: A Feminist Taboo?*, New York: the Feminist Press.

Kaplan, Thomas (1990) 'Britain's Asian Cold War', in Ann Deighton (ed.) *Britain and the First Cold War*

Katzman, David (1978) *Seven Days a Week: Women and Domestic Service in Industrialising America*, New York: OUP.

Keat Gin Ooi (1992) 'Domestic Servants Par Excellence: the Black and White Amahs of Malaysia and Singapore with Special Reference to Penang', *Journal of Malaysian Branch of the Royal Asiatic Society* 65(2).

Keckley, Elizabeth (1868). *Behind the Scenes. or, Thirty Years a Slave and Four Years in the White House*, New York: C. W. Carlton; reprinted New York: Arno, 1968.

Kelly, J. (1979) 'The Doubled Vision of Feminist Theory: A Postscript to the Women and Power Conference', *Feminist Studies* 5:216–27.

Kelly, Liz, Burton, S. and Regan, L. (1994) 'Researching Women's Lives or Studying Women's Oppression? Reflections on What Constitutes Feminist Research', in M.

Maynard and J. Purvis (eds) *Researching Women's Lives from a Feminist Perspective*, London: Taylor and Francis.

Kofman, E. and Sales, R. (1992) 'Towards Fortress Europe', Women's Studies International Forum 15(1): 29–39.

Krueger, Richard (1994) *Focus Groups: a practical guide for applied research*, London: Sage.

Kussmaul, Anne (1981) *Servants in Husbandry in Early Modern England*, Cambridge: Cambridge University Press.

Lamphere, Louise (1987) *From Working Daughters to Working Mothers: Immigrant Women in a New England Industrial Community*, Ithaca: Cornell University Press.

Lega Italo-Filippina Filippini Emigrati (LIFE) (1991) *Filipino Migrant Women in Domestic Work in Italy*, Geneva: ILO.

Leonard Barker, D. and Allen, S. (eds) (1976) *Dependence and Exploitation in Work and Marriage*, London: Hutchinson.

Leonetti, I. and Levy, F. (1978) *Femmes et Immigrees: L'insertion des femmes immigrees en France*, Paris: La Documentation Francaise.

Lim, Lin Lean and Oishi, Nana (1996) *International Labour Migration of Asian Women: Distinctive Characteristics and Policy Concerns*, Geneva: ILO.

Lister, Ruth (1990) *The Exclusive Society: Citizenship and the Poor*, London: CPAG.

Locke, John (1993) *The Second Treatise on Civil Government* (1689), in D. Wootton (ed.) *Locke's Political Writings*, London: Penguin.

Lovell, Terry (1991) 'Dual Systems and the Theory of Patriarchy', in T. Lovell (ed.) *British Feminist Thought: a Reader*, Oxford: Blackwell.

Luxton, Meg (1980) *More than a Labour of Love*, Toronto: Women's Press.

Lycklama, G. and Heyzer, N. (eds) (1994) *The Trade in Domestic Helpers: Causes, Mechanisms and Consequences*, London: Zed.

Mack, Beverley, (1990) 'Service and Status: Slaves and Concubines in Kano, Nigeria', in S. Colen and R. Sanjek (eds) *At Work in Homes*.

Macklin, A. (1992) 'Foreign Domestic Worker: Surrogate Housewife or Mail Order Servant?', *McGill Law Journal* 37(3): 681–760.

Marie, C.-V. (1984) 'De la Clandestinité a l'insertion professionelle réguliere', *Travail et Emploi* 22 (December): 21–9.

Marshall, T.H. (1950) *Citizenship and Social Class and Other Essays*, Cambridge: Cambridge University Press.

Martin, L. and Seagrave, K. (1985) *The Servant Problem: Domestic Workers in North America*, Jefferson NC: McFarland.

Maza, Sarah (1983) *The Uses of Loyalty: Domestic Service in Eighteenth Century France*, Princeton: Princeton University Press.

McClintock, Anne (1995) *Imperial Leather: Race, Gender and Sexuality in the Colonial Contest*, London: Routledge.

Miles, Robert (1989) *Racism*, London: Routledge.

Morgan, David (1993) *Successful Focus Groups: Advancing the State of the Art*, London: Sage.

Morokvasic, Mirjana (1984) 'Migrant Women in Europe: a Comparative Perspective', in Women on the Move, UNESCO.

— (1991) 'Fortress Europe and Migrant Women', *Feminist Review* 39: 69-84.

— (1993) 'In and out of the Labour Market: Immigrant and Minority Women in Europe', *New Community Document* 19(3): 459–83.

Morris, J. (1992) '"Us and Them"? Feminist research, community care and disability', *Critical Social Policy* 33 (Winter 1991/2).

Morris, Lydia (1994) *Dangerous Classes: the Underclass and Social Citizenship*, London: Routledge.

Murgatroyd, Linda, and Neuburger, Henry (1997) *A Household Satellite Account for the*

UK, London: Office for National Statistics.

Neiboer, H. J. (1971) *Slavery as an Industrial System*, New York: Lennox Hill.

Nicholson, Linda (1986) *Gender and History*, New York: Columbia University Press.

Oakley, A. (1974a) *The Sociology of Housework*, London: Martin Robertson.

—— (1974b) *Housewife*, London: Allen Lane.

O'Brien, Mary (1983) *The Politics of Reproduction*. Boston: Routledge and Kegan Paul.

O'Connell Davidson, Julia (1998) *Prostitution, Power and Freedom*, Cambridge: Polity Press.

O'Dy, S. (1995) 'Les soeurs de Sarah' *L'Express*, 26 October 1995.

OECD (1996) SOPEMI 1995 (Annual Report). *Trends in International Migration*, Paris: OECD.

Okin, S. M. (1989) *Justice, Gender and the Family*, New York: Basic Books.

—— (1991) 'Gender, the Public and the Private', in D. Held (ed.) *Political Theory Today*, Cambridge: Polity Press.

—— (1992) *Women in Western Political Thought*, Princeton: Princeton University Press.

Olsen (1983) 'The Family and the Market: A Study of Ideology and Legal Reform', *Harvard Law Review* 96.

—— (1985) 'The Myth of State Intervention in the Family', University of Michigan *Journal of Law Reform* 18: 835–64.

ONS Omnibus Survey (1995) *Time Use Data for Satellite Accounts*, London: Office for National Statistics.

Palmer, Phyllis (1987) 'Housewife and Household Worker: Employer–Employee Relations in the Home 1928–1994', in Carole Groneman and Mary Beth Norton (eds) *'To Toil the Livelong Day': American's Women at Work 1780–1980*, Ithaca, NY: Cornell University Press.

Palmer, Phyllis (1989) *Domesticity and Dirt: Housewives and Domestic Servants in the US 1920–1945* Philadelphia: Temple University Press.

Pateman, Carole (1983) 'Feminist Critiques of the Public/Private Dichotomy', in S. Benn and G. Gaus (eds) *Private and Public in Social Life*, London: Croom Helm.

—— (1988) *The Sexual Contract*, Cambridge: Polity Press.

—— (1992) 'Equality, Difference, Subordination: the Politics of Motherhood and Women's Citizenship', in G. Bock and S. James (eds) *Beyond Equality and Difference*.

Patterson, Orlando (1982) *Slavery and Social Death*, Harvard: Harvard University Press.

Pereira de Melo, Hildete (1984) 'Feminists and Domestic Workers in Rio de Janeiro', in E. Chaney and M. Castro (eds) Muchachas no More.

Perkins, Gillman C. (1903) *The Home: its Work and Influence*, reprinted 1972 by University of Illinois Press, Urbana.

Phillips, Anne (1991) *Engendering Democracy*, University Park, Pa: Pennsylvania State University Press.

Preston-Whyte, E.M. (1973) 'The Making of a Townswoman. the Process and Dilemma of Rural–Urban Migration amongst African Women in Southern Natal', Papers from the First Congress of the Association for Sociologists in Southern Africa, University of Natal, Durban.

Psimmenos, Iordanis (1996) 'The Making of Perphractic Spaces: the Case of Albanian Undocumented Immigrants in Athens City', ERCOMER Conference 1996, Utrecht, Netherlands.

Pugliese, E. (1991) 'Emigrazione e immigrazione', in M. Macioti and E. Pugliese (eds) *Gii immigrati in Italia*, Bari: Laterza.

Quimpo, D. (1994) '"We Serve, we Exist, we Merit Respect": a History of the Filipino Community in France', Paris: Kayumanggi Network.

Rahal-Sidhoum, Saida Marie (1987) 'Un Statut pour l'autonomie des femmes immigrées en France', unpublished report by Collectif Femmes Immigrées, 14 Rue Nanteuil – 75015 Paris.

Rapp, Rayna (1978) 'Family and Class in Contemporary America: Notes toward an Understanding of Ideology', *Science and Society*, 42: 278–300.

Rathzel, Nora (1991) 'Germany: One Race, One Nation?', *Race and Class*, 32, 3 (January–March): 31–48.

Reinharz, Shulamit (1992) *Feminist Methods in Social Research*, Oxford: Oxford University Press.

Rollins, Judith (1985) *Between Women: Domestic Workers and their Employers* Philadelphia: Temple University Press.

Romero, Mary (1988a) 'Day Work in the Suburbs', in Ann Statham, Eleanor Miller and Hans Mauksch (eds) *The Worth of Women's Work: a Qualitative Synthesis*, Albany: SUNY Press.

Romero, Mary (1988b) 'Sisterhood and Domestic Service: Race, Class and Gender in the Mistress–Maid Relationship', *Humanity and Society* 12: 318–46.

Romero, Mary (1992) *Maid in the USA*, London: Routledge.

Rose, Hilary (1986) 'Women's Work: Women's Knowledge', in Juliet Mitchell and Ann Oakley (eds) *What is Feminism?* Oxford: Basil Blackwell: 161–83.

Rothman, Barbara (1989) 'Women as Fathers: Motherhood and childcare under a modified patriarchy', in *Gender and Society* 3(1) (March): 89–104.

Rubery, Jill *et al.*. (1998) *Europe and Women's Employment*, London: Routledge.

Rubin, G. (1975) 'The Traffic in Women: Notes on the "Political Economy" of Sex', in R. Reiter (ed.) *Toward an Anthropology of Women*, Monthly Review Press.

Rudolph, H. (1996) 'The New Gastarbeiter System in Germany', *New Community* 22(2) (April): 287–300.

Ruíz, Vicki L. (1987) 'By the Day or the Week: Mexicana Domestic Workers in El Paso', in V. Ruiz and Susan Tiano (eds) *Women on the US-Mexico Border: Responses to Change*, Boston: Allen and Unwin.

Salt, J., Singleton, A. and Hogarth, J. (1994) *Europe's International Migrants: Data Sources, Patterns, Trends*, London: HMSO.

Salzinger, L. (1991) 'A Maid by any Other Name', Michael Burawoy *et al.* (eds) *Ethnography Unbound*: 139–60. Berkeley: University of California Press.

Sayd, Yakuta (1993) *La mujer immigrante en Cataluña: mujeres marroquíes con problemas*, Barcelona: Comissionat de l'Alcaldia per a la Defensa dels Drets Civils.

Sayer, Derek (1991) *Capitalism and Modernity: an Excursus on Marx and Weber*, London: Routledge.

Schreiner, Olive (1911) *Women and Labour*, London: T. Fisher Unwin.

Schwartz Cowan, R. (1983) *More Work for Mother: the Ironies of Household Technology from the Open Hearth to the Microwave*, New York: Basic Books.

Scott, A. and Morgan, D. (1993) *Body Matters: Essay on the Sociology of the Body*, London: Falmer.

Seccombe, W. (1974) 'The Housewife and her Labour under Capitalism', *New Left Review* 83: 33–24.

Shanley, Mary (1990) *Feminism, Marriage and the Law in Victorian England*, Princeton: Princeton University Press.

Sitaropoulos, N. (1992) 'The New Legal Framework of Alien Immigration in Greece: a Draconian Contribution to Europe's Unification', *Immigration and Nationality Law and Practice* 6(3) (July).

Slavery Still Alive Conference (1995) Report, London: Kalayaan.

Smith, P. (1978) 'Domestic Labour and Marx's Theory of Value', in A. Kuhn and A.M. Wolpe (eds) *Feminism and Materialism*, London: Routledge and Kegan Paul.

Spelman, Elizabeth (1981) 'Theories of Race and Gender: the Erasure of Black Women', in *Quest: a Feminist Quarterly* Vol. V, No. 4: 36–62.

Stacey, Margaret (1981) 'The Division of Labour Revisited or Overcoming the Two

Bibliography

Adams' in P. Abrams, R. Deem *et al.* (eds) *Practice and Progress: British Sociology 1950–1980*, London: George Allen and Unwin.

Stanley, Liz (ed.) (1984) *The Diaries of Hannah Cullwick*, London: Virago.

—— (1987) *Essays on Women's Work and Leisure and 'Hidden' Work*, Manchester: Sociology Department, University of Manchester.

—— (ed.) (1990) *Feminist Praxis: Research, Theory and Epistemology in Feminist Sociology*, London: Routledge .

Steward, David, and Shamdasani, Prem (1990) *Focus Groups: Theory and Practice*, London: Sage.

Sutherland, Daniel (1981) *Americans and Their Servants from 1820 to 1920*, Baton Rouge: Lousiana State University Press.

Thompson, E. P. (1978) *The Poverty of Theory*, London: Merlin Press.

Tiend and Booth (1991) 'Gender, Migration and Social Change', *International Sociology* 6(1): 51–72.

Toharia, Luis (1997) *Labour Market Studies: Spain*, Luxembourg: Office for the Official Publications of the European Commission.

Tucker, Robert C. (ed.) (1978) *The Marx-Engels Reader*, London: W.W. Norton.

Turkovic, Robert (1981) 'Race Relations in the Province of Cordoba, Argentina 1800–1853', unpublished PhD thesis, University of Florida, Gainesville.

Ungerson, Clare (1995) 'Gender, Cash and Informal Care', *Journal of Social Policy* 24 (1): 31–52.

Vasquez, N.D., Tumbuga L. and Cruz-Soriano, M. (1995) *Tracer study on Filipino Domestic Helpers Abroad*, Geneva: International Office of Migration.

Vogel, I. (1973) 'The Earthly Family', *Radical America*, July-October.

Walby, Sylvia (1997) *Gender Transformations*, London: Routledge.

Waerness, K. (1984) 'The Rationality of Caring', in *Economic and Industrial Democracy* 5(2) (May): 185–211.

Walker, Alan, and Maltby, Tony (1997) *Ageing Europe*, Buckingham: Open University Press.

Walzer, Michael (1983) *Spheres of Justice*, Oxford: Martin Robertson and Co.

Wihtol de Wenden and de Ley (1986) in C. Brettell, and R. Simon (eds) *International Migration. The Female Experience*.

Weinert, P. (1991) Foreign Female Domestic Workers: HELP WANTED!, Geneva: International Labour Office.

Whisson, M. and Weil, W. (1971) *Domestic Servants: a Microcosm of the Race Problem*, Johannesberg: SAIRR.

White, Deborah Gray (1985) *Ar'n't I a Woman? Female Slaves in the Plantation South*, New York: Norton.

Women of Europe Supplements (1990) *Childcare in the European Community 1985–1990*, WES (31) August.

Workman, Ann (1985) *Cook, Cat and Colander*, London: Andre Deutsch.

Wrigley, J. (1991) 'Feminists and Domestic Workers', *Feminist Studies* 17(2): 317–29.

Young, Iris (1990) *Justice and the Politics of Difference*, Chichester: Princeton University Press.

Yuval-Davis, Nira (1991) 'The Citizenship Debate: Women, Ethnic Processes and the State', *Feminist Review* 39 (Winter): 58–68.

Index